Visions and Revisions
— *of* —
Eighteenth-Century France

Visions and Revisions
of
Eighteenth-Century France

Edited by

Christine Adams, Jack R. Censer,
and
Lisa Jane Graham

The Pennsylvania State University Press
University Park, Pennsylvania

Library of Congress Cataloging-in-Publication Data

Visions and revisions of eighteenth-century France / edited by
  Christine Adams, Jack R. Censer, and Lisa Jane Graham.
      p.   cm.
    Includes bibliographical references and index.
    ISBN 0-271-01636-1 (cloth : alk. paper)
    ISBN 0-271-01637-X (paper : alk. paper)
      1. France—Civilization—18th century.   2. France—History
  —Revolution, 1789–1799—Causes.   3. Continuity.   4. History
  —Methodology.   5. Political culture—France—History—18th century.
  I. Adams, Christine, 1962–   .   II. Censer, Jack Richard.
  III. Graham, Lisa Jane, 1963–   .
  DC138.V57   1997
  944'.034—dc20   96-31048
                                                                        CIP

It is the policy of The Pennsylvania State University Press to use acid-free paper
for the first printing of all clothbound books. Publications on uncoated stock satisfy
the minimum requirements of American National Standard for Information
Sciences—Permanence of Paper for Printed Library Materials, ANSI Z39.48-1992.

To Robert Forster
colleague, teacher, friend

Contents

Part III: Conceptions of the Public Sphere in Eighteenth-Century France

Acknowledgments

This volume emerged from a series of papers given at a two-day meeting at The Johns Hopkins University in September 1994 to honor Robert Forster's more than thirty years as scholar, mentor, and friend. One of the most eminent scholars of the revolutionary era, Bob Forster has shared his knowledge, insights, and human warmth with the entire coterie of scholars in his field. In particular, he did much to inspire all of the scholarship in this volume. For that, we thank him with deepest gratitude.

We thank Gary Kates and Jon Dewald, who read the entire manuscript and offered many helpful suggestions. We also thank Peter Potter of The Pennsylvania State University Press, who has been extremely supportive. In addition, Marjorie Censer helped with various aspects of the conference that ultimately inspired this whole project.

Introduction

Directions in French History

The eighteenth century has always fascinated students of French history because the Revolution of 1789 is seen as the "political event that cuts French national history in two."[1] Following the arguments of the revolutionary leaders themselves, historians take the year 1789 as a convenient marker to designate the death of the old order and the birth of the modern. These assumptions have shaped the research agenda of French history in the early modern and modern periods. Historians have analyzed the complex workings of Old Regime society, searching for "origins" and clues to the cataclysmic events of 1789.[2] The problem with this approach is that the

---

1. François Furet, "Beyond the Annales," *Journal of Modern History* 55 (September 1983): 400.
2. A synthesis of the most recent work on this topic is provided by Roger Chartier, *The Cultural Origins of the French Revolution*, trans. Lydia G. Cochrane (Durham: Duke University Press, 1991).

eighteenth century is stripped of its historical integrity in the process of being presented as a prelude to 1789. This teleological analysis tends to depict the Old Regime as a straw man waiting to be toppled at the end of the century.

Since 1789, when the revolutionary leaders first coined the term Old Regime, the historiographies of the two periods have reflected and reinforced each other. Thus, a growing dissatisfaction with the prevailing interpretations of the French Revolution has profoundly transformed our attitude toward the Old Regime as well. In the past decade, a consensus has emerged that insists on the need to view the period from 1715 to 1815 as a continuum, within which the French Revolution occupies an important but by no means exclusive position. The concept of continuity has particularly benefited the study of the Old Regime by releasing it from the restricted role of forerunner. In this vision, understanding the Revolution retains importance without excluding subjects that emphasize other dimensions of the historical experience. Indeed, the Old Regime and the Revolution may now be placed in a dialogue with each other as each assumes its distinct identity.[3] This broader scope has allowed historians to push in new and exciting directions, and has made the eighteenth century one of the most vibrant fields in French history today.

The current study of the eighteenth century also reflects more general methodological and theoretical changes in French history. For much of the twentieth century, two interpretative models dominated the field: Marxism and the *Annales*. The two paradigms framed the debates, the questions, and the methods of analysis through the 1970s. Both emphasized economic and demographic history: the Marxists with their neat explanatory framework; and the *Annales* school with its serial, functional, and structural approaches to French history.[4] Both schools dissuaded scholars from studying politics

3. Both Roger Chartier and Tom Kaiser have explored this historiographical issue in the relationship between the Enlightenment and the French Revolution. See Roger Chartier, "Enlightenment and Revolution," in *Cultural Origins of the French Revolution*, 3–20; and Tom Kaiser, "This Strange Offspring of Philosophie: Recent Historiographical Problems in Relating the Enlightenment to the French Revolution," *French Historical Studies* 15 (Spring 1988): 549–62.

4. For a discussion of the traditional theoretical and methodological approaches to French history, see Lynn Hunt, "French History in the Last Twenty Years: The Rise and Fall of the *Annales* Paradigm," *Journal of Contemporary History* 21 (1986): 209–24. For further discussion of the *Annales* approach to history, see François Furet, "Beyond the *Annales*" and the two articles in the fiftieth anniversary issue of *Annales:* André Burgière, "Histoire d'une Histoire: La Naissance des *Annales*," and Jacques Revel, "Histoire et Sciences Sociales: Les Paradigmes des Annales," *Annales E. S. C.* 34 (November-December 1979): 1344–76.

and institutions and both reduced the role of the individual in the larger historical process. In recent decades, however, both the *annaliste* and Marxist historians have so transformed their approaches that the original focus—theoretical or methodological—is scarcely recognizable.[5] The historian has expanded his bag of analytical tools to include those borrowed from neighboring disciplines such as art history, sociology, anthropology, literature, and gender studies, going even further than envisioned by the *annaliste* pioneers of cross-disciplinary studies. No period in French history has benefited more from these forays outside the discipline than the eighteenth century.

New Directions in French History

The following essays introduce the reader to some of the main currents of this new research and indicate where the field of eighteenth-century French history is heading in terms of topics and arguments. The eight essays in this volume highlight fertile areas of current scholarship. First, several authors illustrate a fresh approach to traditional social history. While clearly rooted in the sources and methods of the social historian, these essays—those of Adams, Fairchilds, and Ranum, in particular—extend the boundaries of the discipline in a cultural direction, demonstrating the extent to which the new cultural history has evolved out of the established field of social history.[6] The wide range of source materials and methods of analysis found here reflect the truth of Roger Chartier's assertion that the popularity of cultural history is due in part to cultural historians' having adopted and adapted the problematics and methodologies that assured the success of socioeconomic

5. Lynn Hunt points to Gareth Stedman Jones's efforts to overcome some of the inadequacies of the Marxian model, as well as challenges to the *Annales* paradigm by "fourth-generation *Annalistes*" such as Roger Chartier and Jacques Revel; see her "Introduction: History, Culture, and Text," in *The New Cultural History: Essays,* ed. Lynn Hunt (Berkeley and Los Angeles: University of California Press, 1989), 5–7. Jack Censer, while noting that Marxist historians have moved in new directions, particularly into cultural history, argues that most still operate within the class-based framework established by Georges Lefebvre; see "Commencing the Third Century of Debate," *American Historical Review* 94 (December 1989): 1311–12.

6. For a lengthier discussion of this process, see Lynn Hunt, "Introduction: History, Culture and Text."

history.[7] Thus, while reassuring and familiar, these essays are simultaneously suggestive and original.

The work of several authors in this volume reflect another dominant trends in the historiography of eighteenth-century France. Drawing on Alexis de Tocqueville's classic *The Old Regime and the French Revolution*,[8] many historians now emphasize the connections between the practices of the Old Regime, and the "new order" that emerged with the coming of the French Revolution.[9] Spanning the Old Regime and the French Revolution, these essays reflect in part this revised chronology of the period, a chronology emphasizing continuity more than rupture.[10] Continuity, oddly enough, validates the study of the period before 1789. The Old Regime is not a frail body with embryonic revolutionary tendencies; its problems can be instructive in their own right.

Distancing themselves from the events of 1789 altogether, the essays in Part I focus on issues and concerns of the social world outside the realm

7. Roger Chartier, "Intellectual History or Sociocultural History? The French Trajectories," in *Modern European Intellectual History: Reappraisals and New Perspectives,* ed. Dominick La Capra and Steven L. Kaplan (Ithaca: Cornell University Press, 1982), 24–25.

8. *The Old Regime and the French Revolution,* trans. Stuart Gilbert (Garden City, N.Y.: Doubleday, 1954).

9. François Furet is the best-known historian to grapple with Tocqueville's argument in *Interpreting the French Revolution,* trans. Elborg Forster (Cambridge: Cambridge University Press, 1981). Jack Censer suggests that the Furet/Tocquevillian version of the eighteenth century and the Revolution has become the dominant paradigm in the field of French Revolution history today in "The Coming of a New Interpretation of the French Revolution?" *Journal of Social History* 21 (Winter 1987): 296. His article reviews the Chicago conference out of which a large collection of essays was published in 1987 as *The French Revolution and the Creation of Modern Political Culture,* vol. 1: *The Political Culture of the Old Regime,* ed. Keith Michael Baker (Oxford: Pergamon, 1987). See also Sarah Maza's review article, "Politics, Culture, and the Origins of the French Revolution," *Journal of Modern History* 61 (December 1989): 704–23, for further discussion of both Furet's arguments and the works that appear in the Baker volume. The essays in Jack Censer and Jeremy Popkin, eds., *Press and Politics in Pre-Revolutionary France* (Berkeley and Los Angeles: University of California Press, 1987) also take up Furet's argument and focus on the importance of prerevolutionary political culture in preparing the Revolution. See Censer and Popkin's preface to this work, ix–x. The most recent effort to pursue Tocqueville's analysis precisely where he left off is Isser Woloch, *The New Regime: Transformations of the French Civic Order, 1789–1820s* (New York: Norton, 1994).

10. For examples of this new tendency in historiography, see the essays in part 4 of David G. Troyansky, Alfred Cismaru, and Norwood Andrews Jr., eds., *The French Revolution in Culture and Society* (New York: Greenwood, 1991). Keith Baker maps out discursive continuities in French political culture between the Old Regime and the Revolution in his collection of essays, *Inventing the French Revolution: Essays on French Political Culture in the Eighteenth Century* (Cambridge: Cambridge University Press, 1990).

of revolutionary events. Although important social transformations clearly took place over the course of the eighteenth century, continuity is an important theme. Fairchilds (Chapter 2) focuses on the role of enduring religious beliefs in the rise of a consumer society, while Adams (Chapter 3) considers the strength of sibling relations in the face of a growing emphasis on companionate marriage. Ranum (Chapter 1) analyzes the persistence of aristocratic values and social deference even as prerevolutionary mores were leaning toward egalitarianism.

Continuities in political attitudes and discourse are identified by all of the authors in Parts II and III; for some, this approach leads to links between a vibrant Old Regime and the Revolution. Thus, in his treatment of the political views of Dufourny de Villiers, Chisick (Chapter 5) suggests that the fundamental ideas of revolutionaries like Dufourny were shaped by the political discourses and concerns of the late Enlightenment and did not shift dramatically during the years of the Revolution—even though the Terror may have restricted their practical options. Garrigus demonstrates that racially charged debates over political participation in the French colony of Saint-Domingue did not emerge with the Revolution, as has sometimes been argued, but instead materialized in midcentury disputes over militia participation. Lenard Berlanstein's analysis of the actresses of the Comédie-Française (Chapter 7) reveals that questions about the legitimacy of female participation in the public sphere arose in the context of the absolutist public sphere, and did not erupt only in the early 1790s when revolutionary leaders sought to implement Rousseau's ideas on gender and virtue.

This emphasis on the *longue durée* prevents the authors from falling into a teleological trap. Roger Chartier formulates the teleological position this way: "every historical moment is a homogeneous totality endowed with an ideal and unique meaning present in each of the realities that make up and express the whole; that historical becoming is organized as an ineluctable continuity; that events are linked together, one engendering another in an uninterrupted flow of change that enables us to decide that one is the 'cause,' another the 'effect.'"[11] And by showing what logic this view requires, Chartier suggests that revolution was not the only possible outcome in the context of Old Regime society, and that the events of the latter half of the eighteenth century were not steps on a predetermined road to 1789. These essays refuse to force the unique characteristics of Old Regime history into the uncomfortable prerevolutionary straitjacket. For example, as

11. Roger Chartier, *Cultural Origins of the French Revolution*, 4–5.

Lisa Graham's essay (Chapter 4) suggests, tensions between the police and the people in the reign of Louis XV involved subtle disagreements about royal authority, not a desire to topple the throne that culminated in the execution of Louis XVI in 1792.

It would be foolish, however, to deny the enduring historical fascination with the Revolution to which many of these chapters attest. In these essays, Tocqueville's continuity thesis has been pursued in light of the arguments presented by the German sociologist Jürgen Habermas in his study of *The Structural Transformation of the Public Sphere*.[12] A wide body of literature has emerged in the past decade, influenced by Habermas's argument that the distinguishing feature of French political life in the Enlightenment was the emergence of a public sphere where individuals gathered to exchange ideas and exercise their critical reason.[13] According to Habermas, this public sphere was, by definition, separate from and hostile to the absolutist state. Where the absolutist state was governed by principles of secrecy, exclusion, and hierarchy, the nascent civil society of the public sphere was founded on principles of openness, transparency, and equality. Habermas identified the public sphere with a specific social group, the bourgeoisie, as well as a set of institutions including salons, academies, and Masonic lodges. Habermas's model has been enormously influential because it offered historians a handy solution to the problem of the relationship between the Enlightenment and the French Revolution. Although the technical details of his account have been criticized, the overall schema continues to inspire exciting research.[14] Habermas's framework is an essential guide to the three final

12. *The Structural Transformation of the Public Sphere: An Inquiry into a Category of Bourgeois Society*, trans. Thomas Burger (Cambridge: MIT Press, 1989). This work was originally published in German under the title *Strukturwandel der Öffentlichkeit* (Darmstadt und Neuwied, 1962).

13. See, for example, Joan B. Landes, *Women and the Public Sphere in the Age of the French Revolution* (Ithaca: Cornell University Press, 1988); Dena Goodman, "Public Sphere and Private Life: Toward a Synthesis of Current Historiographical Approaches to the Old Regime," *History and Theory* 31, no. 1 (1992): 1–20; Roger Chartier, *Cultural Origins of the French Revolution*, chap. 2; Sarah C. Maza, *Private Lives and Public Affairs: The Causes Célèbres of Prerevolutionary France* (Berkeley and Los Angeles: University of California Press, 1993); Jack Censer, *The French Press in the Age of Enlightenment* (New York: Routledge, 1994), 209–11; Anthony J. La Vopa, "Conceiving a Public: Ideas and Society in Eighteenth-Century Europe," *Journal of Modern History* 64 (March 1992): 79–116. See also the forum on the public sphere in the eighteenth century in *French Historical Studies* 17 (Fall 1992).

14. The most recent efforts to work within Habermas's framework include Craig Calhoun, ed. *Habermas and the Public Sphere* (Cambridge: MIT Press, 1992); Dena Goodman, *The Republic of Letters: A Cultural History of the French Enlightenment* (Ithaca: Cornell University Press, 1994); Arlette Farge, *Subversive Words: Public Opinion in Eighteenth-Century*

essays of this collection by Garrigus, Berlanstein, and Censer, and influences that of Graham as well.

The essays in this volume draw attention to the renewed interest in politics, which, as with social history, looks very different from its ancestor, institutional history. The definition of politics has been expanded to include not only broader segments of the populace but a wider array of cultural and discursive practices previously ignored. The essays in Parts II and III reflect the revived interest in the ideas and practices that defined the political culture of the era. The political culture of eighteenth-century France is key to understanding both the workings of the Old Regime and the nature of the Revolution itself.[15] One of the difficulties for historians, however, has been successfully defining and employing what Sarah Maza refers to as an "increasingly popular but ever-elusive term."[16] While an abstract definition of political culture, the "set of discourses or symbolic practices" by which societal claims on government are articulated, negotiated, implemented, and enforced[17] may be difficult to visualize, these essays offer a variety of concrete examples of political culture in practice. The works by Graham, Chisick, and Censer in particular analyze the tools and texts used to articulate and shape political opinions, while Garrigus and Berlanstein grapple with the issues of race and gender in shaping political discourse. While all of the authors are sensitive to the "linguistic turn" in understanding political culture, none neglects the social aspect.[18]

Finally, a pivotal issue in this collection is gender. In recent years, gender has moved from the margins to the center of the historian's project. This book attests to the importance of gender as a conceptual and analytical tool

---

France, trans. Rosemary Morris (University Park: Pennsylvania State University Press, 1994); Margaret Jacob, "The Mental Landscape of the Public Sphere," *Eighteenth-Century Studies* 28, no. 1 (Fall 1994): 95–114; James H. Johnson, *Listening in Paris: A Cultural History* (Berkeley and Los Angeles: University of California Press, 1995).

15. Some important works on the political culture of eighteenth-century France include Lynn Hunt, *Politics, Culture and Class in the French Revolution* (Berkeley and Los Angeles: University of California Press, 1984); Keith Michael Baker, *Inventing the French Revolution;* Sarah Maza, *Private Lives and Public Affairs.*

16. Sarah Maza, "Politics, Culture, and the Origins of the French Revolution," 720. Keith Michael Baker, in the introduction to *The Political Culture of the Old Regime* also acknowledges some of the difficulties in arriving at a definition of this term.

17. See Keith Michael Baker, *Inventing the French Revolution*, 4.

18. Keith Michael Baker discusses in detail his more linguistic definition of "political culture" and the power of language in the introduction to *Inventing the French Revolution*, 4–10. For a theoretical discussion of this "linguistic" approach to history, see John E. Toews, "Intellectual History after the Linguistic Turn: The Autonomy of Meaning and the Irreducibility of Experience," *American Historical Review* 92 (October 1987): 879–907.

in current historical study. Many of the essays demonstrate that gender played a critical role in specific political and cultural debates of the prerevolutionary and revolutionary eras.

The importance of gender had been largely ignored until the 1980s when Joan Scott boldly insisted that the "articulation of the meanings of sexual differences was . . . crucial at certain moments in the French Revolution, when citizenship and political participation were being defined." Scott suggested that the category of gender could be particularly useful in understanding even the language of politics and public life, traditionally considered outside the realm of women's history.[19]

Others took up her challenge, most notably Joan Landes in her *Women and the Public Sphere in the Age of the French Revolution.* Landes explicitly used Habermas's public sphere argument as the framework for her own analysis of the eighteenth century. Her work, however, provided a new interpretation of the genesis of the modern public sphere, this time from a feminist perspective. Landes insisted that the bourgeois republic created by the French Revolution was more definitively and exclusively masculinist than the elite cultural spaces of the ancien régime. Since her book, scholars have pursued and, at times, criticized her presentation of the roles and representation of women in eighteenth-century French society.[20] Her careful attention to Rousseau's gendered vision of the virtuous republic has been adopted by other feminist historians, who assert that his vision of separate spheres for men and women—with women relegated to a purely domestic role—was not just peripheral, but rather, central to revolutionary discourse.[21]

Landes's book, while pathbreaking, is controversial among historians. Some have criticized it for a lack of empirical evidence and for a narrow

19. Joan Wallach Scott, "Women's History," 23, and "Gender: A Useful Category of Historical Analysis," esp. 44–50, both in her *Gender and the Politics of History* (New York: Columbia University Press, 1988).

20. Landes, *Women and the Public Sphere.* This work has generated both praise and controversy; see, for example, the forum in *French Historical Studies* dealing with the public sphere in the eighteenth century.

21. Recent efforts to assess the role of women in light of Landes's argument include: Carol Blum, *Rousseau and the Republic of Virtue: The Language of Politics in the French Revolution* (Ithaca: Cornell University Press, 1986); Dena Goodman, *The Republic of Letters;* Madelyn Gutwirth, *The Twilight of the Goddesses: Women and Representation in the French Revolutionary Era* (New Brunswick: Rutgers University Press, 1992); and Dorinda Outram, *The Body and the French Revolution: Sex, Class and Political Culture* (New Haven: Yale University Press, 1989).

and overoptimistic view of the eighteenth-century woman.[22] Whatever the case, the book has served an important purpose. Today, most historians recognize the important role of gender in shaping discourse and reality in the Age of Enlightenment and the Revolution—sometimes along different and even contradictory lines; for many gender has become their focal point.[23]

Several works in this volume consider the tensions in the history of women and gender.[24] Adams, Garrigus, and Berlanstein use gender to frame their analysis of three distinct domains: the family, the plantation colony, and the theater. Berlanstein's article directly addresses the Landes debate in its discussion of the contestation surrounding the appropriate official role of the actresses of the Comédie-Française in 1789. While disagreeing on some elements, he shares her view of the Revolution itself, if not the Old Regime. Garrigus depicts a discourse over public space on the French island of Saint-Domingue during the mid-eighteenth century as colonial whites of the middling classes compared the free men of color with women—wanton and disorderly—in order to discredit their claims to equality. Adams's work, while using gender as a key analytical tool, is also implicitly influenced by recent work in the history of private life, and the delineation of the private in opposition to the public sphere. Most scholars agree that the fiction of two separate, often gendered, spheres of human activity crystallized during the eighteenth century.[25] Thus, at least implicitly, these essays support Landes's view that sexual differentiation was fundamental to the project of the emerging bourgeois culture and society.

Associated with many of the tendencies sweeping through French history is the intellectual spirit labeled postmodernism. A term so inclusive as to escape precise definition, it has been most decisively linked to the "linguistic

22. See for example, Olwen Hufton's critical review of Landes's book in *American Historical Review* 96 (April 1991): 528.

23. See for example, the essays in Lynn Hunt, ed., *Eroticism and the Body Politic* (Baltimore: Johns Hopkins University Press, 1991); Elizabeth Colwill, "Just Another *Citoyenne?* Marie-Antoinette on Trial, 1790–1793," *History Workshop* 28 (Autumn 1989): 63–84; Sarah Maza, *Private Lives and Public Affairs.*

24. For an introduction to this topic, see Lynn Hunt, "The Unstable Boundaries of the French Revolution," in *A History of Private Life*, gen. eds. Philippe Ariès and Georges Duby, trans. Arthur Goldhammer (Cambridge: Belknap Press of Harvard University Press, 1990), vol. 4: *From the Fires of Revolution to the Great War*, ed. Michelle Perrot, 13–45.

25. See Philippe Ariès and Georges Duby, gen. eds., *A History of Private Life*, vol. 3: *The Passions of the Renaissance*, ed. Roger Chartier (Cambridge: Belknap Press of Harvard University Press, 1989), and vol. 4: *From the Fires of Revolution to the Great War*, ed. Perrot.

turn." This latter label refers to a rejection of materialistic explanations of historical causation in favor of more narrowly discursive ones. This point of view, most visibly articulated by François Furet, Mona Ozouf, and Lynn Hunt, influences the work of Garrigus, Graham, and Censer.[26] For example, Garrigus focuses on how the process of whites' labeling free men of color shaped the political futures of both groups in the plantation colony. In constructing such a discourse, which utilized negative connotations of womanhood, white men could denigrate and isolate the opposition. This case study relies clearly upon the deployment of language as a political tool.

One final comment is in order. All of the essays in this volume are influenced by a historiographical shift that extends beyond the field of French history. None of these papers focuses on the familiar or the famous. All use archival evidence to bring to life issues and individuals whose significance lies primarily in their ability to speak for their time. The essays encompass the entire social spectrum of eighteenth-century France yet none of the names, except Sade, is readily identifiable. Even in his discussion of Sade, Orest Ranum explicitly eschews the notoriety of his subject to explore the most mundane of concerns. Thus, like the illuminating microhistorical work of Natalie Zemon Davis, Carlo Ginzburg, and David Sabean, this volume restores human agency, often in its humblest guises, to the historian's project.[27] It suggests that the human subject, whether obscure or celebrated, viewed individually or collectively, lies at the heart of the historian's quest. Thus, Adams demonstrates one family's decision to avoid marriage in the interest of sibling loyalty, while Graham shows how individual subjects devised ways to manipulate the royal police and voice opinions within a restricted field of political action. Censer analyzes the varieties of news available to French subjects who wanted to inform themselves of current affairs. Garrigus offers evidence of how free men of color in Saint-Domingue appropriated Enlightenment arguments to advance claims for political recognition; Chisick analyzes one man's intellectual trajectory

26. Furet, *Interpreting the French Revolution;* Mona Ozouf, *Festivals and the French Revolution,* trans. Alan Sheridan (Cambridge: Harvard University Press, 1988); and Lynn Hunt, *The Family Romance of the French Revolution* (Berkeley and Los Angeles: University of California Press, 1992).

27. See for example: Natalie Zemon Davis, *Society and Culture in Early Modern France: Eight Essays* (Stanford: Stanford University Press, 1975); Carlo Ginzburg, *The Cheese and the Worms: The Cosmos of a Sixteenth-Century Miller,* trans. John and Anne Tedeschi (Baltimore: Johns Hopkins University Press, 1980); and David Warren Sabean, *Power in the Blood: Popular Culture and Village Discourse in Early Modern Germany* (Cambridge: Cambridge University Press, 1984).

through Enlightenment ideals to Jacobin politics. The essays all demonstrate the process of mental bricolage whereby individuals, working with the cultural materials available, sought to comprehend and, sometimes, to change their world.

Eighteenth-Century France in Eight Perspectives

This volume is divided into three parts. The three sections group essays in order to delineate areas of intensive research in this prolific field. Nonetheless, as we have already done, the essays can be recombined to highlight alternate patterns and issues. Nor do the articles in each section hold exclusive right to comment on that selected subject.

Some historians have expressed concern that the fields of the French Revolution and the eighteenth century have "become splintered and atomized in much the same way as scholarly disciplines in general, becoming too narrow for fruitful exchange."[28] We believe this collection refutes such claims by demonstrating that vibrant creativity does not necessarily lead to incoherence. On the contrary, the variety of approaches and topics brings fresh insight to one of the most studied periods of history.

Part I presents three perspectives on the social world of the Old Regime. These scholars are working within the established tradition of social history. What distinguishes their work is the emphasis on questions of *mentalités*, a field of study that derives from the *Annales* tradition. *Mentalité*, a word that does not translate well from the French, suggests the "collective mentality that regulates, without their knowing it, the representations and judgments of social subjects."[29] The term *mentalités* has been criticized for its lack of rigor as an analytical category. François Furet argues that *l'histoire des mentalités* is "linked to the past less by a series of specific questions than by the passionate desire to revivify the emotions, beliefs and mental universe of our ancestors."[30] Still, the effort to uncover what Roger Chartier

28. See Jack Censer, "The Coming of a New Interpretation?" 296.
29. Roger Chartier, "Intellectual History or Sociocultural History?" 23. Michel Vovelle explores the history of *mentalités* in several essays in his *Ideologies and Mentalities*, trans. by Eamon O'Flaherty (Cambridge: Polity, 1990).
30. Furet, "Beyond the *Annales*," 405. For some misgivings about the category of *mentalités*, see Robert Darnton, "Intellectual and Cultural History," in *The Past Before Us: Contemporary Historical Writing in the United States*, ed. Michael Kammen, (Ithaca: Cornell University Press, 1980), 346–48.

labels "the relationship between consciousness and thought" has been fruitful for French social and cultural historians.[31] Whether their sources are quantitative or qualitative, Fairchilds, Adams, and Ranum focus on how individuals experienced and made sense of their everyday lives. Rather than "ejecting the subject (individual or collective) from the analysis and denying any importance to the personal or social relationships that social agents entertain with cultural objects or thought contents,"[32] these authors are always sensitive to the individual in history. As a result, these essays move beyond the traditional methodology in social history, which relied on graphs and statistics to chart larger trends, to a closer reading of the sources for qualitative information that reveals often imperceptible cultural shifts.

To lead off, Orest Ranum focuses on the gritty business of managing an estate. Ranum analyzes the epistolary exchanges between the marquis de Sade and his estate manager. Studiously eschewing the tendency to sensationalize Sade's notorious sexual behavior, Ranum reveals the essentially petty and pragmatic concerns of this representative of late eighteenth-century aristocracy. The marquis's letters are filled with one concern: money and how to get more of it out of his estate. Ranum examines the ways in which Sade relies on verbal abuse in his letters to cajole, threaten, and offend his estate manager, and hints that Sade's care to maintain aristocratic distance from his estate manager may have been a distinguishing feature of the dying noble culture of the late eighteenth century. In this analysis, the author not only comments on the endurance of old habits among the nobility, but also implicitly reminds modern scholars that Sade had a social as well as a literary and sexual identity.

In fact, Ranum's understanding of Sade forces us to rethink our use of Sade as an emblem of attitudes toward women and sex in the late eighteenth century. Scholars interested in gender have used Sade's pornography to indicate the endemic nature of sexism, particularly in the Revolution.[33] Despite his radical materialist philosophy, which emphasized an egalitarian view of the pursuit of pleasure, Sade's correspondence actually reveals him to be a typical aristocratic snob. Ranum's characterization of this individual as a traditional aristocrat seemingly disconnects his sadistic portraits from

31. Chartier, "Intellectual History or Sociocultural History?" 23.
32. Ibid., 30.
33. See for example, "Sade's Family Politics" in Hunt, *Family Romance of the French Revolution*, 124–50; and Lucienne Frappier-Mazur, "The Social Body: Disorder and Ritual in Sade's 'Story of Juliette' in *Eroticism and the Body Politic*, 131–43.

the cataclysmic changes at the end of the century. This new context for Sade makes improbable any alignment of him with the Revolution. Thus, the Revolution is spared the most problematic alliance scholars have attempted to fix upon it when defining the sexist nature of the event. Others, even in this volume, will link the Revolution to sexism, but those inclined to add Sade's outrages to this indictment will have to consider carefully Ranum's material.

To continue this examination of the social world of the Old Regime, Cissie Fairchilds explores the relationship between religious belief and the emergence of a modern consumer economy in eighteenth-century France. Taking Weber's argument that Protestantism promoted capitalism as her point of departure, Fairchilds suggests that the Counter-Reformation played a similar role in staunchly Catholic countries such as France. Using the *inventaires après décès* as her evidence, Fairchilds traces the acquisition of religious objects by French men and women over the course of the eighteenth century. Fairchilds convincingly demonstrates that at least until 1750, religion was a major factor behind consumer demand. Of particular significance in the French case, according to Fairchilds, was the impact of Jansenism on the Counter-Reformation. Ultimately, the spread of Jansenism through the French church in the eighteenth century allowed France, alone of all Catholic countries, to experience a consumer revolution similar to those of Protestant countries such as England and Holland.[34]

The two institutions that defined the private sphere of early modern life were the church and the family. While Cissie Fairchilds concentrates on religion's influence in material decisions, Christine Adams illuminates the family's role in determining domestic arrangements. Adams uses the example of the Lamothes, a professional family in Bordeaux, to explore sibling relations in eighteenth-century France. Based on a close analysis of the letters exchanged among the seven brothers and sisters, Adams suggests that there may have been personal, religious, and economic factors that encouraged celibacy, and that familial relations could substitute for conjugal ones in providing intimacy, support, and affection. While companionate marriages based on genuine affection between spouses may have been glorified in the eighteenth century, Adams's case study, innovative through its attention to sibling relations, reveals that these bonds could occasionally

34. For a broader discussion of the impact of Jansenism in eighteenth-century France, see Dale Van Kley, *The Jansenists and the Expulsion of the Jesuits from France, 1757–1765* (New Haven: Yale University Press, 1975) and *The Damiens Affair and the Unraveling of the Ancien Régime, 1750–1770* (Princeton: Princeton University Press, 1984).

become so strong and satisfying as to substitute for or to preclude marriage altogether.

Abandoning the comforts and concerns of the hearth for the bustle of the Parisian streets, Part II addresses the political culture of eighteenth-century France. Lisa Graham uses police archives to examine the changing nature of political life in Enlightenment France. By scrutinizing the files of individuals arrested for crimes of opinion (*mauvais discours*), she delineates the strengths and weaknesses of absolutism in the critical midcentury decades. Taking Habermas's model of the public sphere and expanding it sociologically and culturally, Graham examines the shifting meanings of the word "public" in the eighteenth century as it emerges in encounters between the police and the people. In particular, she focuses on the crown's efforts to police the public and their access to political information. Graham argues that by the 1750s, French subjects refused to accept their continued exclusion from the decision-making process by asserting their right to formulate and express political opinions. Her study suggests that the monarchy erred in deciding to pursue a policy of repression rather than compromise, an approach that alienated and ultimately antagonized essentially loyal subjects. This revisionist account suggests that long-term hostility toward the monarchy was not the primary motive in these crimes of opinion; rather, it emerged in response to royal repression.

In the loftier realm of political ideals, Harvey Chisick offers an intellectual profile of the Jacobin activist, Dufourny de Villiers. Dufourny was a staunch supporter of the Revolution, and served the cause as a trained engineer, prolific pamphleteer, and dedicated politician. Chisick argues that Dufourny's political views were shaped by the ideals and language of the late Enlightenment, especially the emphasis on morality, political virtue, and an optimistic view of human nature. Chisick's analysis of Dufourny, who maintained his political vision while accommodating himself to the radicalization of the revolutionary government, explicitly challenges François Furet's argument that the seeds of the Terror were inevitably present in the democratic liberalism of 1789. Instead, as Chisick insists, we must recognize that during the revolutionary years a "morally-oriented, generally humanitarian, meliorative and conservative outlook" was harnessed to a violent and bloody struggle. In other words, circumstances drove events far more than an incipient radicalism among Dufourny or those around him.

The essays in Part III clarify conceptions of public space and political power in the late eighteenth century. Habermas provides the theoretical framework that unites these three scholars, whose essays range from issues of race and gender to those of public opinion in prerevolutionary France. Each paper pursues the implications of Habermas's argument, a process that often entails adjusting or correcting the original categories of the analysis.

John Garrigus explores racial tensions in the French plantation colony of Saint-Domingue in the three decades that preceded the Haitian revolution. He asks whether Habermas's concept of an emerging public sphere in Enlightenment France can be applied to the political culture of a slave plantation colony. Garrigus examines the ways in which dominant white authorities used pejorative feminized stereotypes to exclude people of color from the emerging public sphere. He illustrates his argument through an analysis of the debates that erupted when colonial whites resisted efforts by the royal administrators to reestablish the militia in the 1760s. In their efforts to discredit the free men of color who volunteered for militia service, white leaders redefined civic patriotism to mean commercial as opposed to martial service. In addition, they sought to depict the free colored populace as excessively feminized: consequently, disorderly and debauched. Finally, as Garrigus demonstrates, once the Revolution spilled into the colony, militia service proved instrumental in advancing claims for citizenship among the free men of color. For the prerevolutionary period this analysis supports Habermas's concept of a burgeoning public sphere, opened up by nongovernmental elites, but the use of gender as an exclusionary device appears very much like the flaws in the public sphere noted by Joan Landes. Still, in a modification of Landes's gendered analysis, free men of color are able to make use of this newly constructed public sphere for their own purposes, and do not simply face exclusion from it. Garrigus also corrects Habermas by indicating that those same architects of the public sphere are, in fact, deposed during the Revolution.

Leading us back to the center of the kingdom, Lenard Berlanstein plunges us into the animated world of Parisian theater in his study of the actresses at the Comédie-Française. The royal theater was distinguished from other official institutions because women sat on the general assembly, which was the central decision-making body. Women and men were accorded the same deliberative and voting rights. Because they exercised an unusual degree of public power for women in the Old Regime, actresses were a central part of the prerevolutionary debates concerning the appropriate role of women in the public sphere. Berlanstein's analysis makes clear that actresses' power in governing the theater was frequently contested and often outrightly denounced. Royal officials, playwrights, and philosophes complained that actresses enjoyed excessive power and that this was morally detrimental to

French society. This resentment culminated in a petition sent by the actors of the Comédie-Française to the National Assembly in December 1789 demanding that actresses be removed from the general assembly. Such a petition accords both with the Revolution's masculinist conception of the public sphere and with Landes's interpretation of Habermas's model. Although actresses received criticism even within royal space (where Landes believed them secure), the attack by the philosophes and revolutionaries ends up largely as she would predict.

In the final chapter, Jack Censer explores how eighteenth-century French individuals understood politics by examining the kind of information that was most available to them: newspapers and newssheets. He compares a variety of papers and journals in order to assess the differences in news coverage and intended audiences. Censer focuses his analysis of the press on the first five months of Turgot's ministry in 1776 when a series of fundamental and highly controversial governmental reforms were enacted. Censer selects three papers to represent the main positions within the political spectrum. He finds that the crown's official paper, the *Gazette de France*, focused exclusively on the monarchy's perspective. In the less restrained *Courrier d'Avignon*, more attention was given to the opposition's arguments as well as to those of the crown, while the German-based *Courrier du Bas-Rhin* offered the most explicit and complete account. In contrast to the papers, the hand-copied *nouvelles à la main* were the most forthright in presenting a specific interpretation of the events; they also covered the broadest range of topics. Censer concludes that the variations among the media can guide us to a clearer sociological definition of the multiple publics who, in effect, composed Habermas's rather monolithic "public sphere." He further suggests that the monarchy's refusal to loosen the editorial policy of the *Gazette de France* would ultimately be more of a hindrance than a boost to royal authority. Like Berlanstein and Garrigus, he offers amendments to Habermas's conceptualizations and insights for future research.

Tocqueville was the first historian to suggest that "radical though it may have been, the Revolution made far fewer changes than is generally supposed."[35] With this assertion, Tocqueville laid down a challenge for all subsequent generations of French historians. Tocqueville's interpretation stemmed from his overriding concern with salvaging liberty from the dust-

---

35. Tocqueville, *The Old Regime and the French Revolution*, 20.

bin of French history. He argued that the revolutionary leaders, despite their rhetoric of a rupture with the past, had pursued a project of administrative centralization initiated by the Bourbon kings and their ministers. This project was ultimately completed by Napoleon Bonaparte through the creation of the French Empire. The victory of the state came at the price of individual freedom, a concept close to Tocqueville's heart. Still, the desire for freedom was indomitable: "Thus beneath the surface of conformity there was forever stirring in the minds of many Frenchmen a spirit of resistance and a sturdy individualism."[36] This tension between authority and freedom underlies and, consequently, links the Old Regime and the Revolutionary eras. It also underlies this collection of essays, each of which addresses it from a different angle.

Whether the authors focus on domestic or political affairs, on Paris or a plantation colony, they all explore individual efforts to maneuver within an existing set of social conventions and institutional constraints. Thus, each essay pursues the line of inquiry opened by Tocqueville concerning the interplay of authority and liberty as a distinguishing feature of French history. From this perspective, the Old Regime emerges as a site for individuals attempting to redefine their social and political roles equally as important as the Revolution. The Revolutionary era, in turn, becomes a highly charged moment for exploring, but not necessarily realizing, political and social change. The Old Regime is neither so old nor the Revolution so revolutionary as the traditional chronological divisions would have us believe.

The force of Tocqueville's analysis lies in its ability to place the event of the Revolution within the sweep of the *longue durée*, without detracting from the significance of either conceptual category. This allows him to open his study of the French Revolution with an explicit contradiction: "for never was any such event, stemming from factors so far back in the past, so inevitable yet so completely unforeseen."[37] The eight essays in this volume wrestle with this contradiction while revealing its profound truth. In their respective fields of research, each author aims to balance historical causation with careful analysis, the inevitable with the unforeseen. Taken as an ensemble, the volume delineates the texts, discourses, and practices, available to French men and women at different moments in the long eighteenth century and how they appropriated these cultural materials to address specific needs and situations.

36. Ibid., 108.
37. Ibid., 1.

This collection of essays spans a broad range of topics and conceptual issues. Yet, by presenting them together, we emphasize not only the diversity of the field but also its coherence. The book charts the major directions of current research: social history with a focus on individual agency, the evolution of political culture, the workings of gender in history, and critical assessment of Habermas's notion of the public sphere.

By arranging work along such lines of inquiry as well as others suggested in the earlier part of this Introduction, the book identifies a new and productive framework for study. The historiographical narrative that has unfolded over the last several decades concerns the Marxists and their detractors. Put crudely, the first half of this century witnessed the rise of a class-oriented analysis of the Revolution. Challenged initially by Anglo-American scholars for its tendency to see the contemporary world in the past, the thesis came under fire from François Furet, who emphasized the linguistic over the materialistic. This is a profitable discussion that has perhaps been too divisive and predictable and has, to many observers, been overdone. This volume has suggested more collaborative sites on which to advance knowledge of the Old Regime and the French Revolution. These new zones, while sources of continuing debate, are more welcoming to a variety of scholarly contributions.

The questions raised in these essays reach beyond the confines of eighteenth-century France and take us to the heart of the historian's quest for understanding. As the following collection demonstrates, historians sharpen their analysis and acquire deeper knowledge by consulting their neighbors in the humanities. The goal of this exercise is not to lose the integrity of the discipline but to enrich it.[38] Thus, by posing new questions to old documents, we see things we did not see before. Ultimately, as this book demonstrates, borrowing from other fields enhances our ability to analyze the texts and images that are the essence of the historian's craft. We hope that the exploration of this field will prove to be as stimulating and thought-provoking for the reader as it has been for all of us.

---

38. See Lynn Hunt, "The Virtues of Disciplinarity," *Eighteenth-Century Studies* 28, no. 1 (Fall 1994): 1–8.

Part I

The Social World of the Ancien Régime

1

"Mon Cher Avocat"

Social and Verbal Abuse: The Marquis de Sade's Relations with His Estate Managers

Orest Ranum

Bathed in the Provençal sun that Van Gogh has taught the world not only to recognize, but to worship, the upland valley of the Luberon rolls gently between sharp, dramatic, wooded escarpments. Through the valley runs the ancient Via Domitia, now the D 108, the road that joined the Haute Provence towns of Apt and Forcalquier to the Roman Empire. The Pont Julien, one of the four surviving ancient Roman bridges, lies just between the mountain village of La Coste and Apt in the valley below. Just beyond lies Roussillon, the village made famous by Lawrence Wylie's *Village in the Vaucluse.*

When Gaspard François Xavier Gaufridy, *notaire royal* at Apt, like his father before him and his son after him, rode through the fields and vineyard to do business high up in the Château of La Coste, he traveled just sixteen kilometers. The Gaufridy *notaires* must have taken pride in their profession and felt a sense of social prestige from the fact that they were lawyers for the Sade family, whose castle loomed over the whole valley.

The Sade family had come into possession of this eagle's nest and its *terres attenantes* only in the second quarter of the eighteenth century. They enjoyed the income, of course, from the vineyards, olive groves, and wheatfields of the estate, but there was also a certain prestige in being chatelains of one of those *hauts lieux féodaux* that escaped the seventeenth-century state policy of destruction. La Coste postdates the earliest feudal construction at Les Baux, only a few miles away, but not by much. Further proof of the political and social eminence of La Coste may be briefly noted; it was the third castle systematically pillaged by the local inhabitants in the Luberon, and then set fire to in the fall of 1792. From far-off Paris the marquis, who was deeply engaged in a Mountainous Jacobin section at the time, wrote Gaufridy: "Je n'en puis douter, mon ami, il y a une bande de fripons, de scélérats déchaînés contre moi."[1]

The notary had known the marquis since childhood and had supervised the legal arrangements that the late father of the marquis, an officer in the royal armies, failed ambassador, and sometime client of the prince of Condé, had ceded to his son upon the latter's marriage. To the inattentive observer it would seem that the relations between the marquis and his notary were friendly, and respectful of the social distance that separated them. The letters exchanged between Gaufridy and his client (the latter almost always absentee) reveals a relationship that was anything but routine or typical. Or perhaps it was typical in another sense—echoing a refrain that a Toulousain noble, or perhaps the notaries of the Duc de Saulx-Tavanes would have recognized in their own correspondence: "De l'argent, de l'argent, de l'argent, Gaufridy."[2]

A word about the correspondence itself. As late as the 1950s the notarial *étude* of Gaufridy, his associates, predecessors, and successors, had remained virtually intact in quiet and provincial Apt. Some local historians

---

1. Maurice Lever, *Donatien Alphonse François Marquis de Sade* (Paris: Fayard, 1991), 492; subsequent page references are to this text. Lever and Thibaut de Sade are editing a complete edition of Sade's letters. The biography contains lengthy extracts from the correspondence. For further information on this biography, see my review, *American Historical Review* (April 1993): 504–5.

2. The relations between noble landowners and their estate managers has been one of the central themes in Robert Forster's work; see *The Nobility of Toulouse in the Eighteenth Century: A Social and Economic History* (Baltimore: Johns Hopkins University Press, 1960), and *The House of Saulx-Tavanes* (Baltimore: Johns Hopkins University Press, 1971).

had had access to it, and may have taken a letter or two written by the marquis, just to be able to show off his signature, but in the late 1950s the lot of the marquis's letters to Gaufridy were pulled from the *étude*, broken up, and sold in the Paris autograph market.[3]

No matter how much abuse Gaufridy received from the marquis, no matter how embarrassing or even socially degrading the tasks were that the marquis ordered him to do, he never lashed back at his noble client. An evident deference and loyalty prevailed, as well as willingness to feign pleasantness to the point of suggesting that the abuse did not mean anything, or hurt. This description fairly characterizes some forty years of a quite intimate if inegalitarian friendship. Schooled in the law in Avignon, and heir to his *charge*, Gaufridy had some taste for the literary life of his day; he may have been just a bit too gallant with one of the marquis's cousins at one point, but this may only have been a suspicion on Sade's part.

By contrast, the marquis de Sade, son of an ambitious nobleman with enormous literary pretensions, had been born in Paris in the Hotel de Condé. He would grow up to express love for his estates, castles, and servants in Haute Provence in a theatrical, superficial sort of way. There was nothing very special about this perception; indeed, almost all aspects of Sade's ways of viewing the world and his fellow human beings were theatrical and superficial. Sade felt he knew Gaufridy and Provence very well, that they held no surprises; this confidence included tender familiarities about "his" peasants at his estates at La Coste, Arles, Saumane, and Mazan. These expressions of love for Provence were about as sincere and deeply felt as any of the other expressions of sincere thought and feeling by the marquis. And here was the trouble for all who were on friendly or intimate terms with the marquis: words seemed to float from the marquis in an unending flow, with little evident conviction or social authority beneath them. There are numerous expressions of friendship to Gaufridy, and one apology, but never does the domineering tone of the *maître* give way to indicate a genuine friendship of trust and confidence.

The Sade family, despite their lineage to the twelfth century, were not anything more than mere chivalric nobility—not all that illustrious in Haute

---

3. Scholars such as Maurice Lever are still trying to procure these dispersed letters or obtain copies of them in order to complete an edition of them. Currently about three hundred letters addressed by the marquis to Gaufridy are known and edited, but it is evident that no complete edition is currently available. In 1990 Jean-Louis Debauve began the project to study Gaufridy in his own right.

Provence, a region where some of France's oldest families, the Forbins, the Cambis, the Barbantanes, the Simianes, the Caussans, the Adhémar de Monteil, Grimaldi, and Crillon lineages had the greatest prestige. It had been a Crillon heiress that had willed La Coste to the Sades.

The marquis knew the history of his family very well, and he was personally always anxious about the preservation of his *chartier* when he learned that chateaux were being burned in Provence. There are occasional expressions of nostalgia in his letters for those good old feudal days when seigneurs could do anything they pleased on their estates.

We have already noted his expression of love for his peasants. In virtually the next letter, or perhaps six months or a year later, but definitely as early as 1777, he wrote: "I've noticed that the Costains are beggars to broken on the wheel, and certainly I will prove to them some day my scorn for them, and way of thinking. I assure you that if each were roasted one after the other I'd furnish the firewood without raising an eyebrow. . . . Aren't they proving their independence by going off to hunt, or into the mountains. . .?" (459).[4]

His remarks about nobility of the Robe families, and especially that of his wife's, the Montreuils, whose father was a president in the Parlement of Aix, as well as other lower royal officials, were socially degrading and offensive. Likening the Montreuils to "disgusting and dirty toads" (459)[5] may well have made Gaufridy feel uneasy when he read it, or overheard it, for his own social rank was certainly below that of the Montreuils.

Moreover, in private Gaufridy was for the Sades what Sharon Kettering has described as brokers at the level of the central government; that is, he functioned as the intermediary for the marquis and the leaseholders, artisans, household servants, and suppliers of consumer goods for the estate.[6] There was Lions, the *régisseur* in Arles, whom Sade once described to Gaufridy as a "coq d'Inde, Jacobite, et imbécile" (436); there was Reinaud, another *avocat*, Ripert at the Mazan property, and Chauvin at La Coste— all of whom Sade believed he knew well, but who only rarely wrote or negotiated with the marquis directly. Gaufridy could speak in Sade's name

---

4. "Narratives" of abuse are more easily translated than single terms. For recent analyses of abuse in the ancien régime, see Garrioch, "Verbal Insults in 18th century Paris," in *The Social History of Language*, ed. Peter Burke and Roy Porter (Cambridge: Cambridge University Press, 1987); and Le Charny, "L'Injure . . ." *Revue d'Histoire Moderne et Contemporaine* 36 (1989): 559–85.

5. For example, "Il est nécessaire de contenir les vassaux" (297).

6. *Patrons, Brokers, and Clients in Seventeenth-Century France* (New York: Oxford University Press, 1986), chap. 2.

to all these persons, and many others as well; that is, ordering them around and collecting money from them.

Lest we infer that all the *avocats* in Provence were very deferential to nobles in the way Gaufridy was to Sade, it is interesting to note that the marquis remained entirely correct and courteous to Ripert, whom he knew well. Though only an estate manager, and certainly less prestigious socially than Gaufridy, Ripert somehow kept enough social distance between himself and the marquis to put slanderous abuse out of the question, whether about himself, or apparently also about social inferiors. By contrast, when Lions, *régisseur* in Arles informed him that the sheep had not been sheared yet, Sade wrote him: "Je me fous des moutons, moi, mon cher avocat! Croyez vous que mon boucher et mon boulanger se paieront en leur disant Messieurs, mes moutons ne sont pas tondus?" (442).[7]

Sade was not authorized to write to anyone but his wife, and to her only infrequently, during the long years of imprisonment that occurred just prior to the Revolution. The letters surviving from prior to this long internment to Gaufridy are almost exclusively concerned with financial matters. So are most of the letters after the prison term. The formal arrangements for quarterly payments, the extra sums that Sade frequently asks for, and then demands rise in increasingly abusive complaints about Gaufridy's slowness in sending letters of exchange, of negotiating leases. Some of Sade's most recent editors give two or three unending epithets that Sade has fired off to Gaufridy, and then, out of something like social embarrassment, break off with an editorial "etc." The tendency of Sade's editors to want to preserve *bienséance* therefore makes this study of the marquis's abusive language preliminary at best.

After the peremptory passages about how Sade does *not* want information about the condition of fields or repairs on buildings that are urgently needed (442), he simply and categorically states over and over again to Gaufridy that all he wants to know from him is just how much income his estates will bring in and when. These passages suggest that Gaufridy sought to keep his client at least partially informed about the agrarian and human conditions on his estates.

There is also evidence of a growing sense of unreality in the marquis's mind regarding the political and social upheavals in Provence in 1791 and 1792, and beyond. To be sure, when Gaufridy informed citizen Sade that

---

7. Lever suggests that Sade is more Sadian about money than about sex, adding "au reste, les deux choses ne sont pas étrangères."

he should pay this or that sixty livres pension to some parish church or convent, according to the terms of some ancestor's will, Sade asks why, since the financial and legal status of the church had been dismantled. Indeed, ambiguities and contradictions are always evident, and it is possible to characterize the marquis's reactions as typical for someone of his rank and urban upbringing. While Sade could write that the mass executions by the guillotine that occurred almost under his windows were "just," he never seemed to realize that his quarterly payments from Gaufridy would in any way be affected by the Revolution.

As the political climate in Provence became more revolutionary Ripert became so afraid that he no longer signed his letters to Sade. The citizen Sade and principal writer for a *section* advised him to put the word *citizen* in his letters as often as possible, thus giving the impression that he, Ripert, supported the campaign to repress titles and other marks of respect. By this time Sade's own sons were émigrés, a fact easily and quickly known in Provence, and enough in 1793–94 to incur a death sentence to anyone who could be proved to have associated with an émigré. What were Gaufridy's responses to the Revolution?

In August 1794 Gaufridy and his son joined a royalist plot led by a young Provençal aristocrat. With everyone's mail being opened, and rumor and gossip sufficient for a sentence to death, the plot was quickly discovered, so the notary and his son fled to Lyon. Sade wrote them offering to take them in in Paris; at the same time, however, he was furious with Gaufridy for not staying in Provence to look after his estates, and forwarding his income to him (581).[8] Gaufridy headed for Toulon instead of accepting the marquis's lodgings. Louis XVII had recently been declared king in Toulon, where the port had recently been opened to the English fleet. When Gaufridy received the letter containing the caustic criticism of his conduct in fleeing to Lyon, he remarked in his reply that he had felt a "dégoût" in reading what the marquis had written him. Gaufridy feared for his life; Sade never seemed to understand this. The expression of *dégoût* is the only bitterness that Gaufridy expressed to the *maître* in the currently available correspondence.

It has already been observed that Sade seems to have been abusive only to his most intimate relatives and friends. Because of the need to cooperate in hiding incriminating evidence about Sade's sexual offenses—and this in-

---

8. Sade threatened to take Gaufridy to court for negligence, a threat that made no sense at all given the revolutionary climate in Provence at the time.

cluded trying to bribe some wounded or burned servant girl to silence—Gaufridy, Mme de Sade (the marquis's long-suffering spouse), and Mme de Montreuil (his mother-in-law) became a tightly knit circle (266–67 and 303–4). The fact that these persons cooperated, however, and had confidence in and respect for each other, infuriated Sade. Their aims were consistent with his wishes in a general way, but he remained left with a sense of being trapped unless he could keep everyone in a one-to-one relationship with him; that is, to be able to share secrets and confidences with each. To his wife, Sade would describe his mother-in-law as a "bête vénimeuse, monstre infernal, foutue gueuse de mère, maquerelle."[9]

To Gaufridy, Sade would describe his wife veiled in a recollection: "Quand mon pauvre père disait: 'je fais épouser à mon fils cette fille de maltôtiers pour qu'il s'enrichisse, la pauvre homme ne savait pas que ces maltôtiers, ces banqueroutiers me ruinerait" (405). There are many allusions to the moneygrubbing pre-noble origins of his wife's family as tax farmers; here it is possible to discern a continuity in the Sade family of social values and prejudices of the eighteenth-century courtly and sword nobility that were quite free of Sade's own particularity. These phrases were said in a calculated way to hurt his spouse, and perhaps Gaufridy as well, who, while certainly lower in social rank than the Montreuil, was nonetheless on the same social trajectory, from minor legal professional possibly to contracting in the fiscal administration before buying a higher venal office. The legal philosopher, Joel Feinberg, in his *Offense to Others,* refers to insults about one's ancestry, and about one's mother, as of a particularly strong and verbally virulent type of abuse.[10]

True, the letters addressed to Gaufridy after the years of imprisonment are more abusive than the earlier ones, which led Sade himself, his intimate contemporaries, and later scholars to interpret this fact as a terrible consequence of his years of isolation in the Bastille and other prisons. The effects of imprisonment on the conventions of courtesy, respect for others, and socially acceptable behavior in general, are something our own society might well ponder,[11] but in Sade there was already a personal tendency toward peremptoriness, and abusiveness that can explicitly be associated with the social views of persons of his rank.

9. See Lever's summary of epithets about her (345).
10. (New York: Oxford University Press, 1985), 219 and passim.
11. For this author, Erving Goffman's work looms over all these questions. I acknowledge the great influence it has had on some of my work since the late 1960s.

Gaufridy did not seem to have had this distinctively social abuse hurled at him. What Gaufridy received is described by Feinberg and other legal philosophers as the "pure insult."[12] While suggestive, the term *pure insult* implies that there is a vocabulary of abuse that is value-free socially—a distinct possibility in societies both more democratic and egalitarian than was France of the late eighteenth century. The following were used repeatedly by Sade in his letters to Gaufridy, the epithets idiot and imbecile being perhaps the most frequent. In addition, Gaufridy is accused of criminal negligence, of being cruel, of being a hypocrite, a lazy person, an egotist. Such phrases as "you are a hangman, and a *chie culotte*" also appear.[13] Lawyers and estate managers in general are abusively described as *coquins*, *scélérats*, and *gueux*. Gaufridy's son, the notary, is described as a *poule mouillée*, a *monstre*, an *embecile*, and *idiot*, and a *dragon*. Contemporary readers may be tempted to laugh in derision, a quite typical reaction or response from someone living in an egalitarian society and constitutionally guaranteed rights of freedom of expression. Neither Gaufridy nor his son, however, had such an opportunity, and for two reasons: the immediate and devastating laughter of derision can scarely be communicated by letter, and the Gaufridys owed Monsieur le Marquis respect and deference in the ancien régime, no matter how abusive he became toward them.[14] And Sade would often make the ultimate threat: unless Gaufridy managed to do the impossible, he would commit suicide and hold Gaufridy responsible. "Dans cet état de cause, mon cher avocat, plus d'un individu se brûlerait la cervelle, et je ne vous cache pas que j'ai été deux ou trois fois tenté de le faire" (493).

Madame de Sade would continually apologize for her husband's abusive writing, saying that he "doesn't mean it."[15] She also wrote her husband that the police would certainly not release him so long as he continued to be abusive in his letters, since his letters were certainly opened and read by censors.

While it is premature to draw any conclusions from this partial study, some reflections seem in order. First of all, note that there are two, and

12. Feinberg, *Offense to Others*, 222.

13. "Vous êtes un bourreau" seems easy enough to translate. What is lacking, however, is the emotional force that the phrase may have taken on in the Revolution; see Lever, *Sade*, 574.

14. But, as Yves Castan puts it, the century "devenant de moins en moins respectueux"; *Honnêteté et Relations Sociales en Languedoc, 1715–1780* (Paris: Plon, 1974), 87.

15. Mme de Sade wrote her husband: "J'ai beau dire la vérité, qui est que tu ne penses pas ce que tu écris, que c'est de la douleur et le désespoir qui t'emportent dans de certains moments, l'on me répond que l'on ne peut te juger que par tes écrits, et que tant que tu écriras sur ce ton, on pensera très mal de toi" (345). The *on* are the prison and police officers.

only two descents into sexual and scatological insults in the Sade correspondence as we now have it.[16] Joel Feinberg's big book on insult in the twentieth century is largely taken up with insults of these two types. Though certainly vague and inconclusive, might the near absence of the sexual and scatological insult in the marquis's arsenal of insults be revealing of a *longue durée* in the distinctly social and perhaps even class-specific history of the insult? There is absolutely no doubt that not only the eighteenth century, but Sade himself, was familiar with a much larger, more diverse vocabulary of sexual and scatological insults than he used in his letters to Gaufridy. Sade may appear to be passionately out of control in his abusive outbursts—but was he in fact still quite in control and familiar with a still more abusive and vulgar vocabulary that he chose not to use?[17] The marquis always addressed Gaufridy *en maître*, whether in the most friendly or the most abusive of moods.

It would seem that Sade's verbal abuse was of two quite distinct types: the first is the specific social characteristic that is degrading, such as "moneygrubbing financier" about the Montreuil in-laws, for example. The second is the so-called pure insult, such as idiot and imbecile. Thus, despite his claims to libertinism, he may rarely have descended to sexual and scatalogical insults, because these were used more frequently by his social inferiors. And if Feinberg's research may be taken as a sample for the current social foundations of abusive and insulting language, it is evident that we are living in a truly popular, nonaristocratic society and age. The sexual and scatalogical insults of our age are distinctly popular, and perhaps even democratic.

While it is true that the effects of months and years of imprisonment destabilized Sade's personality, I still suggest that in his own vocabulary the arsenal of insults and abusive phrases had a distinctly aristocratic valence. It might also be possible to demonstrate that Sade's theatricality, his saying or writing things just for immediate effect, and with little thought for the long-range consequences of their meaning, had something profoundly of the eighteenth-century courtly society about it.[18]

16. It is significant that the phrase *chie-culotte* is used at a time when Sade is particularly vulnerable and desperate—a further sign of self-control rather than insanity; see the example in Lever, *Sade*, 574.

17. The question of theatricality in Sade's prose and life is too vast a subject to be treated here; an example, however, of a particularly theatrical letter to Gaufridy is found in Lever, *Sade*, 493.

18. The fact that Sade expresses hostility toward court life (for example, Lever, *Sade*, 457) in no way undermines this assertion about the courtly aspects of his speech and conduct. By

---

way of contrast, and concerning someone who really had a great deal to say about politics, Sebastian de Grazia writes about Machiavelli: "Only from his correspondence with friends do we harvest dirty words, and out of hundreds of letters we may find about a dozen such words. Not that our author does not know others. If one of the stiff-necked lords of the Palazzo calls him 'that ribald' we need not return so much as a nod of agreement. But if his friend Buonaccorsi can correspond in a friendly, scurrilous way and if even his patrician, 'more religious than you' friend Vettori can do the same on occasion, we must assume that their expressions were neither new nor shocking nor repulsive to our author. . . . Yet we have no letters from him as foul as theirs"; *Machiavelli in Hell* (Princeton: Princeton University Press, 1989), 374.

2

Marketing the Counter-Reformation

Religious Objects and Consumerism in Early Modern France

Cissie Fairchilds

Historians generally agree that the "consumer revolution"—the transition from a traditional society of scarcity to one of modern mass consumption—occurred first in the middle of the seventeenth century in the Dutch Republic and a few decades later in England.[1] They also agree that it was no coincidence that both these countries were Protestant. Ever since Max Weber, historians have assumed that Protestantism contributed to the con-

1. For the Dutch Republic see Simon Schama, *The Embarrassment of Riches: An Interpretation of Dutch Culture in the Golden Age* (New York: Knopf, 1987) and Jan de Vries, "Peasant Demand Patterns and Economic Development: Friesland, 1550–1700," in *European Peasants and Their Markets: Essays in Agrarian Economic History,* ed. William N. Parker and Eric L. Jones (Princeton: Princeton University Press, 1975), 205–66. For England see Neil McKendrick, John Brewer, and J. H. Plumb, *The Birth of a Consumer Society: The Commercialization of Eighteenth-Century England* (Bloomington: Indiana University Press, 1982); Lorna Weatherill, *Consumer Behaviour and Material Culture in Britain, 1660–1760* (London: Routledge, 1988); and Carole Shammas, *The Pre-Industrial Consumer in England and America* (Oxford: Clarendon, 1990).

sumer revolution by reinforcing the self-discipline necessary for success in early modern capitalism and thus providing the wherewithal to buy consumer goods. They have also cited Protestantism's promotion of literacy, which contributed to modern consumption habits by exposing people to both the pleasures of book-owning and the blandishments of print advertising.[2] And recently sociologist Colin Campbell reversed Weber's Protestant ethic and argued that the emphasis of the eighteenth-century English Protestant sects on feeling and the direct experience of the holy encouraged a cult of sensibility and an ethics of hedonism that gave birth to modern consumerism.[3]

Few have realized, however, that Counter-Reformation Catholicism may also have promoted modern consumption habits in ways similar to but even more effective than Protestantism. France, after all, although Catholic, experienced a consumer revolution very similar to and almost simultaneous with England's,[4] and Counter-Reformation Catholicism may have helped in this. Surely the new individualized and interiorized sanctity of the post-Tridentine church, centering on Christ and the Eucharist rather than the traditional local saints, relics, and pilgrimages, required, in theory at least, every bit as much self-discipline, literacy, and book-buying as Protestant-

2. Levels of literacy and book ownership were substantially higher in Protestant England than in Catholic France in the late seventeenth century, and English newspapers carried more advertisements for consumer goods earlier than French ones did. For literacy figures see Lawrence Stone, "Literacy and Education in England, 1640–1900," *Past and Present*, 42 (February 1969): 69–139; and Roger Chartier, *The Cultural Origins of the French Revolution*, trans. Lydia G. Cochrane (Durham: Duke University Press, 1991), 69. For book-owning see Weatherill, *Consumer Behaviour*, 26 and 27, and Chartier, *Cultural Origins*, 69; for newspaper advertisements, see Stephen Botein, Jack R. Censer, and Harriet Retvo, "The Periodical Press in 18th-Century England and France: A Cross-Cultural Approach," *Comparative Studies in Society and History* 23, no. 3 (July 1981): 464–490.

3. Colin Campbell, *The Romantic Ethic and the Spirit of Modern Consumerism* (Oxford: Blackwell, 1987). The main problem with Campbell's very ingenious hypothesis concerns the timing of the consumer revolution. Weatherill, *Consumer Behaviour*, and Shammas, *Pre-Industrial Consumer*, date it at the end of the seventeenth and beginning of the eighteenth century, long before the heyday of Campbell's cult of sensibility.

4. I have made a detailed comparison of the consumer revolutions in the two countries in an article to appear in the *Economic History Review*. Other works on French consumption patterns include Daniel Roche, *The People of Paris: An Essay in Popular Culture in the Eighteenth Century*, trans. Marie Evans (Berkeley and Los Angeles: University of California Press, 1987); and *La Culture des apparences: Une histoire du vêtement, XVIIe–XVIIIe siècle* (Paris: Fayard, 1989). See also Annik Pardailhé-Galabrun, *La Naissance de l'intime: 3000 foyers parisiennes, XVII–XVIIIe siècles* (Paris: Presses Universitaires de France, 1988); translated as *The Birth of Intimacy: Private and Domestic Life in Early Modern Paris*, trans. Jocelyn Phelps (Philadelphia: University of Pennsylvania Press, 1991).

ism.[5] Indeed, historians have found similar levels of book-buying in post-Reformation Catholic and Protestant households in France, although the books themselves were very different.[6] And of course Catholics, unlike Protestants, bought crucifixes, rosaries, and other religious objects, as well as books. Historians and art historians are beginning to realize that the church's promotion of objects and images as aids to devotion must have had a major impact on consumption habits and therefore on the European economy throughout its long history; indeed, Christianity may be one reason why modern capitalism developed in the West. Werner Muensterberger has argued that religion lies at the root of the acquisitive instinct and has shown that holy relics were the West's first "collectibles," and Richard Goldthwaite has persuasively demonstrated that demand for religious pictures was a major stimulant to the extraordinary efflorescence of the art market in Renaissance Italy.[7]

Yet only with the Counter-Reformation would there develop a true mass market for religious objects. In the Middle Ages and the Renaissance religious objects and images were largely *public*, not *private*. Holy objects resided in holy places, there to be visited and venerated by the faithful. They were not something the average person would aspire to own. Only the wealthy could afford a relic or painting, and even in Renaissance Italy, where a private domestic market for art and other collectibles was most widely developed, wealthy patrons were more likely to commission a painting or donate an altar cloth to a church or chapel than to purchase a holy object for their own use.[8] Before the Counter-Reformation only the reli-

5. The standard work on Counter-Reformation piety is Jean Delumeau, *Catholicism between Luther and Voltaire: A New View of the Counter-Reformation* (London: Burns and Oates; Philadelphia: Westminster, 1977). See also the more recent work by Louis Chatellier, *The Europe of the Devout: The Catholic Reformation and the Formation of a New Society* (Cambridge: Cambridge University Press, 1989).

6. Philip Benedict, "Bibliothèques protestants et catholiques à Metz au XVIIe siècle," *Annales E. S. C.* 40, no. 2 (March–April 1985): 343–70. For the importance of books to the success of the Counter-Reformation see Henri-Jean Martin, *Livre, pouvoirs et société à Paris au XVIIe siècle (1598–1701)* (Geneva: Droz, 1969), 1:6–16; translated as *Print, Power, and People in Seventeenth-Century France*, trans. David Gerard (Metuchen, N.J.: Scarecrow, 1993).

7. Werner Muensterberger, *Collecting: An Unruly Passion: Psychological Perspectives* (Princeton: Princeton University Press, 1994), esp. 62–70; Richard A. Goldthwaite, *Wealth and the Demand for Art in Italy, 1300–1600* (Baltimore: Johns Hopkins University Press, 1993).

8. Samuel K. Cohn, Jr., *Death and Property in Siena, 1205–1800: Strategies for the Afterlife* (Baltimore: Johns Hopkins University Press, 1988). Cohn finds that only with the Counter-Reformation was there widespread private ownership of religious objects and images, which were passed down by bequests to family members and friends (175–76).

gious medals sold as cheap souvenirs at pilgrimage shrines and rosaries, promoted as aids to prayer by the Dominicans beginning in the late fourteenth century, were widely owned, and both paid a price for their popularity: both were widely misused, secularized, and debased. Religious medals, which often bore the initials of their owners, were used as calling cards, loan pledges and even money, while rosaries soon became a standard part of medieval dress for both men and women. Magistrates wore them into court, and soldiers wore them into battle. The debasement of these objects can be traced linguistically. The common French name for a religious medal, *jeton*, was soon used for small coins as well (and lingered into the 20th century as a name for telephone tokens), while the words for rosaries, *chapelet* and *patenôtrier*, were applied indiscriminately to necklaces, bracelets, belts, and beads of all sorts.[9] This secularization and debasement made the late medieval church leery of promoting the private ownership of religious objects.[10] It would take the challenge of Protestant iconoclasm to make the church attempt to see that every Catholic not only owned the religious objects necessary for their devotions but also used them properly.[11]

This determination of church to see that the faithful had the necessary physical aids to their private devotions created an enormous mass market for religious goods—a market so large that it must have stimulated consumer demand in myriad ways and in doing so helped pave the way for the consumer revolution. One can imagine that religious objects were often the first goods apart from the basic necessities of life purchased by the poor,

9. For *jetons*, see *The New Catholic Encyclopedia* (New York: McGraw-Hill, 1967), 9, 547. For the history of the rosary, see ibid., 12, 667–70; for its linguistic debasement see Alfred Louis Auguste Franklin, *Dictionnaire historique des arts, métiers et professions exercés dans Paris depuis le treizième siècle* (reprint of the Paris, 1906 ed., New York: Burt Franklin, 1968), 550–51.

10. A caveat: during what Georges Duby has called the "great vulgarization" of Christianity, beginning in the late fourteenth century, preaching orders like the Dominicans and Franciscans attempted to reach the great mass of believers and encourage them to go beyond participation in the public rituals of the church and engage in private devotions centering on the essentials of Christianity. To this end they encouraged the purchase of—and often distributed free of charge—devotional aids like rosaries. In this, as in much else, they anticipated the Counter-Reformation. See Jacques Chiffoleau, *La comptabilité de l'au-delà* (Paris: Collection de l'Ecole français de Rome, 1980).

11. It should be noted that the church as a body never mandated that believers own religious objects. The decrees of the Council of Trent specified only that images be displayed in churches; see H. J. Schroeder, O. P., trans., *Canons and Decrees of the Council of Trent* (Rockford, Ill.: Tan Books, 1978), 215. But many confraternities required their members to own religious objects for use in their private devotions, and many bishops mandated it throughout their dioceses.

and that once such people were lured into the market they might have purchased secular goods as well, goods produced and distributed through networks that had originated to cater to religious demand. And would not experience of owning the holy have given people a taste of the pleasures of possessing other goods as well? Would not the responsibility of housing the holy have led to a cleansing and reordering of domestic space, which might have stimulated the purchase of the domestic amenities like bookcases and window curtains, which played so important a role in the consumer revolution? And finally, would not the fact that the church invested certain material goods with spiritual meaning make people more appreciative of *all* material goods and more eager to acquire them?

This essay will attempt to trace the impact of the religious demand stimulated by the Counter-Reformation on the consumer revolution in France. Using *inventaires après décès*, inventories of the estates of those who died intestate,[12] it will chart patterns of ownership of religious objects and images and analyze how these related to the spread of the goods and buying habits of the consumer revolution. The inventories for the study have been drawn from four different areas of France during two different periods. The areas that provide the inventories are Paris, sui generis as the center of fashion and pacesetter of innovation in consumption habits; Toulouse, a provincial city known for its Counter-Reformation piety; and two contrasting rural areas, the proto-industrial Aube in Champagne, center of rural hosiery production, and the more purely agricultural Bouches-du-Rhône in southern Provence.[13] The periods are roughly 1710–30 and 1770–90. These dates may seem rather late for tracing the effects of the Counter-Reformation, which after all began early in the sixteenth century, but the consumer revolution, well under way in urban areas by the 1720s, did not penetrate the countryside until the last half of the eighteenth century.[14] In fact the dates are appropriate for religious history as well; while the Counter-Reformation went forward in cities and towns from the 1620s to the 1720s,

---

12. In Paris and Champagne, where inheritance laws followed the *coutume de Paris*, inventories were also taken if a husband or wife died, because the survivor inherited half the community property acquired during the marriage. See Barbara B. Diefendorf, *Paris City Councillors in the Sixteenth Century: The Politics of Patrimony* (Princeton: Princeton University Press, 1983), 222–23. As is always the case with inventories, wealthier segments of the population are better represented than the poor.

13. The sources of the inventories and how the samples were chosen are described in Appendix 1.

14. See my "A Comparison of the Consumer Revolutions in Eighteenth-Century England and France," forthcoming.

new religious practices did not really begin to take hold in the countryside until the eighteenth century, and its conquest of rural areas was not complete until the eve of the French Revolution.[15]

Table 1, below, shows the incidence of all religious objects except jewelry in the inventories of my sample. This probably understates their ownership. Rosaries were often buried with their owners and therefore were not recorded in estate inventories.[16] And religious items, personally precious to their owners, were often specifically left to their loved ones in wills, again escaping an inventory. And if, as often happened with the poor, they were one of the few items of value in a meager estate, they might be sold to pay the expenses of their owners' last illness, and again escape being recorded by the notary. That was what happened to Guilhamette Bernadet's crucifix in Toulouse in 1771.[17]

Table 1   Percentage of Inventories with Religious Objects or Images, 1711–29 and 1771–89

	1711–29	1771–89
Paris	63.3	50.5
Toulouse	67.5	70.8
Aube	19.2	16.5
Bouches-du-Rhône	24.0	30.0
	$N=242$	$N=370$

SOURCES: For the sources for this and the following tables, see Appendix A.

Despite this underrecording, the inventories show substantial levels of ownership of religious goods, especially in Paris and Toulouse. In fact, as Table 2, which traces the prevalence of four of the new household goods of the consumer revolution, shows, at the beginning of the eighteenth century religious items were more commonly found in inventories than any of the

15. For the lateness of the Counter-Reformation in rural areas, see Jeanne Ferté, *La Vie religieuse dans les campagnes parisiennes, 1622–1695* (Paris: J. Vrin, 1962); Louis Pérouas, *La Diocèse de La Rochelle de 1648 à 1724* (Paris: SEVPEN, 1964); Philip T. Hoffman, *Church and Community in the Diocese of Lyon, 1500–1789* (New Haven: Yale University Press, 1984), and Timothy Tackett, *Priest and Parish in Eighteenth-Century France: A Social and Political Study of the Curés in a Diocese of Dauphiné, 1750–1791* (Princeton: Princeton University Press, 1977).
16. Pardailhé-Galabrun, *Naissance de l'intime*, 443.
17. Archives Départementales, Haut-Garonne, 3E11877, inventory of sale of effects of Guilhamette Bernadet, 1771.

Table 2 Percentage of Inventories with
Selected New Household Goods, 1711–29

	1711–29
Mirrors	
Paris	87.0
Toulouse	76.0
Aube	33.3
Bouches-du-Rhône	36.0
Curtains	
Paris	53.5
Toulouse	33.1
Aube	3.7
Bouches-du-Rhône	8.0
Clocks	
Paris	31.0
Toulouse	2.5
Aube	0.0
Bouches-du-Rhône	0.0
Coffee and Tea Utensils	
Paris	21.1
Toulouse	10.7
Aube	0.0
Bouches-du-Rhône	0.0

new household amenities except mirrors. Religious items were, however, like the goods of the consumer revolution, much more common in cities than in the countryside. The dearth of religious items in rural areas in Table 1 is even more striking when we realize that, as Table 3 shows, from 1711 to 1729 *all* of the religious goods in the inventories from the Aube were *nappes pour le pain bénit:* fine embroidered tablecloths used to carry bread blessed by the priest as it was distributed among villages after the service. Every family that could afford it took a turn at donating the bread and kept a fine cloth for the occasion.[18] Thus all the religious items in the Aube were used for the traditional communal religious practices that had always flourished in peasant villages rather than the private devotions of the Counter-Reformation. Only in the 1770s and 1780s do the crucifixes and holy water fonts used for private prayer spread in the Aube. This confirms

18. Alfred Franklin, *La Vie privée d'autrefois* (Paris: Plon, 1901), 23:114–21.

Table 3   Frequency of Religious Items in Inventories, 1711–29 and 1771–89

<table>
<tr><td colspan="3" align="center">1711–29</td></tr>
<tr>
<td>

Paris
1. picture
2. crucifix
3. book
4. reliquary; *bénitier*
5. prie-dieu; other

</td>
<td>

Toulouse
1. picture
2. *bénitier*
3. crucifix
4. book
5. prie-dieu

</td>
<td>

Aube
1. *nappe pour le pain bénit;* no other religious objects

</td>
</tr>
<tr>
<td></td>
<td>

Bouches-du-Rhône
1. picture; *bénitier*
2. prie-dieu; Madonna; book

</td>
<td>

Total
1. picture
2. crucifix
3. book
4. *bénitier*
5. prie-dieu

</td>
</tr>
<tr><td colspan="3" align="center">1771–89</td></tr>
<tr>
<td>

Paris
1. book
2. crucifix
3. picture
4. *bénitier*
5. other

</td>
<td>

Toulouse
1. *bénitier*
2. crucifix
3. picture
4. book
5. prie-dieu

</td>
<td>

Aube
1. *nappe*
2. book
3. *bénitier*
4. crucifix
5. picture; other

</td>
</tr>
<tr>
<td></td>
<td>

Bouches-du-Rhône
1. *bénitier*
2. crucifix
3. other
4. Madonna; rosary; book; picture

</td>
<td>

Total
1. book
2. crucifix
3. *bénitier*
4. picture
5. prie-dieu

</td>
</tr>
</table>

the conclusion of historians of French religion that it was only during the eighteenth century, when well-trained, earnest "bons curés" were in place in nearly every parish, that the new private devotional practices of the Counter-Reformation really took hold in rural areas.[19]

The patterns of ownership of religious objects in inventories confirm what we know about eighteenth-century French religious history in other ways as well. Both Paris and Toulouse show very high levels of ownership of religious objects even as early as the second and third decades, confirming the early triumph of the Counter-Reformation in urban areas. But, as Table

---

19. For the *"bons curés"* and their role in the spread of the Counter-Reformation, see Tackett, *Priest and Parish in Eighteenth-Century France.*

3 shows, the types of religious objects most prevalent in the two cities were different, and this difference grew wider over the course of the eighteenth century. At the beginning of the century pictures were the most commonly owned religious object in both cities. In the later period books had gained first place in Paris, while the holy water font (the *bénitier*) and the crucifix headed the list in Toulouse. Moreover, the proportion of households own-ing religious objects grew over the course of the century in Toulouse, while Paris showed a rather dramatic decline in the later period.

This contrast probably stems from the differing religious histories of the two cities, for each epitomized a different type of Counter-Reformation piety. Toulouse was a center of what might be called an early, baroque, or Jesuit brand of the Counter-Reformation, while Paris was the center of the later or Jansenist variety.[20] This distinction is important: the teachings of these two versions of the Counter-Reformation about the proper use of religious objects—and indeed about the material world in general—differed in ways that had a significant impact on French consumer behavior. Both agreed with the Council of Trent that while religious objects and images were useful for "instructing" and "confirming" believers in the articles of faith, people might misguidedly worship them rather than the holy doc-trines they represented.[21] But the Jesuits emphasized the usefulness of im-ages; the Jansenists emphasized their dangers.

To Louis Richôme, author of *Holy Pictures*, the standard French Jesuit text on the subject, holy images were everywhere.[22] In fact, the whole material universe was a holy image; like modern deconstructionists he viewed material reality as merely a text. Richôme maintained that there were three kinds of holy images: actual pictures, which he called "Dumb Pictures"; written texts, or "Speaking Pictures"; and reality itself, which he termed an "Allegorical Picture," "that is to say, a mystical Picture, con-taining in itself a spiritual sense, known to spiritual people, and hid to the rude." This allegorical interpretation of reality was possible because God

20. For Toulouse see Robert A. Schnieder, *Public Life in Toulouse, 1463–1789: From Munici-pal Republic to Cosmopolitan City* (Ithaca: Cornell University Press, 1989), 90–131; for Pari-sian Jansenism see, *inter alia*, B. Robert Kreiser, *Miracles, Convulsions, and Ecclesiastical Politics in Early Eighteenth-Century Paris* (Princeton: Princeton University Press, 1978), and Robin Briggs, *Communities of Belief: Cultural and Social Tensions in Early Modern France* (Oxford: Clarendon, 1989), 339–64.

21. Schroeder, *Canons and Decrees*, 216.

22. Louis Richôme, *Holy Pictures of the mystical Figures of the most holy Sacrifice and Sacrament of the Eucharist: Set forth in French by Lewis Richôme, Provincial of the Society of Jesus . . .* [London], 1619, fasc. ed. London: Scolar, 1975).

had so constructed the material universe that "any thing or actions" could "represent . . . [holy] mysteries": "So Manna was an holy Picture, not in regard of colours or of words; but of signification; so Circumcision was an action signifying and figuring Baptism" (2–3). The three kinds of pictures were interchangeable (a painting was a "kind of speech to the eye of the beholder," viii), and all were useful for teaching Christian doctrine.

Jansenists also regarded images of the holy as teaching devices, but to them they were regrettable necessities. As Pierre Nicole, author of the standard Jansenist text on holy objects, wrote, pictures were "the books of the ignorant," but actual books were preferable for conveying the doctrines of Christianity.[23] Why? Not only because with paintings believers were likely to venerate the image itself rather than the doctrine it represented but also because the doctrines most frequently represented in religious art, the cult of the saints and of the Virgin Mary, posed theological pitfalls for the unwary. Nicole's writings abound in warnings against believing that saints could work miracles or that Mary could save sinners; he even states that the Calvinist position on the cult of the saints was absolutely correct! (271). For Nicole a Christian's most important duty was to engage in private prayer within the home; by this he meant not reciting the rosary but instead a rather Protestant exploration of the state of one's soul. For this books of theology were useful, but other religious objects were not really necessary.

Thus the two different Counter-Reformations promoted two different patterns of ownership of religious objects. The Jesuit Counter-Reformation favored pictures, the traditional holy image, and encouraged the ownership and display of all sorts of religious objects in a rather indiscriminate profusion, while someone touched by Jansenism would own religious books and perhaps a crucifix, holy-water font, and/or prie-dieu for private prayers. I have traced these contrasting patterns of ownership of religious objects in Table 4.[24] Here the contrasts between Paris and Toulouse, Jansenist and Jesuit devotion, are clearly visible. In traditional Toulouse, as Table 1 shows, the number of households with religious objects actually increased slightly over the course of the eighteenth century. And, as Table 4 shows, the patterns of ownership of these objects matched Jesuit teachings. Although

23. Pierre Nicole, *Instructions théologiques et morales sur l'oraison dominicale* . . . (Paris: Charles Osmont, 1708), 320.

24. I was inspired to try to trace the differing types of devotion through differing patterns of ownership of religious objects by the work of Jean-Louis Bourgeon, "Les marchands parisiens et leur religion vers 1710: niveaux socio-culturels et types de dévotion," in *La France de l'Ancien Régime: Etudes réunies en l'honneur de Pierre Goubert* (Toulouse: Editions Privat, 1984), 1:91–101, although my categories differ slightly from his.

Table 4 Percentage of Inventories with Different
Types of Religious Items, 1711–29 and 1771–89

	1711–29	1771–89
Religious Pictures		
Paris	45.1	16.0
Toulouse	37.5	29.2
Aube	0.0	.6
Bouches-du-Rhône	8.0	3.3
Religious Books		
Paris	19.7	40.4
Toulouse	21.7	22.5
Aube	0.0	7.0
Bouches-du-Rhône	4.0	3.3
"Baroque Piety"		
Paris	25.4	13.8
Toulouse	32.1	30.2
Aube	0.0	0.0
Bouches-du-Rhône	0.0	0.0
"Interiorized Piety"		
Paris	1.4	9.6
Toulouse	21.0	27.0
Aube	0.0	.6
Bouches-du-Rhône	4.0	3.3

the general trend in France was toward a replacement of the religious picture by the religious book, in Toulouse the decline in the percentage of households with religious pictures was relatively slight and the rise in the percentage of households with books was minuscule. Further, the percentage of households with patterns of ownership that I classified as denoting "baroque piety"—that is, having a saint's picture or relic, a reliquary, or three or more religious objects—was very high at the beginning of the century and dropped only very slightly at its end. In Paris, by contrast, Table 1 shows a decline in the proportion of households with religious objects as the skepticism of the Enlightenment spread among the elite and the persecution of popular Jansenism alienated the lower classes from the church.[25]

25. This alienation of the lower classes because of the persecution of Jansenism had political as well as religious repercussions. See Dale Van Kley, *The Jansenists and the Expulsion of the Jesuits from France, 1757–1765* (New Haven: Yale University Press, 1975) and Arlette Farge

And, as Table 4 shows, those who remained pious tended to embrace an austere Jansenism. The percentage of households with religious art declined dramatically over the course of the century, while that with religious books showed an equally dramatic rise. Further, the number of households with evidences of "baroque piety" declined, while those with what I have termed "interiorized piety" (defined as possessing a religious book plus either a crucifix, holy water font, or prie-dieu, or some combination of these, or the combination of crucifix–bénitier–prie-dieu without a book) rose substantially.

Also apparently increasing during the eighteenth century was the "gender gap" in religious practices. Historians have postulated that eighteenth-century France saw a "feminization of piety," as men of the upper classes fled the church and embraced enlightened skepticism and the new forms of sociability, like learned academies and Masonic lodges, which accompanied it, and male peasants were alienated from the church by the officiousness of the Counter-Reformation "bons curés" as they meddled in village affairs.[26] This left religion and the church to women, inaugurating the pattern of tensions between freethinking husbands and fathers and their pious wives and daughters that would mark the French family in the nineteenth century.[27] Our inventories reflect this gender gap, as Table 5 shows. In the early period female-headed households were less likely to have religious objects than were those headed by men, but by the later period this trend was reversed everywhere but in Paris.[28]

Thus our patterns of ownership of religious objects seem to confirm all the clichés of French religious history: the lateness of the rural Counter-Reformation; the piety of Toulouse; the Jansenism and skepticism of Paris; the decline of the picture and the rise of the book; the feminization of piety during the eighteenth century. Indeed, along with pious donations in wills,

---

and Jacques Revel, *The Vanishing Children of Paris: Rumor and Politics before the French Revolution*, trans. Claudia Mieville (Cambridge: Harvard University Press, 1991).

26. Most explanations of the feminization of piety focus on the alienation of men from the church; see, for example, Hoffman, *Church and Community*, 144–46. Yet it may be that the women were even more attracted to the church than formerly, as it promulgated more positive views of female nature and promoted devotional practices in women's domain, the home; see Sara T. Nalle, *God in La Mancha: Religious Reform and the People of Cuenca, 1500–1650* (Baltimore: Johns Hopkins University Press, 1992), 149.

27. Theodore Zeldin, "The Conflict of Moralities: Confession, Sin and Pleasure in the 19th Century," in *Conflicts in French Society: Anticlericalism, Education, and Morals in the Nineteenth Century*, ed. Theodore Zeldin (London: Allen and Unwin, 1970), 13–50.

28. I used female-headed households rather than simply the estates of women because wives' estates included the possessions of their husbands.

Table 5   Percentage of Inventories with Religious Items Broken Down by Gender

	1711–29	
	Male-Headed Households	Female-Headed Households
Paris	65.1	50.0
Toulouse	71.1	52.2
Aube	26.8	0.0
Bouches-du-Rhône	24.0	0.0
	1771–89	
Paris	47.9	47.6
Toulouse	68.1	72.7
Aube	15.2	30.8
Bouches-du-Rhône	24.6	33.3

they are a major indicator historians have used to trace these trends.[29] But should the possession of a religious object be taken as a transparent reflection of religious faith? Perhaps not. Protestants often kept their crucifixes and rosaries after their conversions.[30] Religious pictures might have been bought as decorations, and prie-dieus were used to hide valuables as well as facilitate prayer.[31] Religious goods were goods, after all, and as with all goods the patterns of their ownership reflected the factors of cost and availability as well as personal taste. The impulse behind their purchase need not have been religious; perhaps it was simply the same acquisitive impulse that lay behind the purchase of the earthenware, window curtains, stockings, and pocket watches of the consumer revolution.

A comparison of the patterns of ownership of religious objects with those of the goods of the consumer revolution suggests that this was so. Table 6

29. For the use of pious donations in wills, see Michel Vovelle, *Piété baroque et dechristianization en Provence au XVIIIe siècle: Les Attitudes devant la mort d'après les clauses des testaments* (Paris: Plon, 1973).

30. Ruth E. Mohrmann, "Every day Culture in Early Modern Times," *New Literary History* 24, no. 1 (Winter 1993): 84.

31. Sr. Jean Gaugeal, a merchant in Toulouse, stored his silver in his prie-dieu; that of the notary Jean Roux of Mallemort was stuffed with eleven tablecloths and thirty-nine napkins. Archives Départementales, Haut-Garonne, 3E11913, inventory of estate of Sr. Jean Gauyeal, 10 February 1717; Archives Départementales, Bouches-du-Rhône, 6B 2407, Jurisdiction de Mallemort, Inventaires, inventory of estate of Jean Roux, 1781.

traces the presence in the inventories of goods indicating four distinct patterns of consumption found in Old Regime France. Two of them reflect the innovations of the consumer revolution: the presence of items signifying the eighteenth-century revolution in dress as people expanded their wardrobes and made them more fashionable, and the presence of new household accessories like earthenware and window curtains that made homes comfortable settings for the new domesticity.[32] The other two reflect the persistence of more traditional consumption habits. One tracks goods like sedan chairs, carriages, arms, and large stocks of linen and plate long associated with high social status, while the other charts the presence of items like spindles, scrap iron, and unworked cloth, which denote what I call traditional buying habits: that is, home production and the tendency to stockpile goods and recycle them on the secondhand market rather than make frequent purchases of new items.[33] In Table 6 these four patterns of consumption are traced in inventories with religious objects and in those without. The results are striking. Owners of religious objects consistently showed higher levels of ownership of *all* types of goods, both traditional and innovative, than did people who did not own religious objects. Perhaps then people who owned religious objects purchased them simply because they were available; they seem to have been people who liked to accumulate possessions and had the opportunity and means to do so. Conversely, the absence of religious goods in an inventory may indicate not a lack of faith but simply a lack of funds, or a disinclination to accumulate possessions of any sort.

This is suggested by Tables 7 and 8, which compare the proportions of high- and low-income and high- and low-status inventories with and with-

32. The category "New Clothes" in Table 6 was defined as the presence of three or more of the following in an inventory: watches; other jewelry; five or more pairs of stockings per person; ten or more nightshirts per person; three or more complete outfits per person; lace; canes, snuffboxes, or fans; dressing gowns; and underpants. The category "New Household Goods" was defined as the presence in an inventory of four or more of the following goods: window curtains; mirrors; new types of furniture like tea tables and bookcases; earthenware; porcelain; crystal; clocks; and accessories for tea, coffee, or cocoa.

33. An inventory was classified as containing "Traditional Status Symbols" if it contained two or more of the following goods: carriages; sedan chairs; arms and weapons; silver- and/or goldplate (goblets, salvers, and so forth—not flatware, which was one of the new household accessories of the new domesticity); more than ten pounds of pewter; fifty or more napkins; and twenty-five or more sheets. An inventory was classified as reflecting "Traditional Buying Habits" if it contained three or more of the following: unmade-up cloth; rags; scrap iron; grain; substantial stocks of foodstuffs; a spinning wheel or spindle; flax; unspun thread or yarn; raw silk, silkworms, or flats for silkworms; cheese and butter-making equipment; and cash.

Table 6 Percentage of Inventories with Various Consumption Patterns, 1711–29 and 1771–89

	New Household Goods	New Clothes	Traditional Buying	Traditional Status Symbols
	1711–29			
Paris				
All inventories	56.3	53.6	8.5	71.8
Invent. with rel. items	80.0	64.4	8.9	80.0
Invent. without rel. items	15.4	26.9	7.7	57.7
Toulouse				
All inventories	26.7	21.6	39.2	56.7
Invent. with rel. items	34.6	24.7	45.7	64.2
Invent. without rel. items	10.3	10.3	25.6	41.0
Aube				
All inventories	0.0	11.5	88.5	38.5
Invent. with rel. items	0.0	40.0	100.0	80.0
Invent. without rel. items	0.0	4.8	85.7	28.6
Bouches-du-Rhône				
All inventories	0.0	17.4	40.0	24.0
Invent. with rel. items	0.0	50.0	66.7	50.0
Invent. without rel. items	0.0	5.3	31.6	5.3
	1771–89			
Paris				
All inventories	78.8	92.5	3.2	15.5
Invent. with rel. items	89.6	95.8	6.3	20.8
Invent. without rel. items	52.2	87.0	0.0	8.7
Toulouse				
All inventories	61.4	62.2	38.2	43.8
Invent. with rel. items	69.8	50.7	49.2	54.0
Invent. without rel. items	38.5	61.5	11.5	15.4
Aube				
All inventories	12.7	25.2	68.4	32.0
Invent.with rel. items	26.9	53.8	80.8	53.8
Invent. without rel. items	9.8	16.7	65.9	28.0
Bouches-du-Rhône				
All inventories	23.0	26.3	56.7	26.7
Invent. with rel. items	33.3	44.4	55.6	33.3
Invent. without rel. items	19.0	4.8	57.1	23.8

Table 7 Percentage of Inventories with Religious Items Broken Down by Value of Inventory

1711–29	Less than 300 *livres*	300 *livres* or more
Paris	36.4	61.7
Toulouse	64.4	67.3
Aube	0.0	26.3
Bouches-du-Rhône	13.3	60.0
1771–89		
Paris	50.0	50.7
Toulouse	61.9	76.5
Aube	7.8	26.9
Bouches-du-Rhône	25.0	36.4

Table 8 Percentage of Inventories with Religious Items Broken Down by Social Class

1711–29	elite	nonelite
Paris	73.1	46.7
Toulouse	69.2	60.0
Aube	10.0	25.0
Bouches-du-Rhône	25.0	23.5
1771–89		
Paris	56.3	40.0
Toulouse	75.4	61.9
Aube	24.3	14.0
Bouches-du-Rhône	44.4	25.0

out religious objects. Table 7 shows that the wealthy were, unsurprisingly, much more likely to own religious goods than the poor were, and Table 8 shows that members of the elite were more likely to own them than the lower classes were, although there the gap between the two groups is less pronounced than with wealth. In fact, regression analysis suggests that for all consumption patterns, including the possession of religious objects, wealth was the single most important determinant (see Appendix B). Economists have long emphasized the primacy of wealth as a determinant of consumption, but social historians, intent on using differences in consumption patterns to chart the nuances of social class, have been reluctant to accept that.[34]

Regression analysis also shows the ownership of a religious object as a fairly strong determinant of consumption patterns, especially the new household goods of consumer revolution (see Appendix B). This may reflect more than a simple mathematical correlation; the ownership of a religious object may well have encouraged its possessor to make other purchases. Table 6, then, might be interpreted in another way: inventories with religious objects may reflect larger accumulations of goods than those without, not because their owners were people with the wealth and inclination to buy goods but because owning a religious object had somehow sparked the acquisition of other goods as well.

How might this have worked? One possibility is what historians of consumption call the "first purchase" phenomenon.[35] A rosary or a religious print may have represented a first step into the world of goods for poor or reluctant consumers who hitherto had bought only the basic necessities of life. After all, the motive for buying them was strong, and they were, at least in urban areas, widely available and very cheap. Sometimes religious goods were even free. In Lille in 1640 church schools distributed free to their pupils eight thousand religious prints; twenty years later, more than seven hundred rosaries were given away.[36] Because they were so accessible, religious paintings, prints, and books were often the first such items consumers bought; once initiated into the joys of book or picture ownership, they often bought secular versions as well. Tables 9 and 10 illustrate this. Notice the decline in the percentage of book- and picture-owners with

Table 9 Percentage of Picture Owners with Religious Pictures, 1711–29 and 1771–89

	1711–29	1771–89
Paris	56.4	23.1
Toulouse	67.7	57.1
Aube	0.0	11.1
Bouches-du-Rhône	100.0	33.3

34. See Shammas, *Pre-Industrial Consumer*, 100–111.

35. For the "first purchase" phenomenon, see Paradailhé-Galabrun, *Naissance de l'intime*, 418–19.

36. Alain Lottin, *Lille: Citadelle de la Contre-Réforme? 1598–1668* (Dunkerque: Westhoek-Editions, 1984), 203.

Table 10 Percentage of Book Owners with Religious
Books, 1711–29 and 1771–89

	1711–29	1771–89
Paris	66.7	23.1
Toulouse	64.1	64.5
Aube	0.0	64.7
Bouches-du-Rhône	50.0	33.3

religious books and pictures as secular versions of those items spread during
the eighteenth century.

The purchase of a religious item might have led the consumer to purchase
unrelated secular goods as well. At the very least, buying something religious probably lured consumers into shops where other goods were sold.
As we have seen, religious goods were given away by churches and confraternities, especially in the early days of the Counter-Reformation. They
were also sold at shrines; in the year 1599–1600 the shrine of Notre-Dame-
de-Grâce at Loos sold 2940 silver religious medals, 29,700 glass ones, 7776
crosses, 4880 "tableaux," 3000 holy water fonts, and 1392 rosaries![37] But
in the late seventeenth and eighteenth centuries most religious goods were
made and sold in shops that handled secular goods as well. Someone in
search of a crucifix in eighteenth-century Paris might venture either into
the shop of a master *tabletier* who made them (like Jean Antoine Bonhomme, who stocked more than two hundred but also displayed combs,
chess sets, dice, billiard balls, and other products of the *tabletier*'s craft to
tempt his customers); or he could visit the shop of a *marchand tapissier*
entitled by guild regulations to sell them. Sr. Edme François Gersain's shop
carried more than forty crucifixes but also sold clocks, mirrors, toilet sets,
and other appurtenances of the newly fashionable domestic comfort.[38]

Thus it is not surprising that there was a strong correlation, at least in
urban areas, between the ownership of a religious item and of the new
domestic amenities like clocks and curtains. Religion might have contributed to the spread of the new domesticity in many ways. For example,
inventories show that in the eighteenth century religious items were no
longer hidden in the *ruelles*, or cubbyholes, where people had traditionally

37. Ibid., 264.
38. Archives de la Seine, D4B6, carton 7, dossier 363, Faillité de Jean Antoine Bonhomme,
28 August 1748; Archives Nationales, Minutier Centrale, LX 232, Fonds Caron, 1725, Inventory of the estate of Marie Louise Sirois, wife of Sr. Edme François Gersain, *marchand*.

stored their most precious and personal possessions but instead openly displayed in decorative groups on walls or mantels.[39] Their pleasing effect probably paved the way for the decorative groupings of earthenware vases and clocks flanked by lusterware urns that followed. Inventories also suggest that the church's struggle to make sure that religious items were properly used and not profaned gradually discouraged the traditional practice of hiding silver, jewelry, money, and other valuables in prie-dieus and therefore stimulated the purchase of secular storage equipment.[40] And the Counter-Reformation's emphasis on the home as the site of prayer and meditation might well have inspired the sort of general cleansing and reordering of domestic space necessary for the growth of domestic comfort, a vital factor in the consumer revolution of the eighteenth century. Louis Chatellier has called the Counter-Reformation a vast transfer of holy objects from sacred places to villages, but it was also a transfer of holy objects from sacred places into the home.[41] This domestication of the holy brought with it a sanctification of domestic space, a prime necessity for the rise of domesticity.

Thus the Counter-Reformation may have fueled the consumer revolution in innumerable ways—but only in urban areas. In the countryside it probably provided little stimulus for consumer spending because religious goods, like goods of all sorts, were not readily available. The dearth of religious items in rural inventories may reflect the uphill fight of the *bons curés* against popular religious practices, but it may also reflect the simple fact that such goods were not readily available to rural consumers. Before 1750, when the rise of the country shop transformed rural retailing, the major sources for goods were peddlers and the fairs and markets they frequented. Both peddlers and fairs sold religious objects. In 1654 the peddlers Jehan Hostache and Jacques Garden sold crucifixes as well as textiles, gloves, ribbons, buttons, and lace.[42] Yet both peddlers and fairs were vigorously attacked by the Counter-Reformation church: fairs for their association

39. For the *ruelle* see Orest Ranum, "The Refuges of Intimacy," in *A History of Private Life*, gen. eds. Philippe Ariès and Georges Duby (Cambridge: Belknap Press of Harvard University Press, 1987–91), 3:220–25.

40. The practice of hiding valuables in prie-dieus was very old, and seems to have grown from a desire to secure the magical protection of religion for one's valuables. In the early modern period people evoked other sorts of magic to protect their valuables as well. Inventories of sixteenth- and seventeenth-century German merchants often reveal magic charms tucked in among stocks of goods.

41. Louis Chatellier, *Tradition chrétienne et renouveau catholique dans le cadre du diocèse de Strasbourg, 1650–1770* (Paris: Presses Universitaires de Strasbourg, 1981), 460.

42. Laurence Fontaine, *Le Voyage et la mémoire: Colporteurs de l'Oisans au XIXe siècle* (Lyon: Presses Universitaires de Lyon, 1984), 106.

with the more raucous elements of popular culture and peddlers for the disrespectful way they treated the rosaries and crucifixes they sold.[43] Thus the church itself slowed the spread of religious goods in the countryside, as one aspect of the Counter-Reformation canceled out another.

After 1750 rural areas gained an alternative distribution network with the phenomenal spread of the country shop. This transformed retailing in major market towns like Arcis-sur-Aube. In 1715 its tax roll listed only a few so-called *marchands*, whom the mayor described as "miserable paupers who sell pots and wooden clogs and have no proper shops."[44] But by 1775 Arcis boasted fourteen *marchands*, four general stores, two ironmongers, one grocer, eight tailors, four wigmakers, two secondhand clothing dealers, and one *lingère*.[45] Inventories show that these country shops, which could supply more merchandise less erratically than fairs or peddlers, brought the tobacco and coffee, the cotton textiles and pottery of the consumer revolution to the countryside.[46] But they did *not* bring crucifixes and theological texts. The country store inventories I have found thus far show no sign of religious goods, with the possible exception of the *bénitier*, which may have been included among the oft-mentioned "earthenware not worth describing" listed in inventories. As Table 3 shows, by the 1780s the *bénitier* had become one of the most common religious items in rural areas; it would be found in almost every peasant cottage in the nineteenth century. Its spread shows how little religion contributed to the consumer revolution in the countryside. As Table 11 illustrates, the *bénitier* spread through the reverse of the "first purchase" phenomenon we saw with books and artwork. Peasants first bought earthenware as dinnerware, and only later hung a decorative *bénitier* on their walls.

The stories of the *bénitier* and the country store suggest that after 1750 the consumer revolution was no longer tied to religious consumption but had developed an impetus of its own. This is confirmed by the consumption

43. For the church's attack on fairs and markets, see Perouas, *Le Diocèse de La Rochelle*, 288; for the disrespectful behavior of peddlers toward the religious goods they carried see Mack Walker, *The Salzburg Transaction: Expulsion and Redemption in Eighteenth-Century Germany* (Ithaca: Cornell University Press, 1992), 24. Of course the peddlers Walker discusses were Protestant.

44. Archives Départementales, Aube, C1911, Arcis-sur-Aube, Impôts, 1679–1790, taille roll for 1715; C1194, 1747–89, Mémoire pour les habitans d'Arcys, 6 August 1747.

45. A. D. Aube, C1191, Arcis, Impôts, taille roll of 1775.

46. In 1776 Jean Joseph Lataud of the village of Grans in Provence stocked tobacco, coffee, and printed cottons as well as the usual foodstuffs, needles, and thread of a country store (Archives Départementales, Bouches-du-Rhône, 6B1844, inventory of estate of Jean Joseph Lataud, 26 March 1776).

Table 11 Percentage of Earthenware Owners with
Earthenware *Bénitiers*, 1711–29 and 1771–89

	1711–29	1771–89
Paris	0.0	0.0
Toulouse	20.0	39.1
Aube	0.0	1.7
Bouches-du-Rhône	0.0	10.0

patterns shown in Table 6. From around 1710 to 1730, owners of religious goods were much more likely than nonowners to possess large quantities of goods of all sorts, both innovative and traditional. But in the 1770s and 1780s, nonowners of religious goods made spectacular gains in the ownership of new consumer goods, while their possession of goods indicating traditional consumption patterns shows striking declines. This suggests that in the 1770s and 1780s people without religious goods were not, as they had been in the earlier period, simply devout people who owned few goods of any kind, but instead people who were genuinely secular, with a modern outlook on life expressed in part through the new consumerism. Those who remained religious, by contrast, remained traditional in their consumption patterns as well; although by the 1770s and 1780s their levels of possession of traditional status symbols and the paraphernalia of home production shows some decline, it is not nearly so striking as that registered by the inventories without religious goods.

This secularization, this modernization of attitude was, I think, ironically, the last legacy of the Counter-Reformation to the consumer revolution. Until about 1750, Catholicism probably contributed to consumer demand in numerous ways that historians ignore at their peril. Not only did the Church urge people to invest in certain kinds of goods; it also held a particular attitude toward the material world. Traditional church doctrine, epitomized in France by what I have called the early or Jesuit Counter-Reformation, pictured the material world as the image of and gateway to the spiritual. Material goods not only symbolized the spiritual, they were permeated with it; the material and spiritual were intertwined. This promoted an attitude toward goods that characterized the period from the High Middle Ages to the late seventeenth century: each and every material object was unique, precious and, above all, weighty with symbolic meaning.[47] Ironically, medieval and early modern society, so much more spiritual

47. In this I was influenced by Philippe Ariès, *The Hour of Our Death*, trans. Helen Weaver (New York: Knopf, 1981), 132–37.

and less "materialistic" than our own, in fact gloried in the wonders of the world of goods and in the very materiality of material objects. This led to consumption patterns of enthusiastic and indiscriminate accumulation of as many of these unique and precious objects as wealth, social conventions, and the production and distribution systems of a primitive economy permitted.

The attitude of the later, Jansenist, Counter-Reformation toward the material world was very different. To the Jansenists, the material and spiritual worlds were separate, and only the spiritual mattered. This separation of the material and the spiritual was a necessary precondition to modern consumerism, and not only because when the spiritual impulse waned, people were left to wallow in the abundance of the material world. The separation of the spiritual and material also contributed to the rise of modern consumerism in a less obvious way by robbing material goods of their spiritual content and meaning. Goods did not, of course, cease to have meaning, but the meaning now resided in a series of goods, a system of signs by which individuals constructed a social identity and presented it to the world; it did not emanate from the individual object itself. Individual objects became replaceable, discardable—obviously a necessary precondition for modern consumerism, in which our attachment to specific objects is weak, and we buy and discard continuously as we construct a comfortable material environment for ourselves and send signals about our personality and social status and aspirations to others. Thus the slow spread of Jansenism through the French church in the eighteenth century did what Protestantism had earlier done in England and Holland: separate the material world from the spiritual, and this separation allowed France alone of the Catholic countries of Europe to have a consumer revolution like theirs.

Appendix A

Sources for Inventories

Bouches-du-Rhône, 1711–29 and 1771–89. In this area, where inheritance laws made wills very common, inventories are scarce and more often found in court records than notaries' registers. This group includes all inventories (except for priests' estates) dating from the periods 1711–29 and 1771–89 in the notarial records of the villages of Eygaliers in the Archives Départementales, Bouches-du-Rhône, Series 374E, and in the court records (Archives Départementales, Bouches-du-Rhône, annex in Aix-en-Provence, series 6B) of the following villages: Auriol, Boulbon, Grans, Mallemort, Noves, Saint-Paul-les-Durance, and Saint-Rémy.

Aube, 1711–29 and 1771–89. All the inventories in the Archives Départementales, Aube, Series 2E from notaries practicing in the villages of Méry-sur-Seine, Dienville, Arcis-sur-Aube, Grandes Chapelles, and Plancy in 1711–29 and 1771–89.

Toulouse, 1711–29 and 1771–89. Here inventories are found in the Archives Départementales, Haut Garonne, Series 3E, classified alphabetically according to the last name of the deceased. This group includes every inventory except those of priests found for the years 1711–29 and 1771–89 classified under the letters *A* through *M*.

Paris, 1711–29 and 1771–89. Actually this sample is from the notaries practicing in the rue Saint-Honoré in 1725 and 1785, found in the Minutier Centrale of the Archives Nationales. It includes all inventories found except those of priests, nobles, and the richest members of the professional and office-holding bourgeoisie.

Appendix B

Correlation Analysis, 1711–29

	new goods	new clothing	buying habits	traditional goods
wealth	0.55670 0.0001	0.38844 0.0001	−0.00238 0.9788	0.51343 0.0001
household size	0.06278 0.4832	0.02639 0.7684	−0.08397 0.3480	−0.01928 0.8296
town	0.42626 0.0001	0.26482 0.0026	−0.45680 0.0001	0.40191 0.0001
status	−0.33076 0.0001	−0.19515 0.0279	0.21803 0.0138	−0.39931 0.0001
gender	−0.04363 0.6262	0.06979 0.4356	0.11777 0.1873	−0.07569 0.3977
book-owner	0.35018 0.0001	0.21667 0.0144	−0.04787 0.5931	0.13719 0.1240
literacy	0.27577 0.0017	0.08643 0.3339	−0.13572 0.1281	0.33543 0.0001
old	0.11410 0.2015	0.12675 0.1556	−0.02228 0.8036	0.23902 0.0068
new goods	1.00000 0.0	0.47422 0.0001	−0.21596 0.0147	0.39733 0.0001
new clothing	0.47422 0.0001	1.00000 0.0	−0.17045 0.0554	0.25000 0.0046
religious objects	0.52728 0.0001	0.34990 0.0001	−0.06649 0.4576	0.42843 0.0001
buying habits	−0.21596 0.0147	−0.17045 0.0554	1.00000 0.0	−0.01181 0.8951
traditional goods	0.39733 0.0001	0.25000 0.0046	−0.01181 0.8951	1.00000 0.0
region	0.47855 0.0001	0.33590 0.0001	−0.46045 0.0001	0.39634 0.0001

NOTE: Pearson Correlation Coefficients/Prob>1R1 under Ho:Rho=0
$N=127$

Correlation Analysis, 1771–89

	new goods	new clothing	buying habits	traditional goods
wealth	0.64975	0.61777	0.05268	0.43965
	0.0001	0.0001	0.4107	0.0001
household size	−0.06283	0.18314	0.15262	0.14292
	0.3264	0.0039	0.0166	0.0250
town	0.55486	0.49731	−0.45549	−0.04530
	0.0001	0.0001	0.0001	0.4794
status	−0.53779	−0.50129	0.19599	−0.14648
	0.0001	0.0001	0.0020	0.0216
gender	0.08950	0.18946	−0.07925	−0.02109
	0.1617	0.0028	0.2155	0.7420
book-owner	0.35479	0.38734	−0.08521	0.16050
	0.0001	0.0001	0.1828	0.0117
literacy	0.43515	0.36543	−0.07035	0.20987
	0.0001	0.0001	0.2717	0.0009
old	0.21989	0.17019	−0.12367	0.03362
	0.0005	0.0075	0.0527	0.5997
new goods	1.00000	0.54364	−0.13254	0.17318
	0.0	0.0001	0.0378	0.0065
new cothing	0.54364	1.00000	−0.09644	0.16306
	0.0001	0.0	0.1314	0.0104
religious objects	0.40645	0.32886	−0.05198	0.19709
	0.0001	0.0001	0.4170	0.0019
buying habits	−0.13254	−0.09644	1.00000	0.33389
	0.0378	0.1314	0.0	0.0001
traditional goods	0.17318	0.16306	0.33389	1.00000
	0.0065	0.0104	0.0001	0.0
region	0.53658	0.54851	−0.47439	−0.11233
	0.0001	0.0001	0.0001	0.0787

NOTE: Pearson Correlation Coefficients/Prob>1R1 under Ho:Rho = 0
N = 246

Best Regression Equations for Measures of Consumption, 1711–29

New Goods ($R^2 = .49$) $N = 199$			New Clothing ($R^2 = .28$) $N = 199$		
Variable	estimate		Variable	estimate	
intercept	−0.377	T-test	intercept	−0.072	T-test
WL	0.126	0.0001	WL	0.103	0.0003
BK	0.184	0.0021	NL	0.339	0.0001
CL	0.186	0.0025			
RL	0.177	0.0009			
BH	−0.108	0.0553			
RG	0.066	0.0418			

Traditional Buying Habits ($R^2 = .24$) $N = 198$			Traditional Status Symbols ($R^2 = .35$) $N = 198$		
Variable	estimate		Variable	estimate	
intercept	−0.518	T-test	intercept	0.236	T-test
WL	0.102	0.0004	WL	0.22	0.0001
ST	0.063	0.007	ST	0.066	0.0021
GN	0.301	0.002			
NG	−0.223	0.0001			

Best Regression Equations for Measures of Consumption, 1771–89

New Goods ($R^2 = .57$) $N = 329$				New Clothing ($R^2 = .57$) $N = 297$		
Variable intercept	estimate −0.239	T-test		Variable intercept	estimate −0.282	T-test
WL	0.176	0.0001		WL	0.174	0.0001
ST	−0.05	0.0003		SZ	−0.047	0.0001
RL	0.13	0.001		TN	−0.272	0.007
RG	0.139	0.0001		ST	−0.045	0.004
				RL	0.11	0.02
				RG	0.29	0.0001

Traditional Buying Habits ($R^2 = .34$) $N = 350$				Traditional Status Symbols ($R^2 = .35$) $N = 339$		
Variable intercept	estimate 0.663	T-test		Variable intercept	estimate −0.033	T-test
WL	0.087	0.0005		WL	0.188	0.0001
TN	−0.308	0.002		SZ	0.025	0.04
TR	0.229	0.0001		RL	0.151	0.0008
RG	−0.131	0.01		BH	0.177	0.0003
				RG	−0.125	0.0001

NOTE: WL = wealth; SZ = household size; TN = town; ST = social status; GN = gender; BK = book ownership; LT = literacy; OL = old; NG = new goods; CL = new clothing; RL = possession of religious objects; BH = traditional buying habits; TR = traditional goods; RG = region.

3

Devoted Companions or Surrogate Spouses?

Sibling Relations in Eighteenth-Century France

Christine Adams

On 11 January 1763, Marie de Lamothe wrote to her brother Victor in Paris concerning her activities during the previous month, noting, "I stayed with the family [at Goulards] until our return to Bordeaux, where I have been since then. I left them for four days to go to our dear Muscadet in the company of my *fidel époux* [or faithful spouse]."[1] An unremarkable letter, except that Marie was referring not to a spouse (she was unmarried) but rather, to her elder brother Delphin. Marie's word choice suggests that she was well aware of the fact that she had established a quasi-marital relationship with her brother, and that on a number of levels, she filled the role of wife for him.

In eighteenth-century France, and indeed throughout Europe, the presence of both a man and a woman was generally considered crucial to the

---

1. Lamothe family letters, Manuscripts Division, Library of Congress. Marie to Victor, 11 January 1763.

operation of the household. Early modern households relied upon the contribution of all members of the family in order to run efficiently, and the mistress, in most cases the wife of the master, played a pivotal role in managing the household. Unmarried women, however, especially sisters and daughters, played an essential role in the stabilization of early modern family formations. In cases where their mother died, or their brothers remained unmarried, daughters and sisters could be called upon to serve as surrogate wives, in a sense, to step in and take over management of the household.[2] In an era of high celibacy, especially among elite urban women, this allowed unmarried women to fill an important practical role in their natal families.[3]

However, single women could play an important emotional role in their natal family as well. In the case of the Lamothe family, a professional family in eighteenth-century Bordeaux, relations between the brothers and sisters of the family went far beyond mutual convenience. Their relations were close, intense, even passionate. The letters between brothers and sisters attest to the deep bond that existed among all the Lamothe siblings, male and female.

That intimate ties frequently bound brother and sister is not a new observation.[4] Leonore Davidoff and Catherine Hall, in their analysis of the English middle classes of the nineteenth century observe that "brothers and sisters approached the model masculine-feminine relationship without the explicit sexuality of marriage," and that "the lives of brothers and sisters

2. In the context of Victorian England, Patricia Jalland examines the cases of a number of spinsters who filled the role of mistress of the household for either their fathers or brothers; see "Victorian Spinsters: Dutiful Daughters, Desperate Rebels and the Transition to New Women" in *Exploring Women's Past: Essays in Social History,* ed. Patricia Crawford (Sydney and Boston: G. Allen and Unwin, 1984), 129–70. Louis Pasteur, the nineteenth-century chemist, envisioned a similar role for one or both of his sisters, whose education he had supervised; Patrice Debré, *Louis Pasteur* (Paris: Flammarion, 1995), 46. I thank Elborg Forster, who is currently preparing the English translation for Johns Hopkins University Press, for the reference.

3. Robert Forster, *The Nobility of Toulouse in the Eighteenth Century: A Social and Economic Study* (Baltimore: Johns Hopkins University Press, 1960), 128–30; Margaret Darrow, *Revolution in the House: Family, Class and Inheritance in Southern France, 1775–1825* (Princeton: Princeton University Press, 1989), 109–10; Angus McLaren, *Sexuality and Social Order: The Debate over the Fertility of Women and Workers in France, 1770–1920* (New York: Holmes and Meier, 1983), 12–13. French demographer Jacques Dupâquier found that approximately 14 percent of the generation born in France between 1784 and 1789, immediately prior to the French Revolution, remained permanently celibate; see *La Population française aux XVII et XVIIIe siècles* (Paris: Presses Universitaires de France, 1979), 60–61.

4. For example, Judy Dunn's sociological study, *Sisters and Brothers* (Cambridge: Harvard University Press, 1985) emphasizes the intimacy that binds siblings.

remained closely interwoven, often displaying a depth of warm affection on both sides."[5] Steven Mintz has drawn attention to what he refers to as the "romanticization of sibling love" between Catharine Sedgwick and her brothers and sisters.[6]

In an age that was beginning to accept and even to glorify the companionate marriage, a marriage in which husband and wife had a say in who their spouse should be, and played an active role in choosing someone to be a friend and companion, the brother-sister relationship could be a useful learning experience.[7] As Davidoff and Hall note, in the case of brother and sister, "Their attachment and treatment of each other was explicitly meant to prefigure that of marriage and through it they were to learn appropriate gender behaviour."[8] Some writers compared the love of brother and sister as second only to the conjugal union. Close brother-sister relations reflect another familial ideal developing in the eighteenth century, that of the new domesticated family, a family model that was much less hierarchical, less formal, and more openly loving. Indeed, some historians have argued that the "modern family" began to take root in the eighteenth century, in contrast to the harsher patriarchal model of an earlier era.[9]

The Lamothe family provides us with a case study of sibling relations in eighteenth-century France, and allows us to consider the nature and the intensity of these relations. A rich source of materials, a collection of more

5. Leonore Davidoff and Catherine Hall, *Family Fortunes: Men and Women of the English Middle Class, 1780–1850* (Chicago: University of Chicago Press, 1987), 348 and 350.

6. Steven Mintz, *A Prison of Expectations: The Family in Victorian Culture* (New York: New York University Press, 1983).

7. For a discussion of the rise of companionate marriage in the eighteenth century, see Lawrence Stone, *The Family, Sex and Marriage in England, 1500–1800,* abridged ed. (New York: Harper and Row, 1979), esp. chap. 8; and Randolph Trumbach, *The Rise of the Egalitarian Family: Aristocratic Kinship and Domestic Relations in Eighteenth-Century England* (New York: Academic Press, 1978).

8. Davidoff and Hall, *Family Fortunes,* 348–49.

9. A number of historians have traced the changes in family life that took place in the eighteenth century. The classic statement is that of Philippe Ariès, *Centuries of Childhood: A Social History of Family Life,* trans. Robert Baldick (New York: Knopf, 1962). See also Stone, *The Family, Sex, and Marriage;* Jean-Louis Flandrin, *Families in Former Times: Kinship, Household, and Sexuality in Early Modern France,* trans. Richard Southern (Cambridge: Cambridge University Press, 1979), 135–40; Trumbach, *The Rise of the Egalitarian Family;* James Traer, *Marriage and the Family in Eighteenth-Century France* (Ithaca: Cornell University Press, 1980). Hans Medick and David Sabean have more recently nuanced this rather "Whiggish" view of the history of the family by emphasizing the interplay of both interest and emotion in family interactions. See the introduction and first chapter in Medick and Sabean, eds., *Interest and Emotion: Essays on the Study of Family and Kinship* (Cambridge: Cambridge University Press, 1984), 1–27.

than three hundred personal letters written by the Lamothe family over a period of twenty-five years allows us to examine the familial life, and in particular, the sibling relations of the family members. The bulk of the letters were written to Victor, one of the younger sons of the family, while he was studying medicine in Paris and Montpellier in the 1750s and 1760s. Victor was eventually joined in Paris by his younger brother, Alexandre, a student of law. The letters reveal a devoted and intimate family, closely bound as much by their deep affection as by their sense of duty to the family, siblings and parents.[10]

The head of the Lamothe family was Daniel de Lamothe, a respected barrister at the Parlement of Bordeaux. His wife was Marie de Sérézac, daughter of a former mayor of Castillon, a small town near Bordeaux. Their large family included three lawyers (the eldest, Simon-Antoine-Delphin, Alexis, and Alexis-Alexandre), one doctor (Simon-Victor), one priest (Jules-Bertrand), and two unmarried daughters, Marie and Marianne. The lives of this family were tightly interwoven, as they shared financial resources, emotional support, and a home. While in Bordeaux, the entire Lamothe family lived under the same roof in their townhouse on Rue Neuve.[11]

The personalities of the various members of the family emerge in the letters, both male and female. The gendering of familial roles is evident, even if issues of "appropriate" feminine and masculine behavior were not made explicit in the letters. The males of the family emphasized their public roles, their professional and cultural pursuits, while the family- and church-oriented lives of the women, with their household tasks, religious practices, and charitable work at the hospital, in some ways prefigure the domestic activities of the "ladies of the leisure class" of nineteenth-century France.[12] I shall explore here the many facets of relations within the Lamothe family, and the tight bonds between siblings, as well as the quasi-marital nature of the relationship between the brothers and sisters. In doing so, I examine

10. The collected letters of the Lamothe family are located in the Manuscripts Division of the Library of Congress. This study of the Lamothe sibling relations is part of a larger study on the personal, professional, and cultural lives of the Lamothe family. See Christine Adams, "Bourgeois Identity in Early Modern France: A Professional Family in Eighteenth-Century Bordeaux," (Ph.D. diss., Johns Hopkins University, 1993). Hereafter, the letters will be cited simply by the name of the letter writer and recipient, along with the date. All translations are my own.

11. Jules Delpit, *Notes Biographiques sur les Messieurs de Lamothe* (Bordeaux: Balarac Jeune, 1846), 9–10.

12. See Bonnie G. Smith, *Ladies of the Leisure Class: The Bourgeoisies of Northern France in the Nineteenth Century* (Princeton: Princeton University Press, 1981) for a discussion of the nineteenth-century bourgeoisie.

new ground, as the nature of sibling relations—especially during this crucial period of transformation in both familial relations and domestic ideology—has been neglected by historians.

The passionate attachment of the Lamothe siblings found its first model in warm relations with their father and mother. Mutual love and respect were the foundation of family relations within the household. Although Daniel often appeared strict in his letters, he and his wife were affectionate, even doting parents. The sisters in particular constantly assured Victor that his parents loved them all dearly, and wanted above all to make their children happy.[13] Marianne wrote to Victor, "I know the goodness of their hearts, and how much they want to make their children happy, at least to the degree that prudence and economy permit them to."[14] Marie noted the great pleasure her parents took in showing Victor small signs of affection, such as the *poule dinde* and other little treats that they sent to Paris for him each year.[15] Marie de Sérézac frequently asked her children in Bordeaux to include loving messages on her behalf to her sons in Paris.

At the same time, Daniel Lamothe and Marie de Sérézac inspired adoration in their children, who considered *ce cher père* and *cette chère maman* worthy of the utmost reverence. Marianne wrote to Victor of "our very good and very respectable papa" and affirmed that they must show "respect, affection and the most exacting submission vis-à-vis such parents."[16] Marie and Marianne considered their mother an admirable role model, and Marie assured Victor that "she's a fine mother who well deserves our respect and our love, may God preserve her for many years."[17] Victor planned to display his affection for his father by dedicating his master's thesis to him as "an authentic proof of [his] affection."[18]

This tenderness was replicated between the Lamothe siblings, and the love they expressed for each other was apparently strong and sincere. They all worked hard to preserve peace and harmony in the family. The sisters, Marie in particular, frequently served as intermediaries to repair any potential rifts between siblings and parents.[19] They constantly reiterated their mutual affection. Alexis thanked Victor for one letter, noting that "it was

13. For example, Marie to Victor, 14 April 1760; 4 July 1761. Marianne to Victor, 21 April 1760; 19 October 1760.
14. Marianne to Victor, 20 April 1757.
15. Marie to Victor, 20 April 1757.
16. Marianne to Victor, 24 January 1757.
17. Marie to Victor, 20 October 1757; 18 August 1764.
18. Victor to Delphin, undated 1760.
19. For example, Marie to Victor, 17 February 1759; 27 November 1760; 18 August 1764.

full of sentiments so tender, so beautiful, so touching, so natural, that one would have to be insensitive to tender feelings . . . not to have been extremely moved by it."[20] Shortly after Victor's departure for Paris, Alexandre wrote to him, "It is wonderful to be loved by you, & especially to be linked by ties of blood."[21]

They frequently requested counsel from each other.[22] Victor turned to his brother Alexis for advice on his choice of career, and was thrilled with Alexis's reply "so full of good advice" and "such deep affection."[23] In wifely fashion, the two sisters demonstrated great admiration for the skills of their brothers. They requested medical advice from Victor on many occasions and praised his expertise. They also respected their elder brothers' legal proficiency,[24] as well as Delphin's mechanical cleverness and many other talents.[25] Marie and Marianne were free with advice themselves, counselling Victor on diverse matters, from personal finances and religion to his choice of clothing.[26]

However, despite obvious affection, the familial bonds of the Lamothes were perhaps more complex than the regular assurances of love and trust would indicate.[27] The large difference in age between the children was undoubtedly a factor in their relations. The oldest and youngest sons—Delphin and Alexandre—were fifteen years apart in age. The three youngest children—Marianne, Victor, and Alexandre—were extremely close, and perhaps formed a subset of the larger family. Alexandre wrote letters to Victor filled with affectionate memories of their childhood, while Marianne referred to Victor and herself as "childhood companions" who had shared almond gâteaux.[28] The eldest children of the family—Delphin, Alexis, and Marie—assumed a more parental attitude toward their younger siblings, offering them advice and counsel.

20. Alexis to Victor, 27 October 1763.
21. Alexandre to Victor, 17 January 1757.
22. See, for example, Victor to Delphin, undated 1760.
23. Victor to Alexis, 1–5 October 1755; 25 October 1755. Alexis to Victor, 14 October 1755.
24. Marianne to Victor, 24 January 1757.
25. See for example, Marianne to Victor, 2 December 1758.
26. See for example, Marie to Victor, 2 April 1757; 20 April 1757; 3 September 1757; 10 January 1758. Marianne to Victor, 7 August 1759.
27. Judy Dunn discusses the complex emotions common in sibling relations in *Sisters and Brothers*, esp. chaps. 4 and 5.
28. For example, Alexandre to Victor, 17 January 1757; Marie to Victor, 19 October 1760. Judy Dunn emphasizes that the shared experience of childhood and adolescence are central to the closeness that siblings feel later in life. *Sisters and Brothers*, 136.

Marie, the eldest daughter, showed strong maternal feelings for her two youngest brothers, writing, "I think of you and Alexandre as my two children, I love you with the love of a mother . . . my title of godmother along with my sentiments gives me, I think, much leeway."[29] She urged Victor to confide in her and delighted in his letters.[30] Alexis and Delphin were full of advice for their younger siblings as well, whether concerning career choices, personal comportment, or the need to spend money wisely.

This age difference and the parental attitude adopted by the older children created unequal relations between the siblings, especially when the death of Daniel in 1763 left Alexis and Delphin, the two eldest sons, in charge of the family finances, and consequently, in control of Victor and Alexandre's career decisions.[31] Both Delphin and Alexis sometimes assumed the harsh tone of their father when writing to Victor and Alexandre, especially when discussing money matters.[32] However, the two younger boys were willing to submit to the reprimands of their elder siblings. Delphin and Alexis were always quick to assure them that they spoke only as affectionate brothers who "want very much for you to advance and perfect yourself."[33]

Although their letters always stressed their strong bonds of sentiment, tensions sometimes arose among the seven Lamothe siblings. On occasion, Marie or Marianne scolded Victor for not writing more often, or when his letters seemed too impersonal.[34] Strains also arose between Victor and the priest Jules. The two wrote frequent and loving letters when Victor first left for Paris, but their correspondence became more rare as time passed. At times, Victor resented Jules's reprimands for certain "vulgar" expressions in his letters, and expressed frustration with Jules's *trop grande exactitude.*[35] At one point, Victor did not write to Jules for two years.[36] Jules interpreted this silence as evidence that Victor feared having to account for his moral conduct in Paris.[37] Victor asserted that this was not the case, that "I would be happy to speak to you of how assiduously I try to fulfill my Christian

29. Marie to Victor, 27 November 1760. See also 14 April 1760; 7 September 1762; 11 January 1763; and 22 July 1766.
30. Marie to Victor, 8 May 1759.
31. See the registration of Daniel Lamothe's testament, Archives Départementales de la Gironde, 2C 189, Contrôle des Grandes Actes, Bureau de Bordeaux, 18 February 1772, p. 85; and Delphin to Alexis, 11 March 1763.
32. See in particular Delphin to Victor and Alexandre, 7 June 1763.
33. Alexis to Victor, 9 March 1759.
34. Marie to Victor, 22 August 1758; 17 February 1759; 8 May 1759.
35. Jules to Victor, 24 October 1761; 6 February 1762.
36. Marie to Victor, 18 August 1764. Victor to Jules, 25 August 1764.
37. Marie to Victor, 18 August 1764.

duties,"[38] but in fact it does appear that Victor's religious fervor had lessened during his years in Paris. Jules seems to have sensed this, creating stress in their relationship.

This situation, however, like other potential conflicts in the relations of the Lamothe siblings, was glossed over. Areas of contestation were contained beneath declarations of affection as the brothers and sisters worked hard to maintain their strong bonds. All clearly recognized, for example, that the division of property could create envy and resentment in the closest of families. Following Daniel's death in 1763, and the reading of the will, the members of the family obviously worried that tensions might arise over the unequal distribution of property. The frequent exhortations of Victor and Alexandre's brothers and sisters in letters to them suggest that they feared discontent over Daniel's arrangements. Over and over, they asserted the importance of preserving the goodwill and amity that the family had always enjoyed. Jules entreated, "Let us work together to conserve the unity that has always reigned in our family," while Marianne wrote, "What greater blessing could our tender father give us, my dear brothers, than to wish for us this peace, this unity, this true concord."[39] Delphin appealed to their better natures, noting that "I know that I need not recommend to you peace, unity & concord, you are too well-born, the sentiments you have demonstrated up to this point are too well-placed, & we all have much reason to congratulate ourselves for our amity."[40]

The hidden tensions in the sibling relations of the Lamothes surfaced for a time during Victor's long stay in Paris where he studied medicine for close to ten years. Victor went to Paris in 1756 to study for his medical examinations, which he planned to take in Montpellier. While the family supported Victor's decision to study in Paris, they clearly did not intend for him to stay for long. They expected him to return to practice medicine in Bordeaux after a few years in Paris, and after obtaining his degrees in Montpellier. Victor, however, enjoyed studying and living in Paris, and for a time, he convinced his family that it would benefit his future career to continue his studies there, beyond the three years originally planned. At that time, Daniel acknowledged, "It is with a certain pain, however, that we face a *séjour* that will separate you from your family for such a long

38. Victor to Jules, 25 August 1764.
39. Jules to Victor and Alexandre, undated 1763. Marianne to Victor and Alexandre, 7 May 1763.
40. Delphin to Victor and Alexandre, 11 March 1763.

time."[41] In 1761, Victor went to Montpellier and received his *doctorat* there, but he returned to Paris within a year. The rest of the family chafed at the high cost of his studies in Paris, but were reluctant to order him back to Bordeaux.

Eventually, it became clear to the family in Bordeaux that it would be extremely difficult for Victor to establish a medical career in Paris, where the practice of medicine was carefully controlled and regulated by the *docteurs-régents* of the University of Paris. As a result, they placed increasing pressure on Victor to give up his dreams of practicing medicine in Paris. It was difficult for Victor to renounce his ambitions for a brilliant career in the capital city, but his family was no longer willing to accept his arguments and finance his stay. Alexis told him brusquely that they all believed that the real reason he wished to stay "is fundamentally because of your excessive attachment to Paris," especially since his opportunities for a successful career looked much better in Bordeaux.[42] The family wanted Victor to return home. Apart from the expense of his stay in Paris, they missed him, and wanted him to return to the bosom of his family. In the end, it was probably this argument, as much as the financial strain, that convinced Victor to renounce his plan to stay in Paris and return to Bordeaux in December 1766.[43]

The family letters reveal the closeness of the Lamothe siblings as a group. However, it is useful to explore in more detail the relations between the two sisters and their brothers. Neither Marie nor Marianne ever married, either due to dislike of the idea of marriage, or a feeling of satisfaction and fulfillment in their roles as sister and daughter. It is likely that family discipline, and a desire to keep the patrimony undivided within the family persuaded the two to choose a lifetime of celibacy, but they seem to have made the choice willingly.[44]

Marie and Marianne modeled themselves on their much-loved mother, devoting themselves to the care of their father and brothers, and to the maintenance of the household. Their apparent contentment with their lives

41. Daniel to Victor, 24 July 1758.
42. Alexis to Victor, undated 1766.
43. I discuss Victor's stay in Paris, and the conflict with his family in "Defining *Etat* in Eighteenth-Century France: The Lamothe Family of Bordeaux," *Journal of Family History* 17, no. 1 (1992): 40–43 and in "Bourgeois Identity in Early Modern France," chap. 5.
44. For a discussion of the factors that may have influenced the decision of Marie and Marianne Lamothe to remain single, see Christine Adams, "A Choice Not to Wed? Unmarried Women in Eighteenth-Century France," *Journal of Social History* 29, no. 4 (Summer 1996): 883–94.

and their choice to remain single challenges the traditionally negative stereotype of the spinster that was already emerging in the eighteenth century, and would become firmly fixed by the nineteenth.[45]

Examination of the practical role that the Lamothe sisters played within their family clarifies why they both chose to remain single, and also illustrates their stabilizing role in household formation. Because of the useful role that they could play in their natal families, unmarried sisters, far from being a burden, were sometimes discouraged from marrying.[46] Marie and Marianne, along with their mother, strove to create a comfortable home environment for the male members of the family. They contributed fully to the "family economy" with their labor and their careful attention to the household budget.[47] Despite the fact that the family, as members of the Bordelais elite, always employed servants, Marie de Sérézac and her daughters were constantly busy. They selected and prepared the family's foods, including the small delicacies that they sent to their brothers Victor and

45. Olwen Hufton, in "Women without Men: Widows and Spinsters in Britain and France in the Eighteenth Century," *Journal of Family History* 9, no. 4 (1984): 356, notes that this distasteful image of the spinster was beginning to take shape already in the literature of the eighteenth century. However, it was in the nineteenth century that this stereotype became firmly set, influenced in part by the perception that the number of unmarried females was growing too rapidly, and constituted a major social problem. See Cécile Dauphin, "Single Women," in *Emerging Feminism from Revolution to World War*, ed. Geneviève Fraisse and Michelle Perrot (1990), vol. 4 of *A History of Women in the West*, gen. eds. Georges Duby and Michelle Perrot (Cambridge: Belknap Press of Harvard University Press), 427–28 and 441–42. See also Steven Mintz, *A Prison of Expectations*, 150; and Priscilla Robertson, *An Experience of Women: Pattern and Change in Nineteenth-Century Europe* (Philadelphia: Temple University Press, 1982), 252.

46. Steven Mintz provides support for this view in an interesting vignette from the life of Catharine Sedgwick. He writes: "The decision to remain unmarried was not fully Catharine's. Significantly, in 1827, when Catharine was thirty-eight and a well-known author, her siblings responded severely to rumors of her possible engagement. Her eldest brother, Theodore, articulated the family's objections to a marriage. His sister's present situation was 'certainly a singularly happy one'; she must not, on light grounds change it. Her brothers and sisters were dependent on her for her wise counsel and moral support and would be unhappy if she changed her marital status" (*Prison of Expectations*, 166).

47. The concept of "family economy," in which the family operates both as a unit of production and consumption, dependent upon the contributions of each member, has most often been discussed in the context of the working poor and farm families, but seems to apply to the Lamothe family as well. See Olwen Hufton, "Women and the Family Economy in Eighteenth-Century France," *French Historical Studies* 9 (1975): 1–22; Louise Tilly, "The Family Wage Economy of a French Textile City: Roubaix, 1872–1906," *Journal of Family History* (Winter 1979): 381–94; Hans Medick, "The Proto-Industrial Family Economy: The Structural Function of Household and Family during the Transition from Peasant Society to Industrial Capitalism," *Social History*, no. 5 (1976): 291–315.

Alexandre in Paris. They knitted stockings and slippers. They sewed the family's sheets, handkerchiefs, *serviettes*, shirts, collars, nightshirts and bonnets, *souliers*, and other articles of clothing.[48] They kept informed of Victor and Alexandre's clothing needs in Paris and mailed the necessary items to them.[49] They did the laundry.[50] They shopped for the family's goods, and searched for the best prices, keeping a close eye on the price of staples.[51]

The important role of the women during the vintage in particular is underscored by the fact that their help was considered essential at the family's country homes during the wine harvest. Marie went to Muscadet in the outskirts of Bordeaux with her eldest brother Delphin, while Marie de Sérézac and Marianne accompanied Alexis, the second son, further afield to Goulards, the country home near Sainte-Foy-la-Grande in the Dordogne. In short, their contributions to the household paralleled those of a wife.

Also like wives, Marie and Marianne were informed and consulted on financial matters, especially those relating to the management of the household, and there is every indication that their opinions were respected[52]— although the decisions of their father, and later their brothers, were considered final. Certainly, Marie considered it her duty to stay informed of the family's financial situation, writing to Victor on one occasion, "For a long time now, I've taken note of our expenses and revenues, I find that one cannot know too much about that subject in order to watch expenses."[53]

In only one instance did a major dispute arise over the management of the family's money, in which the two sisters, along with their mother and brother Jules the priest, opposed their two older brothers. Shortly after Daniel's death, Jules raised objections to several loans at interest that his father had made, and persuaded his mother and sisters, more religious than

48. Marie to Victor, 10 December 1757; 4 May 1758; 6 January 1759; 8 May 1759; 7 September 1762; 16 July 1763. Marianne to Victor, 1 April 1758; 10 March 1764. Delphin to Victor, 19 December 1758; 11 August 1759; 8 June 1764; 29 June 1764. Alexis to Victor, 13 November 1764. Alexandre to Victor, 1766.
49. Marie to Victor, 10 December 1757; 4 May 1758; 6 January 1759; 8 May 1759; 7 September 1762; 16 July 1763. Marianne to Victor, 1 April 1758; 10 March 1764.
50. Marie to Victor, 6 December 1764.
51. Marianne to Victor, 24 March 1761; 23 January 1762. Marie to Victor, 6 December 1764.
52. It is evident that their father and brothers relied upon them to help economize and to persuade their brothers in Paris to spend money wisely. See for example, Marianne to Victor, 20 April 1757. Marie to Victor, 1 December 1756; 24 January 1757; 25 November 1761; and passim.
53. Marie to Victor, 23 February 1762.

his brothers, that the family was obliged to return the money in order to redeem the sin of usury. Delphin and Alexis were clearly irritated by Jules's misgivings, but they wanted to avoid the problems that his objections "could give rise to in the family." They felt the need to persuade their mother and sisters to support their point of view by searching out ecclesiastical opinions conforming to their more liberal ideas on investing money.[54] The matter was apparently negotiated and resolved within the family without an open breach.

Marie and Marianne Lamothe focused their attentions and affections on their brothers as would loving wives. Did their brothers give their sisters the same devotion and care? The sisters were obviously important in the lives of their brothers, but the nature of their roles differed, in much the same way as the role of husbands and wives differed in early modern Europe. For wives, husbands (and children) often occupied the central position in their lives. Women viewed themselves, and constructed their sense of self primarily in relation to their (male) family members.[55] On a more practical level, their work centered on home and family as well.[56] Clearly, this was the case for Marie and Marianne. But the situation was very different for their brothers. All of the male members of the Lamothe family led active professional lives, as well as participating in the intellectual and cultural life of the Bordelais community. Their sense of personal identity extended beyond the family, and encompassed their participation in more public activities.[57] Thus, while the sisters were far from insignificant in the lives of their

54. Delphin and Alexis to Victor, undated 1764.

55. Natalie Zemon Davis analyzes several examples of prominent women whose memoirs focused primarily on male family members, their husbands in particular, and suggests that a woman's sense of identity was very much constructed in relation to her family. See her "Boundaries and the Sense of Self in Sixteenth-Century France," in *Reconstructing Individualism: Autonomy, Individuality and the Self in Western Thought*, ed. Thomas C. Heller et al. (Stanford: Stanford University Press, 1986), 53–63. Scholars of autobiography have made a similar point, noting that "where men stress their individualism in their autobiographies, women define their identity in terms of their relationship with others." See the introduction to Shirley Neuman, ed., *Autobiography and Questions of Gender* (London: F. Cass, 1991), 1–11. For further treatment of gender differences in women's autobiography, see the introduction and essays in Estelle C. Jelinek, ed., *Women's Autobiography: Essays in Criticism* (Bloomington: Indiana University Press, 1980).

56. See Elizabeth Fox-Genovese, "Women and Work," in *French Women and the Age of Enlightenment*, ed. Samia I. Spencer (Bloomington: Indiana University Press, 1984), 111–27; Olwen Hufton, "Women, Work and Family," in *Renaissance and Enlightenment Paradoxes*, ed. Natalie Zemon Davis and Arlette Farge (1993), vol. 3 of *A History of Women in the West*, gen. eds. Georges Duby and Michelle Perrot (Cambridge: Belknap Press of Harvard University Press), 15–45, esp. 29–30 and 38–41.

57. See Adams, "Bourgeois Identity in Early Modern France," for a detailed discussion of the professional and cultural activities of the Lamothe brothers. I argue that these activities, along with family, were crucial in constructing the identity of the brothers.

brothers, they were not the center of their existence—as perhaps most wives were not the center of their husband's existence.

The most important indication that Marie and Marianne filled the role of wife to their brothers lies in the fact that none of the Lamothe brothers chose to marry during the lifetime of their sisters. Delphin, the only child of the family to marry, did not do so until 1772, three years after the death of Marie, and four years after the death of Marianne. This situation clearly elevated the status of Marie and Marianne within the familial household, earning them respect, authority, and a central position in the affections of their brothers that a sister-in-law would have usurped.[58]

For the most part, Marie and Marianne appear to have been happy with their choice to remain unmarried and to stay within the family household. They undoubtedly realized that it would create financial difficulties for the rest of the family if they insisted upon marriage or the convent, and the substantial dowry that would accompany either choice.[59] In return, they were assured of the deep affection of their brothers and parents. This included solicitous attention during their many illnesses and some regard for their desires and opinions.[60]

Still, this constant sublimation of their own desires to those of their family may have created certain stresses and strains that no one openly acknowledged. Both Marie and Marianne suffered from ill health for much of their lives, and died young—Marianne at the age of thirty in 1768, and Marie at the age of forty-two in 1769. Their passionate attachment to their brothers led the two sisters to make heavy demands on the affections of their siblings, and to insist upon constant reassurance of their regard.[61] Their brothers clearly stood in as surrogates for the husbands and children they never had. However, familial love and loyalty kept any tensions firmly in the background.

Within the Lamothe family, relations were comfortable and informal, a welcome respite from the rules governing polite society. Jules discussed a

---

58. Several historians have noted the despair that the marriage of a brother could cause for his unmarried sister, as emotional anguish was compounded by loss of family status and marginalization of the sister's role; see Mintz, *A Prison of Expectations*, 164–65, and Jalland, "Victorian Spinsters," 142–43.

59. In his will, opened upon his death in 1763, Daniel de Lamothe left 10,500 livres to Marie and 10,000 livres to Marianne, along with the furnishings of their rooms, silver place settings, and assorted linens and household items. See Delphin to Victor and Alexandre, 11 March 1763. It was surely to the advantage of the rest of the family that the sisters remained at home, and their portions remained part of the family's assets.

60. For example, Marianne to Victor, undated 1765.

61. Lamothe family letters, passim.

visit home to Victor, noting, "My brothers [are] back and forth in their night bonnets and evening gowns," and Marianne observed in one letter that Alexis was sitting by her side, washing his feet.[62] They merrily seized letters that another sibling had begun to Victor, and filled up the pages with their own news.[63] The brothers and sisters frequently socialized as a group, both at home and at Sainte-Foy.[64] For example, Alexis escorted Marie and Marianne on an expedition to see a giant on display at the Place Royal.[65] In short, they were companions and friends.

A letter from Jules to his brothers in Paris describing the family circle evokes an image of cozy domesticity:

> In the morning, I had the pleasure of dining with the family, we made toast and had chocolate, we laughed, we amused ourselves, then I had a few moments in the company of our good papa, Marianne attacked me for letting her win a few games of cards. Imperceptibly, the morning passed, at dinner, we made the conversation as lively as possible, after dinner, we walked, played cards, walked again, etc. No one slept after supper, because we did so well that we always had something to say. There you have a sample of my days which, as you see, were nearly engrossed by pleasure.[66]

Against this idyllic tableau, the Lamothe siblings squabbled at times, and offered didactic and high-handed advice to each other, but they believed that their admonitions were motivated by the best of intentions and came from the heart. Domestic solidarity was laced by strong emotional bonds.

If we accept that the close relations between brothers and sisters could serve as a model, preparing them for a life of domestic harmony with a loving spouse and children, we must acknowledge that, for the majority of the Lamothe siblings, the model did not serve this purpose. Six of the seven chose not to marry, but instead, remained at Rue Neuve, in the bosom of the family. Why?

Perhaps we must consider that in some cases, the relations between brother and sister could go *beyond* substitution for a spouse—that, rather

62. Jules to Victor, 20 April 1757; Marianne to Victor, 6 February 1758.
63. See for example, Jules and Marie to Victor, 24 July 1760.
64. See Christine Adams, "Bourgeois Identity in Early Modern France," 205–10.
65. Delphin to Victor, 17 December 1757.
66. Jules to Victor and Alexandre, 24 October 1761.

than a love second only to that of the conjugal union, the relations between siblings could be even deeper, and more affective than marital relations. The nineteenth-century Englishwoman Catharine Sedgwick rejected marriage, writing to her brothers that she was "satisfied, by long and delightful experience" that she could "never love any body better than my brothers."[67] Did Marie and Marianne believe as well that they could never love anyone more than their siblings? Did their brothers feel the same way?

Despite the new focus on "companionate marriages" beginning to take root in the eighteenth century, a truly companionate marriage was perhaps difficult to achieve. Although the division of spheres was not so rigid as it would become in a later era,[68] men and women were socialized in very different ways. In an age when the writings of Rousseau underlining the fundamental differences between men and women were becoming more and more popular, it may have been difficult for men and women to learn to live together as friends.[69] Theoretically, brothers and sisters, because of the close and informal relations they were privileged to share, could learn about relations between men and women. The Lamothes, with their routine companionship and casual intimacy, were clearly testing a model of gender relations. They could then bring these lessons to a companionate marriage when the time arrived.

However, this is not what happened in the case of the Lamothes, or rather, it happened only in the case of Delphin, who married at the age of forty-seven—less than three years after the death of his last sister. For

67. Quoted in Steven Mintz, *A Prison of Expectations,* 161; see also 164.

68. Bonnie G. Smith, in *Ladies of the Leisure Class,* esp. part 2, argues that for the bourgeois women of France, the ideology of "separate spheres" developed most fully in the nineteenth century.

69. A nearly contemporary observer, Mary Wollstonecraft, railed against the problems, marital and other, that were created by the separate and very different education and socialization of women and men—a problem that she charged was worsened by Rousseau's popular views on the nature of women; see *A Vindication of the Rights of Woman* (London, 1992; first published 1792). Randolph Trumbach suggests that as the ideal of companionate marriage and closer, more intimate relations between men and women began to take shape in the eighteenth century, some married men consciously tried to limit their intimacy, and thus, degree of vulnerability with their wives by visiting prostitutes; see his "Sex, Gender and Sexual Identity in Modern Culture: Male Sodomy and Female Prostitution in Enlightenment London," in *Forbidden History: The State, Society, and the Regulation of Sexuality in Modern Europe,* ed. John C. Fout (Chicago: University of Chicago Press, 1992), 89–106, esp. 105–6. In a different context, that of eighteenth-century Chesapeake plantation society, Daniel Blake Smith notes that the radically different socialization of boys and girls made it increasingly difficult for men and women to communicate; see his *Inside the Great House: Planter Family Life in Eighteenth-Century Chesapeake Society* (Ithaca: Cornell University Press, 1980), chap. 4.

Delphin, this idealized model seems to have worked. His marriage to Marie-Elisabeth de Brulz in 1772 was socially advantageous.[70] Elisabeth, daughter of an *écuyer*, brought as her dowry the noble property of Lyde, along with the sum of 6000 livres.[71] But while Elisabeth's suitability undoubtedly played a role in Delphin's desire to contract their marriage, it is unlikely that economic and social factors were the sole considerations. With his father dead, and as de facto head of the household, Delphin was able to choose his wife freely. It would seem that he selected a woman for whom he had a great deal of affection. Elisabeth moved into the Lamothe family home on Rue Neuve following her marriage, and established a loving relationship with both her husband and brothers-in-law, assuming the role previously filled by the sisters. The letters that Delphin wrote to his wife, as well as his frequent references to her in letters to his brother suggest a happy and tender relationship.[72]

But the other children of the Lamothe family did not marry. Their close and affectionate family life apparently did not prepare them for marriage, and the transfer of their affections to a new conjugal family. The fact that only one member of this family married is highly unusual, for even in the well-disciplined families of the Toulousan nobility and the Montauban elite, at least one daughter usually married, in addition to one son, and among the barristers of Toulouse, most sons, and the majority of daughters married and were generously dowered.[73] It testifies to a force beyond family interest and discipline, and suggests that the consuming and passionate devotion of the brothers and sisters to their parents and one another satisfied their emotional needs, and attenuated their desire for a wife or husband. This focus of affection on the natal family was explicitly encouraged by the patriarch Daniel, who wrote to his son Victor, "We do not doubt that our relatives [are] filled with affection for you . . . but you must give us preference."[74] First loyalties were to the nuclear family.

70. Marie Elisabeth de Brulz was daughter of the *écuyer* François-Marie de Brulz, and niece and goddaughter of André Pierre de Brulz, seigneur of the *maison de Lyde* and *doyen* of the *conseillers* of the Cour des Aides in Bordeaux.

71. Archives Départementales de la Gironde 3E 21696, Contrat de Mariage, Delphin de Lamothe and Marie-Elisabeth de Brulz, 21 June 1772.

72. See the Lamothe family letters of 1773, and those from Delphin to Elisabeth de Brulz written in 1780.

73. Forster, *The Nobility of Toulouse*, 125–36; Darrow, *Revolution in the House*, 105–10; Lenard Berlanstein, *The Barristers of Toulouse in the Eighteenth Century (1740–1793)* (Baltimore: Johns Hopkins University Press, 1975), 65.

74. Daniel to Victor, 24 July 1758. This emphasis on the primacy of the nuclear family, to the exclusion of others, fits nicely with Ariès's model of the modern family that emerged by the eighteenth century; *Centuries of Childhood*, esp. 398–404.

In fact, some members of the Lamothe family, rather than learning the joys of conjugal love from the happy family life on Rue Neuve, internalized extreme negative ideas on marriage. In his last will and testament signed on 3 September 1786, Alexis Lamothe wrote,

> By God's grace, I did not marry: circumstances were opposed to it in my youth, and as I grew older, [and] I was more in control of my own satisfaction, I congratulated myself for having no real inclination for the state of matrimony. The experiences of others that I saw (without speaking ill of it) sufficed to put me off the idea. The bitterness and the many vexations of the married state are rarely compensated by the sweetness and the pleasure that it brings: luckily not everyone feels the same way.[75]

He had expressed his distaste of the married state even more forcefully in an earlier letter to Victor:

> If you only knew how much misery accompanies marriage! the enormous expenses it exposes you to, the time that the care of a household, a wife, children, steals from you, you would not think about it without turning pale.[76]

In light of this repugnance for marriage expressed by Alexis, and apparently shared by Victor,[77] their "substitute" spouses seemed more desirable than real ones. They, unlike their brother Delphin, found it impossible to contemplate replacing their sisters, even after their deaths—especially since a sister-in-law appeared to fill the void left by their sisters. With the Lamothe family, we seem to have a case of intense emotional investment in the family of origin, an investment that made it difficult for the siblings to contemplate marriage, and subsequently, to bring an outsider into the happy family unit. Consciously or unconsciously, the Lamothe siblings had weighed the costs and benefits of marriage, and had evidently determined

75. Archives Départementales de la Gironde 3E 21732, Testament, Alexis de Lamothe, opened 25 March 1790.

76. Alexis to Victor, 22 December 1761.

77. In his will, Alexis commented on the fact that Victor showed no desire for marriage. Archives Départementales de la Gironde 3E 21732, Testament, Alexis de Lamothe, opened 25 March 1790.

that the potential costs outweighed the possible benefits.[78] Furthermore, the strong bonds of the family, and its tendency to operate as a unit in both personal and fiscal matters, restricted the ability of any one member to act independently, even (or perhaps especially) in matters of the heart. The "good of the family" took precedence over the desires of any one individual, and clearly limited individual autonomy.

The example of the Lamothe siblings, while not "typical," forces us to reexamine traditional ideas about the evolution of family life and marital relations. While historians have presented compelling evidence that the "companionate model" of marriage was fast gaining adherents by the eighteenth century, they have paid less attention to the problems that this new model may have posed for young men and women in its nascent stages. Close sibling relations offered an opportunity for men and women to prepare themselves for affectionate relations with a spouse, especially during this crucial period of transition between the old and new styles of marriage. The case of the Lamothes suggests that the model did not always work as planned. Affection and loyalty within their family were so intense that apparently the children were not educated for a life outside the natal family. Perhaps in this case the passionate attachment of sister and brother had gone too far.[79]

78. Alan MacFarlane discusses the explicit "cost-benefit" analysis that went into Charles Darwin's decision to marry, and goes on to note that in a society where celibacy was an option, marriage "was something to be chosen, a conscious decision which could be made early or put off, and there were costs and benefits in any solution"; *Marriage and Love in England: Modes of Reproduction, 1300–1840* (Oxford: Basil Blackwell, 1986), 3–11. I thank Gary Kates for this reference.

79. I thank Toby Ditz for her very helpful comments on an earlier paper concerning the Lamothe sisters, which helped me to formulate some of these ideas concerning the relations of the Lamothe siblings.

Part II

The Political Culture of Eighteenth-Century France

4

Crimes of Opinion

Policing the Public
in Eighteenth-Century Paris

Lisa Jane Graham

More than two decades ago, Richard Cobb drew attention to the fact that
police archives provide abundant information on topics besides crime. Cobb
suggested that the police offer the most reliable guide to the ordinary and
routine elements of popular life in eighteenth-century France because "who
more than a *commissaire* would have heard so much of the spoken thoughts
and insults of the common people?"[1] Several historians heeded Cobb's call
and used police records to shed light on a stratum of beliefs and attitudes
normally hidden from the historian's view.[2] Perhaps no one has been so

*I thank Jack Censer, William M. Kuhn, and Jeffrey S. Ravel for their comments on earlier
versions of this article.
   1. Richard Cobb, *The Police and the People: French Popular Protest, 1789–1820* (London:
Oxford University Press, 1970), 44.
   2. In addition to Cobb's own work, prominent examples of this type of history would
include: Thomas Brennan, *Public Drinking and Popular Culture in Eighteenth-Century Paris*
(Princeton: Princeton University Press, 1988); David Garrioch, *Neighborhood and Commu-*

instrumental in shaping the directions of this new research as Arlette Farge, who has meticulously reconstructed the daily lives, hopes, and expectations of working Parisians. Farge's most recent book, *Subversive Words*, marks the first serious attempt by any scholar to analyze the emergence of public opinion from the ground up rather than from the top down.[3] It is a rich and illuminating work that will provoke debates in the years to come. Historians will no longer be able to accept Jürgen Habermas's dismissal of "the plebian public sphere as a varient that . . . was suppressed in the historical process."[4]

Recent work on the political culture of Old Regime France has consciously framed itself in terms of the argument presented by Jürgen Habermas in *The Structural Transformation of the Public Sphere*. Habermas insists that the distinguishing feature of eighteenth-century French political life was the emergence of a bourgeois public sphere where "private people come together as a public" and "make public use of their reason" (26 and 55–56). Accordingly, scholars have turned their attention to the sites identified by Habermas as constituting this public sphere such as salons, reading clubs, musical concerts, Masonic lodges, and scientific academies.[5] By restricting our focus to Habermas's narrowly defined public sphere, however, we have neglected the majority of the French public.[6] Until Farge's *Subver-*

nity in Paris, 1740–1790 (Cambridge: Cambridge University Press, 1986); Jeffrey Kaplow, *The Names of Kings* (New York: Basic Books, 1972); and Dale Van Kley, *The Damiens Affair and the Unraveling of the Old Regime, 1750–1770* (Princeton: Princeton University Press, 1984). Robert Darnton has relied on police archives to reconstruct the underground publishing world of the Enlightenment, see *The Literary Underground of the Old Regime* (Cambridge: Harvard University Press, 1982) and most recently, *The Forbidden Best-Sellers of Pre-Revolutionary France* (New York: Norton, 1995) and *The Corpus of Clandestine Literature in France, 1769–1789* (New York: Norton, 1995).

   3. Arlette Farge, *Fragile Lives: Violence, Power, and Solidarity in Eighteenth-Century Paris*, trans. Carol Shelton (Cambridge: Harvard University Press, 1993) and *Subversive Words: Public Opinion in Eighteenth-Century France*, trans. Rosemary Morris (University Park: Pennsylvania State University Press, 1994).

   4. Jürgen Habermas, *The Structural Transformation of the Public Sphere*, trans. Thomas Burger (Cambridge: MIT Press, 1989), xviii.

   5. The bibliography here is enormous but Roger Chartier offers a summary in *The Cultural Origins of the French Revolution*, trans. Lydia G. Cochrane (Durham: Duke University Press, 1991), 20–38. Recent efforts to pursue the implications of Habermas's argument include Dena Goodman, *The Republic of Letters: A Cultural History of the French Enlightenment* (Ithaca: Cornell University Press, 1994); James H. Johnson, *Listening in Paris: A Cultural History* (Berkeley and Los Angeles: University of California Press, 1994); and Sarah Maza, *Private Lives and Public Affairs: The Causes Célèbres of Prerevolutionary France* (Berkeley and Los Angeles: University of California Press, 1993).

   6. In a recent review article, Dale Van Kley had drawn attention to the fact that historians inspired by Habermas have ignored his Marxism; see "In Search of Eighteenth-Century Parisian Public Opinion," *French Historical Studies* 19 (Spring 1995): 215–26. Feminist historians

sive Words, scholars have tended to ignore the political contributions of individuals who existed outside of Habermas's public. This oversight becomes apparent when we recall that the crown invested more time, money, and effort in policing the public of the streets, the cafés, and the markets than it did on the salons or the academies. Arguably, if the monarchy was more concerned with this broadly defined public, then we, as historians, should be too.

As Cobb and Farge have demonstrated, this problem is best pursued by trusting the police to guide us through the streets of eighteenth-century Paris. Like Farge, I am convinced that in order to understand the evolution of political life under the Old Regime, we must cast our gaze beyond the perspective of the elites. Throughout the eighteenth century, the royal government found itself engaged in dialogues with various segments of the French populace, among whom magistrates and ministers were the most articulate participants. Police documents offer the clearest record of encounters between the monarchy and its more humble constituents. As Farge has emphasized, the existence of these documents lays bare a fundamental contradiction at the heart of the Old Regime. On the one hand, the crown refused to recognize the existence or legitimacy of public opinion within the polity. On the other, it made the policing of this nonexistent popular opinion a priority of its officials and thereby tacitly acknowledged what was being officially denied (3–4). Although our work shares this initial premise, Farge and I differ somewhat in what we make of it, especially in our understanding of the police.

Farge views the repressive activities of the police as part of a larger process of state-building in early modern France. Inspired by the work of Michel Foucault, with whom she collaborated on a study of the *lettres de cachet,* Farge understands the monitoring and gathering of information by the police as an integral part of a growing bureaucracy seeking to extend its control over the lives of ordinary individuals. In the tracking of public utterances and writings, Farge sees a calculated response on the part of the crown and its agents to discipline its subjects. For her, the police and the people meet on hostile and unequal ground; therefore, the documents must be searched for what they conceal, for what remains unsaid *(indicible)* before the authorities.

have criticized Habermas for ignoring the role of women in the construction of this bourgeois public sphere. A synthesis of these arguments is provided by Dena Goodman, *Republic of Letters,* 53–89.

By contrast, I am inclined to view the police as equal parts enlightened reformers and agents of repression. As David Garrioch has demonstrated, the police were as much products of the Enlightenment as they were opponents of it. Their reports and their proposals are filled with the humanitarian and rational language of the philosophes. Their curiosity and their meticulous recordkeeping were hallmarks of the inquisitive age in which they lived.[7] From this perspective, the policing of *mauvais discours* appears an ad hoc, generally ineffective response to a situation that the police were the first to admit was beyond their control. For every individual caught and used to set an example, a hundred slipped through their net. Police reports convey official exasperation, frustration, and anxiety more than the radiant confidence of a omnipotent state machine.

This interpretation of the police influences my reading of their archives. To begin, I emphasize the extent to which the police and the people were mutually dependent in their struggle for public order and control of the streets. The police were as concerned about popular responses as they were about royal direction. Second, the archives abound with instances of individuals manipulating police officers with imaginary plots and calumnious accusations. This evidence confirms the arguments of Natalie Davis and Carlo Ginzburg that determined individuals find room to maneuver amid enormous political and social constraint.[8] Finally, my account allows space for the persistence of loyalty to the king in the midst of subversive behavior. The language of fidelity was inextricably bound up with expressions of resistance in Old Regime France.

My openness to both sides of the dialogue, the police and the policed, yields more definitive results than those of Farge, because it allows me to identify specific points of disagreement between the police and the populace. Farge refuses to draw decisive conclusions; she explicitly wants to avoid a linear or teleological narrative of public opinion in eighteenth-century France. Where Farge emphasizes multiplicity and mutability of

7. David Garrioch, "The Police of Paris as Enlightened Social Reformers" *Eighteenth-Century Life* 16 (February 1992): 43–59. Jacques Revel makes a similar point in his discussion of the discovery of popular culture in the eighteenth century; see "Forms of Expertise: Intellectuals and 'Popular' Culture in France (1650–1800)," in *Understanding Popular Culture: Europe from the Middle Ages to the Nineteenth Century*, ed. Steven L. Kaplan (New York: Mouton, 1984), 255–73.

8. For example, see Natalie Zemon Davis, *Fiction in the Archives: Pardon Tales and Their Tellers in Sixteenth-Century France* (Stanford: Stanford University Press, 1987) and Carlo Ginzburg, *The Cheese and the Worms: The Cosmos of a Sixteenth-Century Miller*, trans. John and Anne Tedeschi (Baltimore: Johns Hopkins University Press, 1980).

opinion, I search for rhetorical patterns and persistent concerns. Thus, Farge creates a pastiche of cases while I concentrate on a select few in order to explore the interaction between individual grievances and the wider political context. The two styles yield different results, both of which are historically useful. Farge's work is evocative in its breadth and rich detail; mine offers a synthetic analysis that aims for depth.

The fulcrum on which this essay turns is the comparative analysis of a single word: public. The use of this term by the police and the people reveal conflicting definitions of the French polity and the appropriate role of its unprivileged members. My goal here is threefold. First, to examine what the police said and thought about the populace they were charged with monitoring and how these assumptions shaped their tasks. Second, to listen to how the people challenged official assumptions concerning their intellectual capabilities and their political acumen. Third, to offer a case study as an example of how these issues were discussed and resolved. The documents suggest that police officials were hindered in their pursuit of crime by their efforts to map the Old Regime's social hierarchy onto a theory of knowledge and its availability. In the face of mounting evidence to the contrary, the police insisted that knowledge was and should remain the reserve of a privileged few. This last point suggests that by the middle of the eighteenth century, the balance of power between the police and the people was increasingly precarious.

The connection between the police and the public would have made perfect sense to officials of the Old Regime. Within the political vocabulary of French absolutism, the two words were implicitly linked in the crown's struggle to maintain order and ensure "le bien public."[9] It is useful to recall that policing encompassed more than criminal repression in eighteenth-century Paris. In its broadest sense, the verb *police* entailed the maintenance of public order in a burgeoning metropolis and covered all aspects of urban life.[10] For royal officials living in the Age of Enlightenment, the existence

9. Nicolas Delamare, *Traité de la police* (Paris: Michel Brunet, 1705–19), vol. 1, "Lettre au Roy."

10. David Garrioch emphasizes this "enlightened" aspect of Old Regime policing in "The Police of Paris as Enlightened Social Reformers." The bibliography on the police in early modern France is enormous. A good place to start is Marc de Chassaigne, *La Lieutenance General de Police de Paris* (Geneva: Slatkine-Megariotis Reprints, 1975) and Alan Williams, *The Police of Paris, 1718–1789* (Baton Rouge: Louisiana State University Press, 1979). The first chapter of Steven L. Kaplan's analysis of the regulation of the grain trade, *Bread, Politics, and Political Economy in the Reign of Louis XV* (The Hague: M. Nijhoff, 1976) is extremely helpful. So too are his articles: "Notes sur les commissaires de police à Paris au XVIIIe siècle," *Revue d'histoire moderne et contemporaine* 28 (1981): 669–86 and "Reflexions sur la police du

of an extensive police force was a source of pride. Like politeness, policing was a mark of historical progress and cultural advancement. It distinguished civilized societies from primitive or barbaric ones, which lacked such institutions.[11] Yet even a well-policed society experienced demographic pressures, food shortages, and sporadic revolts. Thus, underlying the confidence in police lurked a sense of anxiety concerning the potential for disorder.

This last point is illustrated by the crown's efforts to police all aspects of public life. Royal officials monitored public spaces such as the arcades and gardens of the Palais-Royal as well as public discussions held in cafés and taverns. The police identified these sites with criminal activities ranging from prostitution and robbery to the clandestine trade in seditious literature. By the eighteenth century, the term *public* designated persons, places, and practices that required policing.

This essay marks a preliminary effort to delineate the contours of this other public sphere, where royal subjects were arrested for claiming knowledge that, according to the police, they had no business having. It is based on the files of individuals arrested for crimes of opinion known as *mauvais discours*. These included seditious speech, subversive literature, and conspiracy plots against the monarchy. The cases were treated very seriously because they all involved a verbal misuse or abuse of the king's person. Whether explicitly threatened or implicitly mocked, Louis XV was at the center of each dossier. Although police documents are not impartial records, produced by and for agents of royal authority, they are a unique resource. They capture the minutiae of daily life and the voice of ordinary men and women who do not always cower in the face of authority. Consequently, these criminal records reveal the extent to which members of the Third Estate made use of political information to formulate opinions, both favorable and critical of the monarchy. They allow us to chart the emergence of public opinion as a legitimate participant in the French polity.[12]

---

travail, 1700–1815," *Revue Historique* 261 (1979): 17–77. Also see Erica-Marie Benabou, *La Prostitution des moeurs au XVIIIe siècle* (Paris: Librairie Academique Perrin, 1987).

11. This point is briefly addressed by Daniel Gordon in his "Philosophy, Sociology and Gender in the Enlightenment Conception of Public Opinion," *French Historical Studies* 17 (Fall 1992): 882–911 and his *Citizens without Sovereignty: Equality and Sociability in French Thought, 1670–1789* (Princeton: Princeton University Press, 1994), 9–24.

12. I borrow the idea of a tribunal from Sarah Maza, "Le Tribunal de la nation: Les Mémoires judiciaires et l'opinion publique à la fin de l'ancien regime," *Annales E. S. C.* (January–February 1987): 73–90.

The Police versus the Public

Let us begin by examining the connotations of the word *public* within the
critical vocabulary of the Old Regime. The term shaped assessments of
criminal behavior because public utterances encouraged the spread of perni-
cious ideas. The maintenance of social order rested on the police's ability
to punish individuals who threatened royal authority, whether physically
or verbally. If such crimes went unpunished, the police risked losing credibility in the eyes of the populace. Moreover, leniency or negligence would
encourage the committing of similar offenses in the future.

In their internal correspondence, police officials frequently used the word
public to stress the gravity of an incident or utterance. In these instances,
the adjective *public* identified the site of a crime, while simultaneously establishing the presence of witnesses. Thus, when an individual was observed
criticizing the king or his government in public places, the police moved
quickly to arrest the offender. This last point had a direct impact on official
reactions to the case of Pierre Liebert. Liebert was a thirty-six-year-old
tobacconist who was prone to irreverent remarks when he drank too much
wine. He was arrested on 31 October 1757 after several witnesses had
testified that

> Liebert, in cabarets and other public places, speaks of the king with
> the greatest insolence, despite the protests and salutary warnings that
> are made to prevent him. If this unruly public behavior remains
> unpunished, it will have a bad effect; that is why I think it necessary
> for Liebert to be sent to Bicêtre by royal decree.[13]

Inspector D'Hémery employed the word *public* twice to emphasize the
magnitude of Liebert's crime. First, he used it to locate the incident spatially
and culturally and second, to insist upon the potential impact of the crime.

D'Hémery's reference to "cabarets and other public places" would have
conjured up a specific social milieu for his colleagues. Cramped living quar-
ters drove working Parisians into the streets in search of space and recre-
ation.[14] The expression "public places" designated sites where members of

13. Archives de la Bastille (hereafter AB) 11967, f. 141. Memorandum from Inspector
D'Hémery to Secretary of State Saint Florentin dated 24 October 1757.

14. Several books offer detailed analysis of daily life in eighteenth-century Paris. See Brennan, *Public Drinking and Popular Culture;* Farge, *Fragile Lives,* and *Le cours ordinaire des
choses dans la cité du XVIIIe siècle* (Paris: Seuil, 1994); Garrioch, *Neighborhood and Commu-*

the laboring populace gathered to relax and exchange news. Woven into the fabric of urban life, these included cafés and taverns, parks and gardens, markets and theaters. They fulfilled a similar role for the laboring populace as the salons and reading clubs did for the bourgeois public identified by Habermas. From the police perspective, however, the street was a more problematic public: it was, by definition, unregulated, porous, and heterogeneous. There was a consensus among police officials that both the individuals and the activities identified with such places required careful monitoring.[15] In addition, official concern was heightened by the potentially large audiences such venues provided for disorderly conduct or utterances.

In his report on Liebert, D'Hémery's argument hinged on the phrase, "if this unruly behavior remains unpunished." The king had to respond with a public display of force because he had been publicly attacked by Liebert. D'Hémery implied that the police would be discredited if Liebert went unrebuked because too many people had witnessed Liebert's offensive behavior. Thus, Liebert "was arrested to set an example and also to restrain the populace."[16] This remark reveals the extent to which the success of law enforcement depended upon the police's ability to legitimate their role in the public eye. This concern was an important criterion in determining official assessments of crime and punishment. In Liebert's case, an arrest would signal royal disapproval and effectively deter anybody from imitating such behavior in the future.[17]

Official fears of public places and utterances can only be understood within the framework of the Old Regime's criminal *mentalité*. Police officers viewed a *mauvais discours* like a contagious disease. They saw themselves as doctors with a moral obligation to protect the body social from

---

nity in Paris 1740–1790; and Daniel Roche, *The People of Paris: An Essay in Popular Culture in the Eighteenth Century,* trans. Marie Evans and Gwynne Lewis (Berkeley and Los Angeles: University of California Press, 1987).

15. Two studies address this concern for different sites, see Benabou, *La prostitution et la police des moeurs au XVIIIe siècle;* and Jeffrey S. Ravel, "The Police and the Parterre: Cultural Politics in the Paris Public Theater, 1680–1789" (Ph.D. diss., University of California at Berkeley, 1991).

16. AB 11967, f. 119. Phelypeaux's (secretary for D'Argenson) summary of the case.

17. This motive of arresting someone because of its public impact emerges in the case of Pidansat de Mairobert. Mairobert was arrested in July 1749 for reciting verses that mocked Louis XV and Madame de Pompadour. On 1 July 1749, the chevalier de Mouchy who was observing Mairobert remarked in his report: "Mairobert does not seem to me to be a man of importance but he is so widely known in public places, that the example [of his arrest] will be known," AB 11683, f. 55.

ideological infection. The germs in question were subversive ideas and unsolicited opinions. Members of the Third Estate were particularly susceptible because they supposedly lacked the education and critical judgment necessary for effective resistance. Individuals with unrestrained tongues, such as Liebert, had to be promptly removed in order to minimize the risk of infection.

The metaphor of disease shaped official attitudes toward the task of policing Old Regime Paris. It also clarifies why relatively harmless disgruntled subjects were periodically treated with severity. Such views were apparent in official responses to the case of Valérie de Brulz du Tilleul, the daughter of a wigmaker. Arrested in 1761 for denouncing a plot to kill Louis XV, Madame du Tilleul failed to provide any proof to substantiate her allegations. Once the police verified that Du Tilleul was lying, they hesitated before setting her free. Inspector D'Hémery suggested that she be released from prison but exiled from the realm as a precaution: "this woman is dangerous and garrulous, it would be inconvenient to leave her in France even if she were confined in an asylum because of her wicked tongue which would make an impression on evil or weak minds."[18] D'Hémery's recommendation convinced his superiors and Du Tilleul was banished from France. Du Tilleul was relatively fortunate; others in her situation were often locked away indefinitely.

The police believed that individuals who lacked formal education were more impressionable than their intellectual superiors. As in D'Hémery's report on Du Tilleul, police officers repeatedly used the phrase "faire impression" to describe the process whereby dangerous ideas embedded themselves in weak minds. The expression, borrowed from the technical vocabulary of the printing industry, conjures up the image of pressing words onto a blank page. Under such circumstances, therefore, it was imperative to minimize the risk of exposure. The danger of words had been legally recognized more than a century earlier when Cardin Le Bret, under Richelieu's aegis, had expanded the definition of *lèse-majesté* to include verbal and written criticism of the king's person.[19] Words had become more threatening than daggers in the ensuing century with the rise of literacy and the rapid expansion of printing. Official fears regarding *mauvais discours* were dramatically confirmed in 1757 when a domestic servant named Robert

18. AB 12139, Memorandum from Inspector D'Hémery to Secretary of State Saint Florentin, dated 2 May 1762.

19. William F. Church discusses Le Bret's treatise *De la Souveraineté du Roi* in *Richelieu and Reason of State* (Princeton: Princeton University Press, 1972), 272–76.

François Damiens stabbed Louis XV. For the police, Damiens was evidence of the ineluctable connection among a weak mind, public information, and crime. Moreover, Damiens's success in executing his crime raised serious doubts about the police and their competency. As a result, there was a crackdown on *mauvais discours* in the aftermath of the assassination attempt. Damiens's horrific execution was both punishment for regicide and an official display of force after having been caught offguard.[20]

Thus, police officials used the word *public* in two explicit ways. First, it was an adjective designating a set of places frequented by commoners where opinions and ideas were freely exchanged. Second, as in the case of Liebert, the notion of "publicness" was used to determine the risk factor of an act or utterance. It distinguished private instances of delinquency from those enacted in front of witnesses. Consequently, it influenced official decisions regarding criminal procedure and punishment. Its exclusively pejorative connotations were linked to the police's understanding of their social task. The disease metaphor helps explain the harsh reactions to offenses such as the unguarded remarks of a tongue loosened by wine. Yet, the disease analogy also draws attention to an acute sense of vulnerability on the part of the police vis-à-vis the populace. It reflects underlying concerns about the crown's ability to maintain social order in the middle of the eighteenth century. The various criteria that crystallized in the word *public* reveal the degree to which the police and the public were mutually dependent.

Public places required policing and public crimes demanded immediate punishment. Yet the word appeared on both sides of the dialogue between the police and the people. Where the public was a source of anxiety for the police, it became a source of power for the people. In the hands of royal subjects, the public would assume a more aggressive role as the purveyor of information. Despite the elaborate censorship laws, literacy was rising and the market in unofficial literature was flourishing by the middle of the century. The police were unable to stem the tide of seditious literature, which ranged from philosophical treatises and political tracts to pornographic *libelles*.[21] Thus, Louis XV's subjects had access to more information than those of his predecessors. Within this context, the public became an

20. For a discussion of the Damiens affair, see Van Kley, *Damiens Affair;* and Pierre Rétat, ed., *L'Attentat de Damiens: Discours sur l'événement au XVIIIème siècle* (Lyon: Presses Universitaires de Lyon, 1979). Farge analyzes the impact of the Damiens affair on the Parisian police (*Subversive Words,* 161–75).

21. See Chartier, *Cultural Origins of the French Revolution;* and Darnton, *Forbidden Best-Sellers of Pre-Revolutionary France* and *Literary Underground of the Old Regime.*

acknowledged source of rumors, news, and opinions regarding current affairs.

The Politics of Information

In order to complete this analysis of the word *public* we must now consider the ways in which members of the French populace used the term in their encounters with the royal police. In the mouths of Louis XV's subjects, the public was transformed from a witness into an agent. In their efforts to excuse and justify their misdemeanors, French men and women referred to the public as a legitimate source of information and approval. These rhetorical strategies helped validate popular demands for access to information and the right to formulate political opinions.[22] This reliance on the public by criminal offenders marked an important shift from the public as audience to the public as tribunal. Traditionally, the monarchy had summoned the public to witness displays of royal authority in the form of ceremonies, processions, and executions.[23] By the middle of the eighteenth century, the crown's spectators became independent actors who often refused to adhere to the prescribed roles of the official script.[24]

To begin, when the accused identified the public as a source of information, they were subtly shifting partial responsibility for their crimes back onto the police. Individuals summoned for questioning frequently asserted that they could not be held responsible for repeating something they had read or overheard in the streets. As the pro-Jesuit pamphleteer, Jean Louis Langlois asserted in a justificatory letter he wrote from the Bastille in 1768, "I thought it was permissible to discuss things that were circulating freely in public print."[25] Langlois was explicit in describing the itinerary of information that ended up in his pamphlets: "when he did not have work to do, he frequently went over to the palace [Palais-Royal] where he heard people

22. Farge identifies "an ever-growing conviction that people had the right to know and to judge" in the eighteenth century (*Subversive Words*, 36).
23. See Farge, *Fragile Lives*, esp. 169–225; and Michèle Fogel, *Les Cérémonies de l'information dans la France du XVIème au milieu du XVIIIème siècle* (Paris: Fayard, 1989).
24. This notion of an official script is borrowed from James Scott, *Domination and the Arts of Resistance: Hidden Transcripts* (New Haven: Yale University Press, 1990).
25. AB 12264, f. 62. Letter from Jean Louis Langlois dated 7 August 1768 written from the Bastille.

he did not know discussing current affairs and on the subjects of which appeared parlementary *arrets* and he returned home with his head full of all this material . . . and started writing down what his imagination suggested."[26] Langlois insisted that he could not be punished for reading a text if the police had failed to suppress it. By recognizing the plausibility of arguments such as Langlois's, royal officials acknowledged their limitations as agents of censorship and constraint. This process is clarified if we look more closely at the example of Fidel Amable Chauveau.

Chauveau was a young shopkeeper's assistant who had grown up in Picardy. In 1741, at age sixteen, Chauveau went to Paris in search of work. Since moving to the metropolis, he had relied on letters to keep in touch with his friends and family back home. On 3 January 1757, Chauveau decided to send his uncle greetings for the new year. His uncle, Sieur Sabinet, was the canon of the College of Saint-Furey in Peronne. In closing his missive, Chauveau included the following lines: "I will inform you as a piece of news that the king and his parlement are embroiled in protracted disputes, in a short while you will hear of something terrible that will take you by surprise I cannot say anything more for the moment."[27] Chauveau was referring to the ongoing struggle between the king and his law courts concerning the controversy over the refusal of sacraments to Jansenists.[28] Rumors were circulating in late December 1756 that Louis XV intended to exile the unruly magistrates if they continued to oppose his will. Unfortunately, Chauveau's allusion coincided with Damiens's attempt to stab Louis XV—two days after Chauveau sent his letter. Sieur Sabinet took the letter to the police and Chauveau was immediately arrested as a suspected accomplice of the regicide.

When questioned about his cryptic allusion, Chauveau insisted that "he had meant by his reference to a terrible thing that the suppression of the Parlement would cause a revolution in the kingdom and that he never thought nor was aware that there could be a villain who would dare to make an attempt on the life of His Majesty."[29] Commissioner Rochebrune

26. AB 12264, fols. 36–37. Interrogation of Langlois by Commissioner Rochebrune at the Bastille on 6 November 1765.

27. AB 11979, f. 80. Fidel Amable Chauveau to Sieur Sabinet, Chanoine de la Collegial de Saint Furey à Peronne, 3 January 1757.

28. For a more detailed account of these disputes, see Jean Egret, *Louis XV et l'opposition parlementaire, 1715–1774* (Paris: Armand Colin, 1970); Jeffrey Merrick, *The Desacralization of the French Monarchy in the Eighteenth Century* (Baton Rouge: Louisiana State University Press, 1990); and Van Kley, *Damiens Affair.*

29. AB 11979, f. 98. Interrogation of Chauveau by Commissioner Rochebrune on 14 January 1757.

was initially unswayed by Chauveau's excuse. He was troubled by the tenor of Chauveau's letter because "if he [Chauveau] had not known of some terrible event that was going to happen, he would not have written in such an affirmative tone as he had" (f.98). Chauveau explained that the king's decision to arrest several magistrates last December

> had prompted different rumors among members of the public that the Parlement had to be suppressed . . . that he had heard as much from 20 people whose names now escape him; that the accused had written according to the crazy ideas of the public [*suivant les idées folles du public*] and that the tenor of the letter would not be detrimental to him if it had been written after the fifth of the present month. (f.98)

Thus, Chauveau claimed that he had merely related news to his uncle that was already circulating in the streets of Paris.

Five months later, after the trial and execution of Damiens, the police released Chauveau from prison. Their decision reflected the calmer political climate as well as their inability to substantiate the case with additional evidence. In his final report on the case, Secretary of State D'Argenson conceded that "this young man had no knowledge whatsoever of Damiens, and that in his letter he had only been referring to the troubles with the Parlement, believing that it would be exiled by the king, as the rumor was then circulating at the time."[30] Ultimately, the police could not deny the plausibility of Chauveau's explanation within the political context of late 1756. In releasing Chauveau, the police tacitly acknowledged their inability to control public access to and use of political information.

The most important aspect of Chauveau's case is that it provides an example of how an individual could shift responsibility for a suspicious act onto an omniscient public as part of a credible defensive strategy. His success in justifying his actions before the police rendered more likely the possibility of this strategy being used in the future.

The existence of the public as a source of ideas, rumors, and opinions allowed French subjects to challenge prevailing assumptions about the limited mental capacity of commoners. In several instances, individuals who appeared before the police claimed full responsibility for their actions, even

30. AB 11953, f. 404. Memorandum of 12 June 1757 signed by Phelypeau, secretary for D'Argenson.

when their personal liberty was at stake. They were both proud and defiant in their assertions. This burgeoning self-confidence is especially vivid in the case of Marie-Magdeleine Bonafon. Bonafon was a chambermaid at Versailles who was arrested in 1745 for writing a *roman à clef* entitled *Tanastès*.[31] *Tanastès* satirized Louis XV's illness at Metz in 1744 as well as his relationship with his notoriously unpopular mistress, Madame de Châteauroux. From a police perspective, the novel was brimming with allusions to sensitive political issues and disrespect for the king and members of the court.

Although Bonafon readily admitted to being the author of the offensive text, Lieutenant General of Police Feydeau de Marville refused to believe that she had written *Tanastès* unassisted. He asserted that "there are certain facts in this work of which she could not naturally have been aware given her station in life."[32] Marville was convinced that as a domestic servant, Bonafon lacked the knowledge and education necessary to write such an incisive satire. He pressed her "to identify the *mémoires* she had relied on in writing *Tanastès* and the person who had provided them to her" (f. 80). Despite Marville's persistence, Bonafon was adamant "that nobody had provided her with any *mémoires* and that she had written entirely out of her imagination" (f. 80). Even though her literary precociousness had landed her in the Bastille, Bonafon refused to disclaim her creation.

Bonafon confirmed official fears concerning the public when she was asked to identify the sources of her satire. She explained that "she composed her work on her own, that she had relied on her imagination, she admits nonetheless that having her head filled with all the public discussions [*tout ce qu'on disoit dans le public*] during and after the king's illness, she had sought to apply these discussions to her work, unaware of the consequences of her actions and without any evil intentions."[33] Bonafon established a direct connection between a public supply of information and her own

31. The relevant documents for this case are located at the Bibliothèque de l'Arsenal, AB 11582. The Bibliothèque Nationale has a copy of *Tanastès* in two volumes, Y2 75132. For a more extensive discussion of this case, see Lisa Jane Graham, "If the King Only Knew: Popular Politics and Absolutism in the Reign of Louis XV, 1744–1774" (Ph.D. diss., Johns Hopkins University, 1994), 76–150.

32. AB 11582, f. 80. Interrogation of Bonafon by Lieutenant of Police Feydeau de Marville on 4 September 1745.

33. AB 11582, f. 57. Interrogation of Bonafon by Lieutenant of Police Feydeau de Marville on 29 August 1745.

literary activity.[34] She used her pen to criticize royal government and suggest ways to reform it.

Unlike many individuals incarcerated for seditious literature, Marie Bonafon was treated with relative leniency. She convinced the police that her intentions had not been malicious, explaining that "as she reads a great deal she had acquired a taste for writing, and moreover she had hoped that in occupying herself with this she might earn a little extra money."[35] Her tenacious insistence on her loyalty to the king was rewarded in February 1747 when she was released from the Bastille and transferred to a Bernadine convent at Moulins. In 1759, after a decade of good behavior as reported by the mother superior to the lieutenant general of police, Marie Bonafon regained her liberty with a small annual pension from the crown.

In the 1750s and 1760s, French subjects frequently made references to "the crazy ideas of the public," "public rumor," or "public knowledge" when being interrogated by the royal police.[36] Commissioners found these phrases frustrating precisely because they limited their ability to assign blame and impose punishment. With reluctance, they were forced to recognize that information was available to the populace and could be manipulated as individuals saw fit.

In fact, royal subjects who appeared before the police were bold in proclaiming their intellectual autonomy, as was, for instance, Jean Antoine Le Fevre. Le Fevre was arrested in February 1757 for writing letters requesting a personal audience with Louis XV. His alleged motive was his desire to warn the king that his life was in danger. Le Fevre had come to Versailles to press his suit and soon became a nuisance. Despite ministerial efforts, Le Fevre refused to reveal his secrets to anybody but Louis XV. His obsti-

---

34. This same connection is made by other individuals arrested for *mauvais discours*. See, for example, Antoine Allegre, AB 11729, fols. 180–81; Jean Louis Langlois, AB 12264, fols. 36–37; Pierre Denis De La Rivoire, AB 12395, fols. 130–31; Jean Baptiste Manem, AB 11981, f.90. The cases of Allegre and La Rivoire are analyzed in my *If the King Only Knew: On the Margins of Absolutism in Eighteenth-Century France* (Charlottesville: University Press of Virginia, forthcoming).

35. AB 11582, f. 55. Interrogation of Bonafon by Lieutenant General of Police Feydeau de Marville at the Bastille on 4 September 1745.

36. Other cases in which individuals identify the public as a source of information that had inspired their crime include: Marc Antoine Sanlir, December 1757, Joly de Fleury (hereafter JDF) 2074, f. 168; Louis François, June 1758, JDF 2076, fols. 205 and 223; Adrien Antoine Tournemine, April 1769, JDF 2076, f. 11; Jean Michel Le Roy, April 1759, JDF 2076, f. 64; Jacques Mirlavaud and Claude Horsel, July 1757, JDF 2076, f. 165; Claude Antoine François Paratre, January 1757, JDF 2077, f. 50.

nacy led to his arrest. Commissioner Le Clerc du Brillet rebuked Le Fevre
for his behavior: "Did he not know that nobody speaks to the king concerning affairs of state except through the channels of his ministers and why
had he refused to declare to Saint Florentin . . . what he had to reveal?"[37]
To which Le Fevre boldly replied that

> finding himself in this situation for the first time in his life, he was
> ignorant of the rules, *that the freedom to think and act does not
> depend on us* [my emphasis], . . . that he found himself disobeying
> the law in spite of himself, . . . repeats that he is a subject loyal to
> his king and would fear to appear as anything else in his eyes. (f. 156)

With this retort, Le Fevre explicitly denied the legitimacy of the police's
efforts to restrict his personal freedom.[38]

During his interrogation, Le Fevre eventually revealed what he had hoped
to confide to Louis XV. He reiterated concerns raised in the *mémoires* he
had addressed to the king. Le Fevre urged Louis XV to mend his ways and
to read the parlementary remonstrances that his minsters hid from his eyes.
There the king would learn of the widespread misery of his subjects
throughout the kingdom. Le Fevre was an ardent apologist for the magistrates, with whom the king was currently embroiled in the dispute over the
refusal of sacraments to priests suspected of Jansenism. He implored Louis
XV to respect the laws of the land and warned that the king's authority
was being abused by his ministers. Commissioner Brillet was dumbfounded
by this eloquent and informed tirade. He refused to believe that Le Fevre
had composed this speech without help but Le Fevre reassured him that
"he had not had any assistance other than that he derived from his reading,
his application and his understanding *(lumières)*.[39]

In his notes on the case, Brillet indicated that Le Fevre's declaration "was
a strong apology for the conduct of the parlements, it was a rhapsody
drawn from the remonstrances of the different parlements that had been
published."[40] Once again, the police were confronted with a chain of events

37. AB 11965, f. 156. Interrogation of Jean Antoine Le Fevre by Commissioner Le Clerc
du Brillet at the Bastille on 11 February 1757.
38. A similar theme pervades Ménétra's autobiography in his attitudes toward individuals
and officials who sought to restrict his personal autonomy; see Jacques-Louis Ménétra, *Journal
of My Life*, trans. Arthur Goldhammer (New York: Columbia University Press, 1986).
39. AB 11965, f. 162.
40. Ibid., f. 152. Noted at the top of the transcript of Le Fevre's interrogation by Commissioner Le Clerc du Brillet at the Bastille on 11 February 1757.

that began with printed matter, moved through the formulation of opinions, and culminated in a criminal act. Moreover, they were forced to admit outright that information was circulating over which they had no control. Print had a leveling effect: it dispelled the mystery that had traditionally surrounded the royal person and his decisions while simultaneously supplying ordinary individuals with the material necessary to think about these decisions for themselves. The supply of printed matter increased steadily throughout the eighteenth century and eroded the carefully constructed hierarchies of *état*, knowledge, and authority that were the bedrock of the Old Regime. Official expressions of bewilderment and exasperation in the criminal dossiers reflect these broader cultural charges. The old criminal categories no longer made sense but there was nothing yet available to replace them.

By the late 1750s, the police and the people disagreed over what constituted appropriate behavior for the unprivileged subjects of a royal state. These differences are evident in the uses of the word *public* by the respective parties. The popular reliance on information confirmed police fears of ideological infection and disease. For members of the Third Estate, however, the public was not inherently hostile to royal authority. As Le Fevre insisted, "all that distinguishes the most loyal subject, the intentions of the most upright heart, the most inviolable love for my sovereign was the mainspring of my actions."[41] Definitions of loyalty included the obligation to reveal abuses to a misguided or errant sovereign.

The public in its various guises did, however, challenge the exclusivity of Old Regime politics by legitimating individual thought and freedom of expression in advancing the claim that the "public" already possessed information that the police regarded as "privileged." Police officials condemned such activities yet were unable to arrest an entire populace. These conflicting theories of knowledge, mapped onto and reinforcing a hierarchical social vision, alert us to a significant source of tension between the crown and its subjects in eighteenth-century France. The implications of this struggle can be explored through the case of Jean Baptiste Manem.

The Boundaries of Silence

Police commissioners were no more successful quelling discussions in the streets than the crown was repressing those erupting in its parlements. In

41. AB 11965, f. 153.

both instances, efforts to contain debate backfired and encouraged an escalation of contestatory activities. Until recently, the disputes in the law courts have attracted far more attention than the *mauvais discours* circulating outside the judicial corridors. As the case of Jean Baptiste Manem demonstrates, even an undistinguished member of the Third Estate could become a royal nuisance when he refused to be quiet. Just as the magistrates ignored Louis XV's *loi de silence*, so too did Manem resist official efforts to stifle his voice.

Jean Baptiste Manem was fifty-two when he was arrested in March 1757.[42] Both his parents were dead and he lived off a small income that he collected from the inheritance, some annuities, and the rent on an apartment in Marseille. His father had been a merchant and Manem had invested in some unsuccessful trading ventures before moving to Paris in 1743. Manem had frequently left the capital and spent time living in England, Holland, and Prussia. Since 1752, the police had been observing Manem and were particularly suspicious of his activities while he was abroad.

In 1753, Manem began sending anonymous letters to ministers and members of the French court warning of a conspiracy to destroy the monarchy and establish a republic based in Marseille. The letters said that members of the "cabale" had infiltrated the court and that Louis XV was surrounded by assassins. Moreover, the king's mistress, Madame de Pompadour, was to be the first victim. The letters were unsigned but they instructed the recipients that "in order to extricate herself from this difficult situation Madame de Pompadour need only contact Monsieur Manem who is the only person informed concerning these various intrigues because he refused to participate when he was invited by the instigator in Marseille."[43] The individuals who received the letters turned them over to the police. Although the allegations were vague, threats to the king's life could not be ignored. The police placed the letters in a file and started monitoring Manem's activities. Unaware that he was being observed, Manem was disappointed that his letters had failed to prompt a response. The kingdom was in danger, and Manem was eager to reveal his secrets.

Undeterred by ministerial silence, Manem decided to test his luck at the Prussian court. He believed an enlightened sovereign would be more receptive to what he had to say. In 1753, Manem went to Prussia where he

---

42. The documents concerning the case of Jean Baptiste Manem are located at the Bibliothèque de l'Arsenal, AB 11981.

43. AB 11981, f. 98. Undated letter entitled "Extrait d'une lettre de Fontainebleau à Paris par Monsieur le C de . . . à Madame la . . ."

addressed several *mémoires* to Frederick the Great. He predicted that a revolution was imminent in France and offered his services to the Prussian king. He hoped to enlist Frederick's aid to warn Louis XV and prevent the revolution. According to the French police, Manem was in turn ignored and ridiculed by Frederick. Still frustrated, Manem returned to France at the beginning of 1757 just in time for the Damiens Affair. He continued addressing letters to members of the court, suggesting that Damiens had been "a failed strike by the cabale." Manem's allegations concerning regicidal plots were more alarming in the wake of Damiens's attempt to stab Louis XV. Official concern escalated in the ensuing weeks and prompted a flurry of arrests. On 9 March 1757, Manem was taken to the Bastille for questioning.

At the Bastille, Manem admitted that he was the author of the letters. The police were especially troubled by the question of motive and pressed Manem to account for his actions. Manem insisted that in writing the anonymous letters, "his goal was to arouse the curiosity of those who received the said letters, so they would summon him for an audience."[44] He was searching for attention and perhaps a small financial reward for the services he sought to render the crown.[45] Manem conceded that although his actions had been imprudent, his intentions had never been malicious. He vaguely repeated that he had "something useful to say and . . . he wanted to arouse their curiosity to see him and hear what he had to say."[46] He claimed he had been swept away by "his zeal for the general welfare of the realm" (f. 191). He apologized for raising a false alarm but not for the desire to obtain a royal audience that had prompted it.

The discussions between Manem and Commissioner Rochebrune revealed specific points of disagreement between the police and the populace. The monarchy presided over a society that derived comfort and security from rigid boundaries between persons and estates. These boundaries reinforced the raison d'être of the Old Regime: hierarchy and privilege. Manem had been foolish to think he could ignore these distinctions. In rebuking Manem for his arrogance, Commissioner Rochebrune could barely conceal his scorn: "If it is reasonable to think that persons at the court the superiority of whose knowledge is commensurate with that of their birth would

44. AB 11981, f. 91. First interrogation of Manem by Commissioner Rochebrune on 18 March 1757.
45. AB 11981, f. 3. Internal police memorandum, no date.
46. AB 11981, f. 190. Third interrogation of Manem by Commissioner Rochebrune on 29 March 1757.

show blind interest in a man whom they did not know and who was exces-sively praised in some anonymous letters . . ."[47] For the police, one of the most disturbing aspects of Manem's behavior was his failure to respect the boundaries of his intellectual as well as his social *état*. Thus, social hierarchy was reinforced and mapped onto epistomology in the criminal vocabulary of the Old Regime.

Manem's actions were considered subversive from the crown's perspec-tive for several reasons. As Commissioner Rochebrune explained:

> he should have rejected his imaginary conspiracy theory because it threatened the interests of the state, that it was a malicious scheme to send anonymous letters against the state to persons of the highest distinction in which he presented himself as a knowledgeable states-man capable of resolving all the troubles of the realm and finally that it was a crime of *lèse majesté* to send mémoires against France . . . to the king of Prussia . . . without the permission of the king of France, and moreover, the accused is inexcusable for having lapsed in his duty to . . . the king and his family in having falsely announced the general extinction of the entire royal family.[48]

Manem had overstepped his role as a loyal and obedient subject. He had refused to accept his invisibility in the eyes of the monarch and his minis-ters. Absolutism in its most traditional sense, as Keith Baker has demon-strated, was not public politics. Notions of participation and contestation were foreign to the French monarchy's definition of government. The king was, in his person and his office, the guarantor of "le bien public."[49] The kingdom was expected to address the king through a legally defined set of corporate and institutional channels. These assumptions explain why the royal police were alarmed by Manem's actions. Manem had attempted to operate as an independent agent, explicitly ignoring official constraints. Deluded into believing that he could "enlighten His Prussian Majesty, the ministers and members of the French court" with his limited understanding of contemporary politics, Manem had committed an act of high treason.[50]

47. AB 11981, f. 191. Second interrogation of Manem by Commissioner Rochebrune on 29 March 1757.

48. AB 11982, f. 203. Interrogation of Manem by Rochebrune on 30 March 1757.

49. Keith Michael Baker, "Public Opinion as Political Invention" in his *Inventing the French Revolution: Essays on French Political Culture in the Eighteenth-Century* (Cambridge: Cam-bridge University Press, 1990), 167–202.

50. AB 11981, f. 266. Third interrogation of Manem by Commissioner Rochebrune on 19 May 1757.

Manem failed to convince royal officials that despite his lies, "his intentions were straightforward and in good faith." Commissioner Rochebrune was unswayed by Manem's excuses and reminded him:

> In society each citizen should occupy himself with his own affairs or with his work and that if the accused had political views which could be of some service he should have had his discoveries printed rather than resorting to circuitous channels and anonymous letters to depict the talents he believed he possessed and finally that the ministers to whom he had addressed himself . . . had made clear by their silence that he was not as enlightened in such matters as he imagined himself to be.[51]

The tone of Rochebrune's harangue was both stern and sarcastic. Manem, as a member of the Third Estate, should busy himself with work rather than waste time and energy meddling in politics. Moreover, Rochebrune implied that it was unlikely Manem had anything important to contribute. Rochebrune's suggestion that it would have been preferable for Manem to opt for publication rather than anonymous threats is puzzling. It may have been sarcastic: Manem never would have found a publisher because nobody was interested in what he had to say. At the same time, it can be read as an explicit admission of police weakness in the war being waged on printed matter. If commoners insisted on voicing opinions, it was easier to monitor them through the publishing industry, which was closely policed, than in random acts of anonymous scribbling. In any case, Manem should have deferred to the king's ministers, whose silence indicated that his ambitions were unfounded.

Manem, however, refused to accept the reprimand without qualifications. Manem asserted that "he had relied on this manoeuver simply because there were no alternatives."[52] He asserted that "this silence on the part of the ministers had misled him and that a word from them would have clarified what he should have done."[53] He had been forced to break the law because his initial efforts had failed to prompt any response. As Manem explained, he lacked the social connections and official titles that commanded recogni-

---

51. AB 11981, f. 266. Third interrogation of Manem by Commissioner Rochebrune on 19 May 1757.

52. AB 11981, f. 96. Interrogation of Manem by Commissioner Rochebrune on 30 March 1757.

53. AB 11981, f. 267. Interrogation of Manem by Rochebrune on 19 May 1757.

tion. Consequently, "he had imagined that the anonymous letters he was writing . . . would make it seem that he was well connected and would attract the attention of the nobles who received the said letters" (f. 267). This argument underlines a deeply felt sense of frustration and resentment. Now that the populace was more politically informed because of rising literacy and increased availability of printed matter, it refused to accept government as "le secret du roi." Individuals such as Manem wanted the opportunity to communicate their opinions to their leaders and to be treated as if they counted. Through his anonymous letters, Manem was crying out, "I am here." Yet, under the Old Regime, members of the Third Estate were part of a juridical category that conferred neither political nor civil status.[54]

The interrogations reveal that Manem had criticized specific ministers and decisions in some of the letters. For example, he had denounced France's recent decision to sign a treaty with Austria. When summoned to justify this critical remark, Manem offered an apology laced with ambiguity:

> He confessed that it was inappropriate for him to criticize govern-
> ment affairs and that in using the expression, "it is said" [*on dit*], he
> was not speaking personally and for himself, moreover there were
> few persons who in considering previous wars and the expenses
> France had incurred trying to destroy the House of Austria would
> not have been a bit surprised by such an abrupt alliance.[55]

Thus, Manem knew that he was not supposed to comment upon the king or his policy, especially if he were being critical. Yet, in acknowledging his lack of discretion, he implicitly reaffirmed his right to formulate an opinion, even on affairs of state, because the public to which he belonged and shared with Chauveau, Bonafon, Le Fevre, and Langlois, already knew and dis-cussed such things.

Although Manem quickly admitted that he had lied about the conspiracy plot, the police remained troubled by the case. They were convinced that "there is something fundamentally evil here."[56] A threat to the king's life,

54. For a discussion of the Third Estate as a juridical category, see William Sewell, *A Rhetoric of Bourgeois Revolution: The Abbé Sieyes and "What is the Third Estate"?* (Durham: Duke University Press, 1994), 41–65.

55. AB 11981, f. 199. Interrogation of Manem by Commissioner Rochebrune on 30 March 1757.

56. AB 11981, f. 104. Undated internal police memorandum.

whether real or imagined, constituted a crime of *lèse-majesté*.[57] The decision to lie about such a serious matter was in itself revealing. It suggested a degree of indifference toward the king that officials found profoundly unsettling. This concern emerged during Manem's first interrogation when Commissioner Rochebrune asked: "Is it not very criminal to have invented that the King and the Dauphin were to be assassinated in order to raise deadly misgivings in the persons who received such a letter and whether it is permissible for a subject to play with his King and the presumptive heir to the throne in such a way?"[58] Manem did not answer Rochebrune's query, knowing full well that it was strictly forbidden to "play" with the king. He had tested royal authority and would pay for his recklessness with his liberty and his sanity.

During his extended incarceration, Manem continued to write to the king and his ministers, imploring them to give him an audience. These letters reveal that Manem had precise notions about how kingship was supposed to operate. In 1758, he addressed a *mémoire* to Louis XV with the following reminder:

> For affairs of much less importance than those contained in the enclosed mémoire . . . great princes, the greatest kings and emperors, even Louis XIV himself never scorned the advice of simple commoners. The accessibility of these rulers was, on the contrary, one of the sources of their grandeur at the same time that it contributed to the security of their throne.[59]

This principle, that the grandeur of kings rested directly on their willingness to listen to their humblest subjects, underlay the myth of monarchy even in the Age of Reason. The sovereign's distance from his people was counterbalanced by his imagined accessibility. What distinguished this trope of "the king's ear" by the eighteenth century was that individuals were more informed about current affairs than ever before and this knowledge legitimated a desire to speak. Manem never realized his dream of an audience

57. For a discussion of *lèse-majesté*, see Church, *Richelieu and Reason of State*. Also extremely useful is the article by Ralph Giesey, Lanny Haldy, and James Millhorn, "Cardin Le Bret and Lese Majesty," *Law and History Review* 4 (Spring 1986): 23–54.

58. AB 11981, f. 91. First interrogation of Manem by Commissioner Rochebrune on 18 March 1757.

59. AB 11981, f. 325. Cover letter from Manem to Louis XV dated 29 October 1758.

with the king nor was he ever released from confinement. He spent the rest of his life in prison and his mind deteriorated under the strain.

Manem's case illustrates a pattern of delinquent behavior that flourished in the last three decades of Louis XV's reign. Manem's exchanges with Commissioner Rochebrune captured the tensions between the police and the people in a tumultuous political era. His dossier reveals a sense of frustration that had no means of expressing itself except through crime. The police were exasperated by their inability to check the proliferation of lies and false threats. Moreover, they were alarmed by the disrespect for the king that such crimes manifested in their use and abuse of his name and his person. Ultimately, the most disturbing aspect of Manem's case may have been that it forced the police to confront the breakdown of a social and epistomological hierarchy to which they, as officials of the Old Regime, were deeply attached. The democratization of knowledge, and thereby of opinion-making, marks a critical stage in the evolution of political life under the Old Regime. If the crown had found a way to accommodate these changes rather than branding them as criminal, it may have secured more loyalty and less enmity from members of the tribunal that would eventually judge it.

The traditional politics of absolutism were subjected to serious challenges from various segments of Old Regime society in the turbulent decades of the 1750s and 1760s. By the end of Louis XV's long reign, the crown had suffered an irretrievable loss of power and prestige. Government as "le secret du roi" gave way to what Keith Baker has termed "a politics of contestation."[60] This essay suggests that the process of contesting royal authority can be traced on more than one level. The police archives provide a new angle from which to approach the changes in French political culture that occurred in the Age of Enlightenment.

Several historians have traced the evolution of public opinion through encyclopedias, judicial *mémoires,* and philosophical treatises. The word *public,* however, also occupied a significant place in the dialogue between police officers and members of the Parisian populace. It was imposing itself upon the crown as a legitimate source of information and ideas. This public did not correspond to the institutionalized public sphere identified by Habermas as providing the foundations of a democratic civil society. Rather,

60. Baker, *Inventing the French Revolution,* 172.

it manifested itself in individual acts of delinquency that forced the police to recognize, with some reluctance, that it existed and was gaining strength.

The cases of Chauveau, Langlois, Bonafon, and Manem confirm the views of those scholars who argue that the availability of information was fundamental to the erosion of the Old Regime's hierarchy of knowledge and power. Moreover, the police were noticeably afraid of this change: it encouraged delusions of grandeur, like valets donning their livery to pass themselves off as noblemen, and it often spilled over into crime. Individuals blended written with spoken utterances, literary with nonliterary activities, to articulate their opinions and grievances. Whether used as a source of creative inspiration, factual information, or personal legitimation, the notion of the public helped royal subjects stake claims and demand recognition as individuals in the emerging civil society. Although their efforts failed to achieve substantial political change, they cannot be ignored. They testify to a new assumption that the Third Estate should have knowledge formerly belonging only to the privileged orders. This assumption would fuel a desire to become politically engaged, if only to protect this right.

5

An Intellectual Profile of a Jacobin Activist

The Morality and Politics of Dufourny de Villiers (1789–1796)

Harvey Chisick

In this essay I shall show how a relatively little-known Jacobin activist, Louis-Pierre Dufourny de Villiers, understood and practiced politics.[1] Dufourny, while finding a place in certain specialized studies of the Revolution, is generally overlooked.[2] But beyond describing the career and, more par-

---

1. I thank Leah Rozen, Menahem Kellner, Deborah Hertz, Lisa Graham, and Jack Censer for their helpful comments on an earlier version of this essay.
2. Dufourny does not appear in most standard one-volume histories of the Revolution, such as those of Mathiez, Lefebvre, Soboul, Sydenham, Furet and Richet, Sutherland, or Doyle. Exceptionally he does figure in J. M. Thompson's *The French Revolution* (Oxford: Blackwell, 1943). Dufourny is not, however, overlooked in the great multivolume histories of the Revolution, such as those of Michelet and Jaurès, and he is mentioned in the basic studies of Jacobinism by Clarence Crane Brinton, *The Jacobins: An Essay in the New History* (New York: Macmillan, 1930); Ferenc Fehér, *The Frozen Revolution: An Essay on Jacobinism* (Cambridge: Cambridge University Press, 1987); and L. Jaume, *Le Discours jacobin et la*

ticularly, the mentality of Dufourny, I shall consider what his experience in the Revolution tells us about its political culture, and whether the paradigm of political culture currently being elaborated by scholars such as François Furet, Keith Baker, Lynn Hunt, and Roger Chartier[3] can adequately explain the main features of the mentality of a highly devoted and active Jacobin and revolutionary.

Dufourny was born in 1739 (it is not known with certainty where) and died peaceably in Paris in 1796. By training and profession he was an engi-

démocratie (Paris: Fayard, 1989). There is no biographical notice on Dufourny in Roger Caratini, _Dictionnaire des personnages de la Révolution_ (Paris, 1988); Albert Soboul et al., Dictionnaire historique de la Révolution française (Paris: Presses universitaires de France, 1989); the biographical section in Colin Jones, _The Longman Companion to the French Revolution_, (London: Longman, 1988); Samuel F. Scott and Barry Rothaus, _Historical Dictionary of the French Revolution, 1789–1799_, 2 vols. (Westport, Conn.: Greenwood, 1985); or, understandably, François Furet and Mona Ozouf, eds., _A Critical Dictionary of the French Revolution_ (Cambridge: Belknap Press of Harvard University Press, 1989). His extensive activities during the Revolution do, however, result in incidental mentions of Dufourny in the reference works of Jones, Soboul, and Furet and Ozouf, while his overlapping roles in the Jacobins and the popular movement have caused him to appear in the basic works of Soboul, Guérin, and R. B. Rose on the sans-culottes. I am aware of no books or articles on Dufourny, and of only a few biographical notices on him. One, of no more than a few lines, is in M. J. Guillaume, _Procès-verbaux du Comité d'Instruction publique de la Convention nationale_, 7 vols. (Paris: Imprimerie nationale, 1891–1907), 2:xviv. Another appears in Roman d'Amat and R. Limousin-Lamothe, eds., _Dictionnaire de biographie française_, 17 vols. (Paris: Letouzey et Ane, 1932–86), 9:col. 1449. Gerard Walter's edition of Jules Michelet's _Histoire de la Révolution française_, 2 vols. (Paris: Gallimard, 1985–87), 2:1372–74, has the most extensive notice, and suggests that both because of his relation to the popular movement and his role as an administrator of the Department of Paris, Dufourny merits study. The most recent notice is in Jean Tulard, Jean-François Fayard, and Alfred Fierro, _Histoire et dictionnaire de la Révolution française, 1789–1799_ (Paris: R. Laffont, 1987), 775–76. Dufourny's name is sometimes spelled, both in manuscript and in printed sources, as Dufourni. Louvet calls him an Italian, and the name could certainly been of Italian derivation. Jean-Baptiste Louvet, _Mémoires: Quelques notices pour l'histoire et le récit de mes périls depuis le 31 mai 1793_, ed. Henri Coulet, (Paris: Desjonquères, 1988), 55.

3. See François Furet, _Interpreting the French Revolution_, trans. Elborg Forster (Cambridge: Cambridge University Press, 1990); most of Keith Michael Baker's articles on the subject have been collected in _Inventing the French Revolution: Essays on French Political Culture in the Eighteenth Century_ (Cambridge: Cambridge University Press, 1990); Lynn Hunt, _Politics, Culture, and Class in the French Revolution_ (Berkeley and Los Angeles: University of California Press, 1984) and _The Family Romance of the French Revolution_ (Berkeley and Los Angeles: University of California Press, 1992); and Roger Chartier, _The Cultural Origins of the French Revolution_, trans. Lydia G. Cochrane (Durham: Duke University Press, 1991). Of considerable importance is the collection _The French Revolution and the Creation of Modern Political Culture_, vol. 1, _The Political Culture of the Old Regime_, ed. Keith Michael Baker (Oxford: Pergamon, 1987), vol. 2, _The Political Culture of the French Revolution_, ed. Colin Lucas (Oxford: Pergamon, 1988), vol. 3, _The Transformation of Political Culture_,

neer. In 1789 he lived in Paris on the left bank on the rue des Mathurins, close to the present-day juncture of the Boulevards Saint-Germain and Saint-Michel, and was chief engineer of the capital. The only trace I have been able to discover of Dufourny before the Revolution is a letter from Sartine, then minister of the marine, of September 1778 thanking Dufourny for submitting a number of memoirs on ways to improve French shipping, and informing him that they had received due consideration but could not be implemented.[4] We here find Dufourny in the familiar pose of the pragmatic patriot, duly submitting his projects to the constituted authorities, and, it is reasonable to suppose, hoping to benefit from his service to them. Virtually nothing else is known of his activities before 1789. From the convocation of the Estates General until his death seven years later, however, he was an indefatigable and resourceful advocate of the Revolution who strove both to convince the public of the justice and necessity of the movement, and actively to defend it against its enemies.

For the most part, I shall draw here on the roughly twenty pamphlets Dufourny published between 1789 and 1796[5] to show how he thought about politics. I shall argue that while his practical positions shifted from moderate reformism to militant Jacobinism and support of the Terror, his basic political assumptions and values remained constant. While Dufourny was exceptional in the consistency and integrity of his political views, his outlook and mentality were altogether typical of the generation that reached maturity in the years before 1789.

Before coming to Dufourny's political ideas, it is worth making a number of preliminary points. First, while an indefatigable publicist from the spring of 1789 on, so far as I have been able to determine, he published nothing

1789–1848, ed. François Furet and Mona Ozouf (Oxford: Pergamon, 1989), and vol. 4, *The Terror*, ed. Baker (Oxford: Pergamon, 1994).

4. Bibliothèque Historique de la Ville de Paris (BHVP), MSS N.A. 481, fols. 176–77.

5. Dufourny signed all his pamphlets that I have been able to find. From 1792, in addition to his name, he used the title "l'homme libre" as proudly as any old-regime aristocrat used his title of baron, duke, or count. The Bibliothèque Nationale has most of his pamphlets, but the Bibliothèque Historique de la Ville de Paris has a number lacking in the holdings of the larger library. I have been unable to find a copy of a pamphlet entitled *Constitution Philadelphique*, which Dufourny says he had published between July and November 1789. Dufourny, *Invitation aux districts à former des comités fraternels. Invitation aux bons Citoyens à verser dans le sein des Infortunés une partie du quart des revenus et des autres dons patriotiques. Observations sur les causes de la misère, son acroissement et ses remèdes. Lues en l'Assemblée du District des Mathurins le 11 Novembre 1789. Par M. Dufourny de Villiers. Suite des Cahiers du quatrième ordre et de la Constitution Philadelphique* (Paris, 1789), 5–6.

before that time. It is well known that during the Revolution formerly frustrated or marginal writers, such as Brissot and Marat, achieved prominence.[6] Dufourny, however, was unable to bring his views to public notice under the Old Regime, and found a public voice only with the Revolution. Dufourny's career after 1789 indicates in dramatic fashion how the Revolution opened the way to publication and political participation to at least a section of the population that had formerly been completely excluded from the realm of politics.[7]

Second, although I shall be drawing mostly on Dufourny's published works here, it would be inaccurate to give the impression that he was exclusively or even primarily a writer, for he had a remarkably extensive and varied political career during the Revolution. Today Dufourny is best known as an activist of the Jacobin Club in which he held numerous offices. Most prominently, he became president of the club following the crisis of the Champ-de-Mars in mid-July 1791 when a large-scale secession of moderates, who then formed the Feuillant Club, seriously challenged the influence of the original society.[8] In a speech delivered at the Jacobins on 3 August 1791, when the worst of the crisis of the previous month was over, the new president of the club, Pétion, congratulated Dufourny on his comportment and noted "how sensible the society is of his zeal and of the distinguished manner in which he carried out his duties at such a difficult and tempestuous time."[9] Dufourny was subsequently twice elected vice president of the society, in May 1792 and March 1793, and he often took the chair of meetings in the absence of regularly elected officials.[10] He further

6. Robert Darnton has brought attention to this phenomenon in his now classic article, "The High Enlightenment and the Low-Life of Literature in Eighteenth-Century France," *Past and Present*, no. 51 (1971): 81–115.

7. For a similar instance see Harvey Chisick, "The People, Poverty and Politics in the Pamphlet Literature of the Early French Revolution—The Case of Jean-François Lambert," *History of European Ideas* 17 (1993): 289–317.

8. Bouche, who had begun the month as president of the Jacobins, but who had left that club for the Feuillants, wrote the *Moniteur* to complain that he was still being associated with the original society. Dufourny politely replied that this was only because Bouche had neglected to inform the Jacobins of his decision to leave. *Réimpression de l'Ancien Moniteur, seule histoire authentique et inaltérée de la Révolution française depuis la réunion des Etats généraux jusqu'au Consulat, mai 1789–novembre 1799 avec des notes explicatives* (Paris, 32 vols., 1850–54), 9:226.

9. Translations are my own unless otherwise indicated. *Discours prononcé dans l'assemblée de la société des Amis de la Constitution de Paris séante aux Jacobins, par M. PETHION, Président, le 3 aout 1791*, 2. Bibliothèque Nationale (BN) Lb[40] 2239.

10. As, for example, on 21 March, 30 April, and 20 July 1792. A. Aulard, *La Société des Jacobins: Recueil des documents pour l'histoire du Club des Jacobins de Paris*, 6 vols. (Paris, 1889–97), 3:446 and 548, and 4:120. Hereafter cited as *J*.

functioned as secretary of the society in August 1791 and June 1792, was elected to the important comité de correspondance for the period 16 November 1791 to 15 February 1792 and again the following October, and was elected the club's archivist on 5 November 1792 (*J*, 3:101, 4:35, 3:253, and 4:360 and 459). He was also twice chosen to serve as *defenseur officieux* in the club's quasi-judicial proceedings (*J*, 4:122 and 192). On one occasion Dufourny and Robespierre were appointed to revise an address of Billaud-Varenne. We gain some notion of the vigor and scope of the work of the two commissioners from Billaud's complaint that "these changes have so much changed [*défiguré*] this work that it is impossible to recognize it" (*J*, 3:602). Though Dufourny was ultimately caught up in the vicious factional infighting in the Jacobins in the spring of 1794 that resulted in the purging first of the extreme-left followers of Hébert and then of the moderate Dantonists, and was denounced himself following Danton's fall, there can be no doubt that from the summer of 1791 until the spring of 1794, he was a highly active and influential member of the club. A measure of the respect that he enjoyed at the Jacobins is reflected in Isnard's praise of him in December 1791 for his contributions to the Revolution, and in Thuriot's comment at the end of 1792 on the "services that the patriot Dufourny has rendered to liberty and to the Jacobins" (*J*, 3:291 and 4:579).

In addition to being chosen repeatedly for positions of responsibility in the club's administrative apparatus, Dufourny also played a pivotal role as a liaison between the club and other revolutionary organizations. On 2 May 1792, for example, he read a petition of the Jacobins to the Legislative Assembly (*J*, 3:553). In November of the following year he was given the floor of the Convention and on behalf of the Jacobins harangued the deputies at length on the importance of maintaining the Terror.[11] In February 1794 Dufourny was again allowed to address the Convention and this time asked that the term *régir* and its derivatives, offensive to republican sensibilities because of its connotations of domination, be extirpated from the French language. His request was put forward by a deputy as a motion and formally adopted.[12] Dufourny was part of a deputation sent by the Jacobins to the Committee of General Security to protest the arrest of their fellow club member, the artist David; on another occasion he criticized Cambon's treatment of Pache at the Committee of Public Safety (*J*, 5:474 and 379).

---

11. *Moniteur* 18:421–23. Dufourny reported back to the Jacobins on the outcome of this mission; *J*, **5:509**.

12. *Moniteur* 19:565. At this time Dufourny was himself a *régisseur des poudres*.

During 1791 and 1792 Dufourny reported to the Jacobins on the activities and decisions of the Paris Commune, with which he maintained close relations.[13] He served as engineer of the revolutionary Commune after 10 August 1792,[14] and was chosen by the Commune at the end of August 1792 as a commissioner of the central government to the Seine-Inférieure to help raise volunteers for the army and to improve morale.[15] Dufourny was accompanied on this mission by Albitte, a fellow Jacobin and the deputy for the Seine-Inférieure, and by Saintex, a fellow Cordelier.

Important as Dufourny's role in the Jacobins was, his revolutionary activities were not confined to that club. On the one hand, as an interested and responsible citizen he was active at the grassroots level of politics from the outset of the Revolution, and his abilities and affiliations led to his repeatedly being given special responsibilities in a variety of contexts. On the other hand, his professional expertise, both with respect to engineering and the fine arts[16] resulted in his being appointed to committees of the Legislative Assembly and Convention and to agencies responsible for organizing the war effort.

Like many middle-class revolutionaries, Dufourny began his apprenticeship in politics in the district assemblies, whose formal role was restricted to electing a representative to the Estates General and to drafting a *cahier de doléances*, but which refused to disband once these tasks had been accomplished and continued to function as local assemblies dealing with a wide range of issues. They have been described as "a remarkable experiment in direct democracy."[17] Dufourny was a member and then president of the District des Mathurins. Remaining active on the local level, he several times

---

13. *J* 3:260, 432–33, and 2:538–39. After Thermidor, Cambon complained that Dufourny was "toujours avec la maudite députation de Paris." *Moniteur* 22 (November 1794): 608.

14. F. Braesch, *La Commune du dix août 1792: Etude sur l'histoire de Paris du 20 juin au 2 décembre 1792* (Paris: Hachette, 1911), 264, 279 and 796.

15. On his return, Dufourny described his mission at the Jacobins; *J*, 4:368–73. While having been chosen for the commission by the Commune, Dufourny received his official appointment from Danton in his capacity as minister of the interior. This is a good example of the fragmentation of authority and overlap in functions after the second revolution of 10 August 1792 among the Assembly, which had legislated the call-up of the volunteers, the Commune and the Jacobins.

16. In the list of electors of the section Thermes-de-Julien to choose the deputies of Paris to the Convention, Dufourny's profession is given as "artiste ingenieur." Archives Nationales (AN) BI14.

17. Soboul, *Dictionnaire historique*, 362. On these important agents of political education see G. Garrigues, *Les Districts parisiens pendant la Révolution française* (Paris: Editions Spes, 1932); and R. B. Rose, *The Making of the Sans-Culottes: Democratic Ideas and Institutions in Paris* (Manchester: Manchester University Press, 1982).

acted as commissioner of the Section of Thermes-de-Julien to the Paris
Commune on the question of the relation of cannoneers to the National
Guard, in which he himself served as a volunteer;[18] after 10 August 1792
he was chosen by his section as an elector, and by acclamation to a quasi-
judicial *juré de jugement*.[19] Having moved across the river to the Arsenal,
Dufourny then became active in that section.[20]

Dufourny's links to the popular movement are not altogether clear. He
was active in the sections as well as in the Jacobins, and he was, moreover,
the founding president of the Cordeliers, which was from the outset more
radically democratic than the Jacobins.[21] His prominent membership in the
Comité de l'Evêché, which planned the coup of 31 May–2 June 1793 that
purged the Girondins from the Convention, and subsequent emphasis on
the importance of this *journée*[22] also suggests that Dufourny may be seen
as one of the rare revolutionaries who could function effectively both in
the educated and relatively well off setting of the Jacobins and in the popular
milieu of the sans-culottes. Both Soboul and Guérin, however, tend to
regard him as an interloper and not an integral part of the popular movement.[23] While there is not space to treat Dufourny's relation to the popular
movement here, an examination of his writings suggests that his consistent
and strong demands for unrestricted direct democracy and subsistence-
oriented economic policies place him close to the sans-culottes.[24]

18. S. Lacroix, *Actes de la Commune de Paris pendant la Révolution*, 2d ser., 9 October
1790–10 August 1792, 9 vols. (Paris, 1900–1914; AMS Press, New York, 1973), 4:460 and
7:29.

19. AN BI14 and W253, dossier 44.

20. Albert Soboul, *Répertoire du personnel sectionnaire parisien en l'an II* (Paris: Sorbonne,
1985), 388.

21. Lacroix, *Actes de la Commune de Paris*, 6:644. The basic work on the Cordeliers is
still Albert Mathiez, *Le Club des Cordeliers pendant la crise de Varennes et le massacre du
Champ de Mars* (Paris: Champion, 1910).

22. On the uprising see Morris Slavin, *The Making of an Insurrection: Parisian Sections and
the Gironde* (Cambridge: Harvard University Press, 1986). In a post-Thermidorian pamphlet
Dufourny called for the establishment of a monument and a festival to commemorate the
journée of 31 May 1793; *Sentinelle, prends garde à toi* (Paris, 1794), 12.

23. Soboul describes Dufourny as "one of the most stubborn adversaries of the sectional
societies" and claims that he "pursued the popular movement with tenacious hatred." Albert
Soboul, *Les Sans-culottes parisiens en l'an II: Mouvement populaire et gouvernement revolu-
tionnair, 2 juin 1793–9 thermidor An II* (Paris: Clavreuil, 1958), 277 and 368. In Guérin's
view Dufourny consistently supported the central authorities against the autonomy of the
sections. When the section clubs were criticized in the Jacobins in January 1794 it was "Dufourny—toujours lui—qui mena l'attaque." Daniel Guérin, *La Lutte des classes sous la première républiquie, 1793–1797*, 2 vols. (Paris: Gallimard, 1968), 1:88.

24. Soboul notes the closeness of Dufourny's economic views to those of the sans-culottes
in September 1793, but treats this as an indication that such demands had become general by

As noted above, following the uprising of 10 August 1792, Dufourny was chosen by his section as an elector for the city of Paris for the elections to the Convention. Though entrusted by his fellow electors with the position of secretary and made part of a commission that was sent to the Assembly, he was not, despite repeated attempts, elected to the Convention.[25] He was, however, chosen by this body as a member of the administration of the Department of Paris, and served as president of the department for a considerable part of 1793.[26] It was as president of the department that Dufourny appeared before the Convention in November 1793 to invite its members to attend the Festival of Reason in Notre Dame.[27] It was also in this capacity that he attended the meetings of both the Committee of General Security and the Committee of Public Safety.[28] Among the factions within the coalition of forces supporting the Revolution, Dufourny expressed support for Marat and Robespierre,[29] but was more closely linked

---

then (*Les Sans-culottes parisiens,* 470). Yet Dufourny had been writing in substantially the same terms since 1789.

25. E. Charavay, *Assemblée électorale de Paris, 2 septembre 1792–17 frimaire an II. Procès-verbaux de l'élection des députés à la Convention* (Paris: Cerf, 1905). The roughly one thousand electors of Paris were responsible for selecting more than twenty deputies to the Convention, and so had great influence. Almost all deputies for Paris were chosen from among the electors themselves.

26. He was elected on 4 January 1793; Charavay, *Assemblée électorale,* 264. He was still serving as an administrator of the Department of Paris when arrested in the spring of 1794.

27. In effect he asked for the full and compulsory attendance of all deputies in order to demonstrate the unity of the republic. Charlier, the deputy for the Marne and an advocate of extreme terror, turned the request into a motion, which was duly passed. *Moniteur* 18:399 (mispaginated 299).

28. *J,* 6:48–49. This information forms part of the denunciations of Dufourny by Vadier and Robespierre.

29. In December 1792 Dufourny opposed the exclusion of Marat from the Jacobins, admitting that he was sometimes extreme, but arguing that he had served the Revolution well and that Robespierre espoused the same principles but expressed them with more restraint (*J,* 4:614). Marat refers to Dufourny several times in the *Ami du Peuple.* In his number of 12 March 1791 he speaks disparagingly of Dufourny's earlier pamphlets, and criticizes his most recent one, *Invitation à tous les citoyens assembleés en sections 1°. A manifester leur reconnoissance pour l'Assemblée Nationale qui vient de supprimer les droits d'entrées . . .* (Paris, 1791), which praised the Constituent Assembly for eliminating taxes on food brought into cities (*droits d'entrées*). In his 17 November 1790 number Marat praised Dufourny for a motion he had made in the assembly of the District of the Mathurins criticizing Lafayette, and for his firmness in facing down two of Lafayette's supporters. The number of 2 June 1791 of the *Ami du Peuple* named Dufourny as one of the patriots Marat wished to found a Société des vengeurs de la loi he was proposing be established; Jean-Paul Marat, *Oeuvres politiques, 1789–1793,* 10 vols., ed. J. de Cock and C. Goëtz (Brussels: Pôle Nord, 1989–95), 4:2,497, 3:1,778, and 5:2,966. Marat and Dufourny both belonged to the Cordeliers as well as the Jacobins, and so had frequent occasion to meet.

with Danton. Little wonder, then, that he was denounced by Robespierre in the Jacobin Club on 5 April 1794, the day Danton was executed. Dufourny's revolutionary career now took a harsher turn. He was arrested, and while in jail lived in constant fear for his life. He survived until the fall of Robespierre, and was released toward the end of July 1794. Too far to the left to be above suspicion in the atmosphere of Thermidor, he was arrested for a short time in September 1794, and then again in May 1795. This time he remained imprisoned for nearly five months. Though Dufourny's experience in the courtrooms and jails of the Revolution in 1794 and 1795 is an important part of his political experience, it is not one that can be treated here.

Because he was an engineer, Dufourny was also able to serve the Revolution in more specialized capacities. As chief engineer of Paris he visited the Bastille on 15 and 16 July 1789 to determine whether there was subterranean communication between it and Vincennes, and to verify that there were no more prisoners in the fortress.[30] As has been noted above, he continued to serve as city engineer of Paris for the revolutionary Commune after 10 August 1792. No doubt his professional qualifications led to his appointment as head of an office whose function was to collect saltpeter for the manufacture of gunpowder.[31] Together with Guyton de Morveau and Fourcroy he also taught a course in making gunpowder.[32] During Year II he was appointed to a Commission provisoire des arts of the Convention with the task of inventorying scientific instruments.[33] Further, regarded as an expert on architecture and the fine arts, Dufourny served on the Commission des Monuments of the Legislative Assembly, and was reappointed to the Commission pour la Conservation des Monuments, des arts et des sciences

30. *Procès-verbal des Séances et Délibérations de l'Assemblée générale des Electeurs de Paris,* fols. 302–5. AN C*I1.

31. Dufourny was initially appointed to head this office as an interim measure on 12 September 1792. F. A. Aulard, *Recueil des Actes du Comité de Salut Public avec la Correspondance officielle des Représentants en Mission et le Registre du Conseil Executif Provisoire,* 28 vols. (Paris, 1889–1933), 1:51–52. A year later it was Dufourny who, still in a position of responsibility, wrote a pamphlet describing the means of collecting saltpeter which, at the direction of the Committee of Public Safety, was to be sent to every Commune in France. This is the *Instruction pour tous les citoyens qui voudront exploiter eux-mêmes du Salpêtre, Envoyée dans toutes les municipalités par le comité de salut public de la Convention nationale, conformément au décret du 14 frimaire de l'an 2e de la République* (Paris, 1793).

32. M. J. Guillaume, *Procès-verbaux du Comité d'Instruction publique de la Convention Nationale,* 4:189.

33. Ibid., 3:323, 327, and 329.

by the Convention in October 1792.[34] He had also been presented by David
in the autumn of 1793 as the first of a jury of fifty artists, connoisseurs,
and politicians who were to judge competitions of painting, sculpture, and
architecture.[35] At the beginning of 1794 he was put forward for membership
in the Commission des Arts; in his work for this Commission he consistently opposed vandalism directed against works of art or monuments associated with the Old Regime.[36] In January 1795 Dufourny showed sound
historical sense in proposing the creation of a collection of books, pamphlets, engravings, and posters that would be of interest for the "moral and
political history of the Revolution."[37] Dufourny's services to the Revolution
did not go unrewarded. The position of head of the Department of Paris
was a paid one, and the remuneration for serving on the Temporary Commission of Arts was itself 2,000 livres a year.[38] Unlike some other figures
whose economic standing improved as a result of serving in the new bureau-
cracies and government agencies, Dufourny was regularly employed and
reasonably well off before 1789.

The final point to be made before we proceed to a consideration of Dufourny's political views concerns the models available to him in thinking
about human nature, society, and the state. Perhaps the key paradigm of
Enlightenment thought derived from Newton's physics. Newton demonstrated that the movements of all inanimate celestial and terrestrial phenom-
ena were subject to a few basic, simple, mathematically demonstrable laws.
Over the eighteenth century, scientists and thinkers, believing that the law-
fulness and regularity observable in nature could also be discovered in human affairs, sought to establish sciences of man and society.[39] Dufourny
certainly believed in the orderly working of nature, and drew the appropriate deist conclusion from it. Unlike many of his contemporaries and
colleagues in the Jacobin Club, however, he did not believe that self-interest
worked as a sort of moral equivalent of gravity or that when subjected to
the workings of a market mechanism it resulted in the general good. Nor
did he believe that competing interests somehow would automatically be

34. Ibid., 1:8.
35. Ibid., 2:830–31.
36. Louis Tuetey, *Procès-verbaux de la Commission temporaire des arts*, 2 vols. (Paris:
Imprimerie Nationale, 1912–17), 1:42, 116, 468–69, 583, and 2:128.
37. Ibid., 2:54 and 98.
38. Ibid., 1:ix.
39. See Peter Gay, *The Enlightenment: An Interpretation*, 2 vols. (New York: Knopf, 1966–
69), 2:chaps. 4 and 7; and Georges Gusdorf, *Les Principes de Pensée au siècle des lumières*
(Paris: Payot, 1971), part 2, chaps. 1 and 2.

harmonized by a hidden hand.[40] Consequently he rejected the doctrine of free trade advocated by the physiocrats and Adam Smith, but strenuously opposed by the working population. Popular opposition to Turgot's liberalization of the grain trade in 1774 was perceived by net consumers of grains as an infringement on the government's obligation to regulate the supply and price of grains so as to keep them at manageable levels, and ensuing shortages resulted in a series of popular uprisings known as the "flour wars."[41] During the Revolution the working population consistently demanded regulation of the grain trade and the price of bread, the policy of the Maximum representing a notable achievement for it.[42] Most middle-class members of the revolutionary assemblies favored the more recently formulated policy of economic liberalism. In that he supported the continued regulation of the prices of grain and bread, Dufourny was in a minority on this issue in his district assembly, the Jacobin Club, the administration of the Department of Paris and other forums in which his colleagues were well educated and economically well off. On the other hand, these views would have been welcome to the sans-culottes of the sectional assemblies.

The paradigm of Enlightenment thought relating directly to man derived from Locke's *Essay Concerning Human Understanding*. About Locke's epistemology Dufourny says virtually nothing. But his ethical assumptions and firm belief in the basic goodness of humanity derived from the English philosopher. The combination of Locke's view of humans as pure potential at birth, his assumption that they are physiologically (that is, naturally) predisposed to avoid pain and to seek pleasure, and his assertion that pain is properly regarded as an evil and pleasure as a good, together form the

40. Jacob Viner, *The Role of Providence in the Social Order: An Essay in Intellectual History* (Princeton: Princeton University Press, 1972), chap. 3.

41. On the flour wars see Steven L. Kaplan, *Bread, Politics, and Political Economy in the Reign of Louis XV*, 2 vols. (The Hague: Martinus Nijhoff, 1976), chaps. 11–13; Florence Gauthier and Guy-Robert Ikni, eds., *La Guerre du blé au XVIIIe siècle: La Critique populaire contre le libéralisme économique au XVIIIe siècle* (Montreuil: Editions de la passion, 1988); V. S. Ljublinski, *La Guerre de farines: Contribution à la lutte des classes en France, à la veille de la Révolution*, trans. F. Adiba and J. Radiguet (Grenoble: Presses Universitaires de Grenoble, 1979); George Rudé, "La Taxation populaire de mai 1775 dans la région parisienne," *Annales Historiques de la Révolution Française* 28 (1956): 139–79; and more recently Cynthia A. Bouton, *The Flour War: Gender, Class, and Community in Late Ancien Régime French Society* (University Park: Pennsylvania State University Press, 1994).

42. On the maximum see Albert Mathiez, *La Vie chère et le mouvement social sous la Terreur*, 2 vols. (Paris: Payot, 1927); and Soboul, *Les Sans-culottes parisiens*. Convenient summaries of this set of policies are available in the various dictionaries of the Revolution cited above.

basis of a positive and optimistic evaluation of human nature.[43] The doctrine of the natural goodness of man is generally associated with Rousseau,[44] and was widely shared by most of those favoring significant reform.

A third model that Dufourny used extensively was the social contract. He informed his countrymen in 1790 that they "no longer had any other title, neither of union, nor of property, nor of cohesion but their new social contract [*pacte social*]," and he insisted on the moral and rational basis of this new contract.[45] Whatever the reservations expressed by Montesquieu, Hume, Smith, and others about the historicity or conceptual usefulness of the social contract, for men engaged in rethinking the nature of political right and reshaping the institutions under which they lived, the appeal of contract theory as the basis of political association made this one of the dominant metaphors of political discourse at the time.[46]

Coming, finally, to Dufourny's political views, I wish to argue that the political outlook of the late Enlightenment was characterized by a thor-

43. John Locke, *An Essay Concerning Human Understanding*, 2 vols., ed. A. C. Fraser (New York: Dover, 1959), 1:92–93, 121, 160–63, 303, and 340–41. In this connection see Ernst Cassirer, *The Philosophy of the Enlightenment*, trans. Fritz C. A. Koelln and James P. Pettegrove (Boston: Beacon, 1966), chap. 3, and Paul Hazard, *The European Mind: 1680–1715* (New York: Meridian, 1967), part 3, chap. 1.

44. Rousseau takes Locke's view that man is physiologically predisposed to avoid pain and seek pleasure a step further by giving it a social dimension, and arguing that human beings identify with the pain of others. This position is not an attribution of moral qualities to man in the state of nature, but an extension of Locke's views of pleasure and pain as dominant motives and of the efficacity of the psychological mechanism of association. Thus, one person wincing as another strikes his or her foot on a rock does not entail a moral judgment, but a physiological reflex (assuming that the observer has himself experienced pain of a similar sort, and so can identify with the experience of the other person). Rousseau calls pity "the sole natural virtue" and describes it as "a disposition that is appropriate to beings as weak and subject to as many ills as we are; a virtue all the more universal and useful to man because it precedes in him the use of all reflection; and so natural that even beasts sometimes give perceptible signs of it." J.-J. Rousseau, "Discourse on the Origin and Foundation of Inequality," in *The First and Second Discourses*, ed. Roger D. Masters, trans. Roger D. Masters and Judith R. Masters (New York: St. Martin's, 1964), 130.

45. *Les Droits des peuples défendus contre la politique & contre les titres odieux de leurs antiques oppresseurs. Ou La Liberté réclamée pour les Avignonois & Comtadins pardevant l'assemblée nationale, Et s'il y a lieu, Pardevant le Tribunal éternel de l'immuable Raison, & avec le seul titre de l'inaliénable liberté des individus et des peuples* (Paris, 1791), 8–9, and *Des Droits des Avignonois à la plus entière liberté, et la déclaration des droits des nations* (Paris, 1790), 13.

46. There is an extensive literature on this subject, especially as relates to Rousseau. See, for example, Bronislaw Baczko, "Le Contrat social des français: Sieyès et Rousseau," in Baker, *The Political Culture of the Old Regime*, 493–513; and Jacques Guilhaumou, "Le Langage du Contrat Social. Première institution du savoir politique jacobin," in *Peuple et pouvoir: Essais de lexicologie*, ed. M. Glatigny and J. Guilhaumou (Lille: Presses Universitaires de Lille, 1981),

oughgoing moralism. By "moralism" I understand a view of human affairs that ascribes primary and decisive force to individual volition and that, further, recognizes and asserts a set of socially binding values, which in this context includes virtue, patriotism, and *humanité*, as well as liberty, equality and, rather belatedly, fraternity. Dufourny's political outlook owes much to the classical republican tradition,[47] and, indeed, is in significant ways archaic. But it differs from classical republicanism in being underpinned by Lockean psychology, which tends toward universalism and egalitarianism.

As a political stance, the moralism of Dufourny and his contemporaries was eclipsed by two forces that are generally and rightly associated with the Enlightenment: the sciences of society and a politics of interest. Montesquieu, Turgot, Condorcet, the physiocrats, Adam Smith, Adam Ferguson, and other Enlightenment figures sought regularities in history that could be formulated as sociological or political laws. With the achievements of Malthus (first version of *An Essay on the Principle of Population*, 1798), Darwin, and Marx, the emphasis in social and historical analysis shifted away from the autonomous, morally grounded individual to great impersonal forces that, working through biological drives or largely unconscious proclivities, determined the well-being and even existence of whole populations. And though the Enlightenment certainly began the rehabilitation of self-interest,[48] it was not until after the Revolution that a political system based on parties frankly advocating the furthering of sets of particular inter-

---

127–52. More generally, Lynn Hunt describes the revolutionaries as involved in "the great adventure of the modern Western social contract" (*Family Romance of the French Revolution*, 4). Why Hunt includes Machiavelli and Montesquieu as contract theorists together with Hobbes, Locke, and Rousseau is unclear.

47. See J. G. A. Pocock, *The Machiavellian Moment: Florentine Political Thought and the Atlantic Republican Tradition* (Princeton: Princeton University Press, 1975); and his "Virtues, Rights and Manners: A Model for Historians of Political Thought," in *Virtue, Commerce, and History: Essays on Political Thought and History, Chiefly in the Eighteenth Century* (Cambridge: Cambridge University Press, 1985), 37–50; and Alasdair MacIntyre, *After Virtue: A Study in Moral Theory* (Notre Dame: University of Notre Dame Press, 1984), 236–38.

48. A. O. Hirschman, *The Passions and the Interests: Political Arguments for Capitalism before Its Triumph* (Princeton: Princeton University Press, 1977); and Roger Mercier, *La Réhabilitation de la nature humaine: 1700–1750* (Villemomble: Editions "La Balance," 1960). Nannerl Keohane points out that self-interest and amour propre were at the basis of much political thought from Machiavelli through the seventeenth century, but that it was only in the eighteenth century that the notion of enlightened self-interest, which formed an effective basis for social and political cooperation, emerged; *Philosophy and the State in France: The Renaissance to the Enlightenment* (Princeton: Princeton University Press, 1980), 22, 380–82, and 427–38.

ests achieved broad acceptance in the West. Under the Old Regime there was administration and there was court intrigue, but there existed no politics in a sense that a classical Greek or a member of a modern democracy would recognize. This perhaps is why contemporary scholars intent on uncovering some form of political activity under the Old Regime regard public opinion and its expression as inherently political.[49] With the Revolution, we do find a clearly recognizable political life emerging. But revolutionary politics were emphatically not party politics, and they conceded no legitimacy to private or partial interests.[50] The explanation for this is to be found in a combination of factors that include the continuing vitality of the classical and republican traditions; the influence of Rousseau, who himself articulated and modified these traditions;[51] the commonsense appeal of an ideology that makes the public good the object of politics; and the immense optimism, goodwill and public-spiritedness of the early years of the Revolution. It is largely because the political ideology grounded in the moral autonomy of the individual was eclipsed so soon and so effectively after the 1790s by the emerging social sciences on the one hand, and by liberal party politics on the other, that it has received less attention that it deserves.[52]

A recent historian of Jacobinism has spoken of the "moralization of politics" and the concomitant "politicization of morals" that characterized the

49. See, for example, Keith Baker, "Politics and Public Opinion under the Old Regime: Some Reflections," in *Press and Politics in Pre-Revolutionary France*, ed. Jack R. Censer and Jeremy D. Popkin (Berkeley and Los Angeles: University of California Press, 1987), 204–46; and Mona Ozouf, "Public Opinion at the End of the Old Regime," *Journal of Modern History* 60, supp. (1988): S1–S21.

50. Hunt, *Politics, Culture, and Class*, 43–44. William Doyle asserts that under Rousseau's influence the generation of the Revolution regarded political parties as "abhorrent"; *Oxford History of the French Revolution* (Oxford: Oxford University Press, 1989), 235. Isser Woloch brings attention to a similarly grounded consensus against the active seeking of public office; *The New Regime: Transformations of the French Civic Order, 1789–1820s* (New York: Norton, 1944), 70.

51. See *Of the Social Contract*, 2.2 and 3.5.

52. This deeply entrenched tradition was not, of course, completely submerged in the nineteenth century, nor is it to this day. Utopian socialists continued to think and write in terms of the morally autonomous individual, which is one reason that Marx and Engels dismissed them as utopian. Romanticism, too, placed great emphasis on the individual, but it emphasized emotion, imagination, the irrational, and heroicism, and tended to be more concerned with the individual's responsibilities to himself than to the body politic. It is also true that most legal systems hold the individual responsible for his or her actions, and so posit a significant degree of moral autonomy. The point, however, is that from the nineteenth century the ideal of the morally autonomous individual was no longer the dominant cultural model that it had been previously. On Proudhon's basically moral outlook, see John Bowle, *Politics and Opinion in the Nineteenth Century: An Historical Introduction* (London: Oxford University Press, 1966), 160 and 167; and on romanticism, Howard Mumford Jones, *Revolution and Romanticism* (Cambridge: Belknap Press of Harvard University Press, 1974).

club.[53] It is questionable whether for Dufourny any such distinction could be made. In his view acceptable politics were simply the actualization of a universal morality. He held the Declaration of the Rights of Man in religious reverence and was convinced of its universal relevance and applicability. For Dufourny the principles contained in the Declaration were all that men on earth knew and all they needed to know. In his lexicon the term *politics* became one of denigration. He defined politics as the "monstrous offspring of the perfidy of tyrants and of the weakness of the oppressed" and asserted that they could not exist among a free and sovereign people.[54] He further informed his countrymen that they could no longer appeal to "old titles of ownership nor to old treaties which are the product of crime, trickery and violence; and besides your constitution forbids it; your present social contract is no longer the result of the atrocious right of conquest, nor of any purchase, or series of exchanges of any territory: all these illegal and illegitimate titles have been eliminated by the first act of your liberty [Declaration of Rights]."[55] Dufourny made these statements in defending the rights of the Avignonese to sovereignty and arguing against the incorporation of Avignon and the Comtat Venaissin into France on the grounds, first, that "a people is the sole proprietor of its territory so we must accordingly declare all foreign territory inviolable,"[56] and second, that liberty is a prime good that the Avignonese would not wish to compromise and that the French did not have the right to infringe on.[57]

Like most of his educated contemporaries, Dufourny regarded nature not only as an orderly and coherent structure, but also as an ethical standard. Where he differed from them was in the strength of both his conviction that natural law applied directly to human affairs was an adequate guide to politics, and his belief in the efficacy, as distinct from the rightness, of this morality. The power of morality as a motive force in politics is asserted by Dufourny in the preface of the first pamphlet he published in 1789 and is reasserted in his other pamphlets down to the Thermidorian regime. In the *Cahiers du Quatrième Ordre*, Dufourny referred to the "moral goal of every society" and asserted that

> we must search for the means to join the Prince and the Nation so intimately that there results one will, one force and power, which

53. Fehér, *Frozen Revolution*, 57.
54. Dufourny, *Des Droits des Avignonois*, 3.
55. Ibid., 13.
56. Dufourny, *Supplément à la Défense des Droits des Avignonois, des Comtadins et autres peuples à la plus entière liberté* (Paris, 1790), 10.
57. Dufourny, *Droits des Avignonois*, 12–13; *Supplément*, 2–3 and 11.

alone constitute a monarchy; we must found on the moral excellence of the Government, and not on luxury and on valets, the true splendor of the Throne, in order that in destroying all that satisfies . . . the pride and greed of the Great and the Rich, we on the contrary defend the weakest, help the poorest, and increase by the happiness of all individuals the general felicity of society; in this way we obtain that collective force, that moral power, which, alone capable of arousing fear, can inspire our enemies with terror, and conserve peace.[58]

Elsewhere Dufourny spoke of the "absolute power of morality,"[59] and after Thermidor he denounced extreme terrorists (he himself had supported the Terror as a necessary war measure)[60] for having been traitors to the fatherland and to morality.[61] Like Sieyès, he believed that "morality must determine all the relationships which bind men to each other, both in their private interests and in their common or social interest."[62] Dufourny's concept of morality was, I would argue, typically Enlightenment; universalist, utilitarian, and overoptimistic in assuming a tendency to beneficence in nature and to goodness in man. Where this engineer who never published a line before 1789 differed from many of his contemporaries and colleagues in the Jacobin Club was in the intensity of his beliefs and in the integrity of his applications of them.

For Dufourny the universal scope of moral values could be restricted neither by social nor by national boundaries. Dufourny was one of the earliest, most radical, and most consistent spokesmen of popular democracy. While most Jacobins and members of the enlightened community followed Sieyès in regarding property, education, and leisure as criteria for

58. Dufourny, *Cahiers du quatrième ordre, celui des Journaliers, des Infirmes, des Indigens, &.c., L'Ordre sacré des Infortunés ou Correspondance Philantropique entre les Infortunés, les Hommes sensibles, et les Etats-Généraux. Pour suppléer au droit de députer directement aux Etats, qui appartient à tout françois, mais dont cet Ordre ne jouit pas encore*, No. 1, 25 Avril 1789 (Paris): iv–v.
59. Dufourny, *Invitation aux districts*, 22.
60. With less than enthusiasm Dufourny wrote, "In the course of our Revolution certain acts caused blood to be spilled and tears to flow; but if they made tyrants draw back, and however atrocious they may have been, if they saved the people, they are legitimate." *Allégeance! Justice! Vengeance!* (Paris, 1795), 15. The title may be misleading in that Dufourny does not call for vengeance here, but warns against it.
61. Dufourny, *Sentinelle, prends garde à toi*, 5.
62. Emmanuel Joseph, Sieyès, *What is the Third Estate?* ed. S. E. Finer, trans. M. Blondel (London, 1964), 120.

participation in the political process,[63] Dufourny criticized this position from the outset. He argued that in addition to their utility, the very humanity of the poor and working population entitled them to political representation.[64] Political thinkers, especially patriotic ones, do not always judge members of other polities by the criteria they apply to their own. Dufourny did. He demanded that international relations be conducted "in accordance with the fraternal affection among all men, the equality of rights, the liberty proper to each people, and the reciprocal obligations among them."[65] If liberty were a good thing for France, Dufourny argued, it was no less desirable for the people of Avignon, and the French were bound by the principles of their own Revolution to respect the independence and liberty of other peoples. Dufourny was certainly consistent here, and having been worsted in the Jacobin Club, took his case for the independence of Avignon to the public in a number of pamphlets. Dufourny's objections notwithstanding, Avignon was annexed by France in September 1791, with the support of Robespierre and a solid majority of the Jacobins. Dufourny's vision of international politics appears clearly in one of these pamphlets in which he refers to "the pact that you [the French] are about to finish declaring to all peoples, that of a universal peace."[66] Elsewhere he wonders whether the Festival of the Federation will remain a national holiday, or

63. Sieyès, *What is the Third Estate?* 78. The qualification for participating in district assemblies, a *capitation* payment of at least six livres was, of course, intended to restrict political activity to the *honnêtes gens*. The most recent treatment of Sieyès is William Hamilton Sewell, *A Rhetoric of Bourgeois Revolution: the Abbé Sieyès and What Is the Third Estate?* (Durham: Duke University Press, 1994).

64. Dufourny, *Cahiers*, 13. He reiterated the right of the people to participate in politics in his *Invitation au Districts*, 10. Dufourny repeatedly called for the elimination of the distinction between active and passive citizens (*Invitation au Districts*, 32; *Droits du peuple*, 16). In more concrete terms, he asked that district and section meetings be open to all without regard to wealth (*Adresse aux citoyens sur le meilleur plan de municipalité, Conclu de la déclaration des droits de l'Homme et du Citoyen* (Paris, 1790), 38, and noted with satisfaction that some districts had not enforced the six livres minimal *capitation* payment for admission to their meetings (ibid., 35). Dufourny was also explicit about his preference for direct over representative democracy (ibid., 23–24 and 49, and *Droits des Avignonois*, 10). Dufourny's advocacy of democracy in a broad and inclusive sense deserves further study. Particularly noteworthy is his willingness to apply his arguments to flesh-and-blood working people and his avoidance of treating the "people" as an abstraction that could be made to serve his own class or political objectives.

65. Dufourny, *Supplément à la défense des droits des Avignonois*, 14. The fraternity of nations was a logical consequence of the primal unity of humanity that Dufourny elsewhere described as "a great being which had but one soul . . . this collective soul"; *Le Gateau des rois* (Paris, 1790), 2.

66. *Droits des Avignonois*, 13.

whether it would eventually become "the festival of the apotheosis of man" and "a preliminary to universal peace."[67]

The second main feature of Dufourny's political vision is its irenicism and aversion to conflict. Though his basic assumptions about human nature and social organization led him to believe in the desirability and feasibility of far-reaching reform, Dufourny believed and repeatedly argued that such reforms must be carried out peacefully. On numerous occasions in the first years of the Revolution, he conjured up the threat of popular or peasant uprisings, but he did so in order to convince his educated and better-off contemporaries of the need to meet the pressing and legitimate demands of the working population for subsistence, employment, and enfranchisement. He feared social conflict and tried to avoid it in any way that did not compromise the principles of the Revolution. What he sought was the harmony of town and country and of different classes so that "the rich man, embraced by the poor and reintegrated into fraternity, will form one family and one nation together."[68] Dufourny's statements on the desirability of universal peace just cited indicate that his moralized political vision was not restricted to his own country, but comprehensively embraced all mankind in a harmonious unity. Though he ultimately worked energetically for the war effort of the Republic, in his continued commitment to irenicism Dufourny stood apart from the mainstream of revolutionary Jacobinism.

A third distinctive feature of Dufourny's political outlook is the importance he attached to public opinion. According to Dufourny, the Declaration of the Rights of Man ultimately derived its legitimacy from its having been submitted to public opinion.[69] Beyond this, Dufourny maintained, the National Assembly recognized that "the strength of the nation resides entirely in public opinion,"[70] and that "it is public opinion alone [*opinion générale*] that can make laws."[71] At the beginning of September 1793 Dufourny appealed to the public in a pamphlet entitled *Opinion publique ranime-toi, discute, prononce, éclaire, forme la volonté générale; dicte à ses rédacteurs les bases de loix définitives sur les denrées, sur la propriété, sur le*

67. Dufourny, *L'Homme libre aux hommes dignes de l'être, Pétition Présentée à l'Assemblée nationale, le 10 Juillet, l'an quatrième de la Liberté* (Paris, 1792), 9. On this aspect of Dufourny's thought, see my "La Notion de Paix perpétuelle pendant la Révolution: La Vision irénique de Dufourny de Villiers," in *J.-J. Rousseau: Politique et Nation. IIe Colloque International de Montmorency* (forthcoming).

68. Dufourny, *Invitation à tous les citoyens assemblés en sections* (Paris, 1790), 2–3.

69. Dufourny, *Adresse aux Citoyens sur le meilleur plan de municipalité*, 7 and 12.

70. Ibid., 11.

71. Dufourny, *L'Homme libre à tous les hommes dignes de la liberté*. This document is a folio-sized poster. BN Lb[41] 4804.

OPINION PUBLIQUE,

RANIME-TOI,

DISCUTE, PRONONCE, ÉCLAIRE,

FORME LA VOLONTÉ GENERALE;

DICTE A SES RÉDACTEURS LES BASES DE LOIX DÉFINITIVES SUR LES DENRÉES, SUR LA PROPRIÉTÉ, SUR LE COMMERCE, SUR L'ACCAPAREMENT ET SUR LES DROITS DES CONSOMMATEURS; PRÉPARE L'O-BÉISSANCE A LA LOI PAR L'ÉVIDENCE; SOUFFLE AUX REPRÉSENTANS DES HOMMES LIBRES TOUTE L'AUDACE DES GRANDES VÉRITÉS, ET ALORS ENFIN LA CERTITUDE DES SUBSISTANCES ASSURERA L'IM-MUABILITÉ DE LA LIBERTÉ.

OPINION PUBLIQUE,

Comme Citoyen, comme Magistrat du Peuple, je t'offre une suite de principes, je t'offre des germes de decrets; assez d'autres limeront des reglemens : examine sévè-rement, prononce, épure, adopte & fais le bonheur du genre humain.

L. P. DUFOURNY,
Président du Département de Paris.

Premier Septembre 1793,
l'an 2e. de la République française une & indivisible.

HOMMES LIBRES,

Lorsqu'a peine fortis des cachots de l'efclavage, vous balbutiez comme des enfans, les vérités fondamentales, vous étiez encore opprimés par cette constitution mo-

A

Title page of Dufourny's 1793 pamphlet on public opinion. Courtesy, Bibliothèque nationale de France, Paris.

commerce, sur l'accaparement et sur les droits des consommateurs; prépare l'obéissance à la loi par l'évidence; souffle aux représentans des hommes libres toute l'audace des grandes vérités, et alors enfin la certitude des subsistances assurera l'immuabilité de la liberté. Opinion publique, comme citoyen, comme magistrat du peuple, je t'offre une suite de principes, je t'offre des germes de décrets; assez d'autres limeront des réglemens: examine sévèrement, prononce, épure, adopte & fais le bonheur du genre humain.[72] The pamphlet contained a number of proposals that were to form the base of Jacobin economic policy during the period of their close cooperation with the sans-culottes, and reflected the virtually limitless hope that Dufourny naively invested in the public.

A year later, in September 1794, Dufourny was arrested on the authority of the Thermidorian Committee of General Security on the grounds that "the public voice designates Dufourny as an agitator of the people."[73] Against this calumny Dufourny appealed to the "true public voice," asserting "I call first to the public voice that has been outraged: *Public opinion, avenge yourself!* I then present myself before its tribunal."[74] Precisely what the complex construct of public opinion in fact thought of Dufourny at this time we do not know. The Committee of General Security seemed convinced that his arrest was unjustified, as it released him a short time later. What is clear from this incident is that the appeal to public opinion remained a powerful rhetorical device, and that retaining the credibility to speak in its name could decide one's fate. Dufourny, in any case, gave no indication that his faith in public opinion was shaken. But the need to distinguish between a true and a false public opinion shows how potentially variable and dangerous this usage could be.[75]

In practical terms Dufourny's respect for public opinion found expression in his advocacy of freedom of the press, at least for papers that in principle accepted the Revolution.[76] He took this position in his first pamphlet of 1789 and maintained it consistently.[77] His defense of this principle against

---

72. BN Lb⁴¹ 3278.

73. *L. P. Dufourny persecuté de nouveau* (Paris, 1794), 2. BHVP, imprimé 109461. This is the precise wording of the warrant for his arrest issued by the Committee of General Security. AN F⁷ 4686. Dufourny obviously had access to this document.

74. *L. P. Dufourny persecuté*, 2.

75. In his debate on the status of Avignon Dufourny had also argued that public opinion had been misled. *Droits des Avignonois*, 8 and *Droits des peuples*, 3.

76. While the commissioner of Paris to the Seine-Inférieure in the late summer of 1792 Dufourny by his own account suppressed a number of anti-revolutionary papers; *J*, 4:372.

77. In October 1792, he called for "the indefinite liberty of the press"; Dufourny, *L'Homme libre à tous les hommes dignes de la liberté*, 4.

a managed press (justified by its advocates in terms of the military crisis of 1793–94) at the Jacobin Club contributed to bringing about his arrest by the hard-line terrorists.[78] I suggest that Dufourny placed such emphasis on the power of public opinion not because, as it has become fashionable to maintain, public opinion was a new principle of authority, but because in his thoroughly moralized vision of politics moral suasion was the ultimate and most appropriate form of political activity.

If this characterization of Dufourny's politics as an extension of his moral values is valid, it raises two questions. First, how characteristic of the period was his political vision? Second, how came this advocate of social harmony, universal peace, and irenic reform to help implement, and then defend, the Terror of 1793–94?

To the first question, I would answer that Dufourny's extension of morality into politics is altogether typical not only of Jacobin activists,[79] but also of the climate of opinion of the last decades of the Old Regime. Common sense suggests that a man with idiosyncratic views would have been unlikely to have been selected by his peers for positions of leadership and responsibility as Dufourny repeatedly was.[80] Historians of Jacobinism as different as Crane Brinton and Ferenc Feher have commented on the heavily moralistic tone of the rhetoric of the clubs. What most historians of Jacobinism have overlooked is that this was a characteristic not restricted to Jacobins and their sympathizers. During the last decades of the Old Regime it was generally and pervasively believed that France faced a moral crisis, more particularly a crisis of moral disaggregation. The main elements of this putative crisis were beliefs that the moral fabric of France was being eaten away by egoism, luxury, and corruption, and that these forces were depopulating the country.[81] It is questionable whether France was any more corrupt in the 1770s and 1780s than it was before or after, and it is a matter

---

78. *J*, 6:355, 368, and 394.

79. It seems that Robespierre was oriented and driven by moral imperatives in which he believed, much in the way Dufourny was. Vadier, on the other hand, appears to have been motivated by more personal and material considerations. See Alfred Cobban, "The Fundamental Ideas of Robespierre," in *Aspects of the French Revolution* (New York: G. Braziller, 1968); and Martin Lyons, "M.-G.-A. Vadier (1736–1828): The Formation of the Jacobin Mentality," *French Historical Studies* 10 (1977): 74–100.

80. The Jacobins remind Brinton of the Puritans, and he finds in their concept of virtue "a collection of eighteenth-century stereotypes in which sentimentality and humanitarianism have a large part" (*Jacobins*, 175 and 179); Fehér, *Frozen Revolution*, 57.

81. See Harvey Chisick, *The Limits of Reform in the Enlightenment: Attitudes toward the Education of the Lower Classes in Eighteenth-Century France* (Princeton: Princeton University Press, 1981), chap. 4.

of record that the population of the country was then growing robustly. The point, however, is that the great majority of educated contemporaries believed that they were experiencing demographic contraction, and that the causes of the crisis they faced, and of which depopulation was but one concrete manifestation, were moral in nature.[82] The appropriate response to a crisis of moral disaggregation was a set of socially cohesive values, such as altruism, humanitarianism, patriotism, and virtue. These values were central to the discourse of the late Enlightenment, and did not need to wait for the Jacobins and Robespierre to give them currency. Indeed, this language, often inflated,[83] was common to Jacobins and non-Jacobins alike.

Roger Chartier has recently suggested that "a passion for regeneration" in France dates from the spring of 1789.[84] This is probably to draw too sharp a line. Concern about corruption, luxury, egoism, and the decline of moral standards during the last decades of the Old Regime has been commented upon by both contemporaries and scholars.[85] The comments by contemporaries were made not simply as lamentation, but in order to increase awareness of problems so as to deal with them. As L.-S. Mercier wrote, "I describe vices and unhappiness only because this description can become the remedy for men I do not believe to be absolutely depraved, but rather inattentive, distracted, or too much given to their pleasures."[86] Books, pamphlets, and journals asserted the primacy of morality, lamented

82. Ibid.

83. A rhetoric of moral concerns and imperatives easily becomes heated. But this is not to say that it is necessarily radical. Indeed there is no contradiction in using highly charged rhetoric for moderate or conservative purposes, especially if the intention is monitory. The typical structure of biblical prophecy entails the description or threat of dire punishment followed by a pivotal "if" clause—if the people does not mend its ways—and an exhortation to do so. See Abraham Joshua Heschel, *The Prophets* (New York: Harper and Row, 1962), 312–13. Dufourny's warnings of the danger of imminent revolution if the people were not treated in a more considerate and humane way can fairly be seen as having similar intent.

84. Chartier, *Cultural Origins*, 113.

85. The writer most closely associated with the denunciation of corruption at the time and the attempt to work out a viable morally based politics in response is Rousseau. See, for example, Jean Starobinski, *Jean-Jacques Rousseau: Transparency and Obstruction,* trans. Arthur Goldhammer (Chicago: University of Chicago Press, 1988), chap. 2; Judith N. Shklar, *Men and Citizens: A Study of Rousseau's Social Theory* (Cambridge: Cambridge University Press, 1985), 103; and Carol Blum, *Rousseau and the Republic of Virtue: The Language of Politics in the French Revolution* (Ithaca: Cornell University Press, 1986), 25–26. It should be borne in mind, however, that Rousseau did not and could not have created interest in these issues. His great popularity in the closing decades of the Old Regime was in large part a result of his ability to articulate and address the latent concerns of a large portion of the educated French public.

86. Louis-Sébastien Mercier, *Tableau de Paris,* 2 vols. ed. Jean-Claude Bonnet (Paris: Mercure de France, 1994), 1:868.

a perceived increase in corruption (especially in towns), debated the causes for what was believed to be happening, and offered reformist solutions.[87] It has recently been argued that "deprived of a political outlet, the critical conscience of the Enlightenment politicized everything in the name of morality."[88] Certainly it is difficult to distinguish moral from political categories at this time. Thinking primarily in moral terms and convinced of the efficacy of moral agency, the literate public of the last decades of the Old Regime carried over these convictions into the Revolution. Far from having to invent moral categories of discourse with the convocation of the Estates General, the men and women of 1789 continued to speak in the categories to which they were accustomed.

In an excellent recent study, Thomas Adams describes a pamphlet by Jean-François Lambert, entitled *Cahier des Pauvres*, that in many ways recalls Dufourny's *Cahiers du Quatrième Ordre*, as "giving a foretaste of Jacobin preoccupations and the Jacobin rhetoric of virtue."[89] Now Lambert, despite his rhetoric of virtue in 1789, which Adams is quite right to note, never became a Jacobin. Indeed, in 1791 he denounced the Jacobins in the same moralizing language he had used to urge reform two years earlier.[90] The point is that a rhetoric of moral crisis was general in the last decades

87. See, for example, Warren E. Roberts, *Morality and Social Class in Eighteenth-Century French Literature and Painting* (Toronto: University of Toronto Press, 1974); André Morize, *L'Apologie du luxe au XVIIIe siècle: Etude critique sur "Le Mondain" et ses sources* (Geneva, 1970); Jack Censer, *The French Press in the Age of Enlightenment* (London: Routledge, 1994), 65–67 and 70–78; Joan Landes, *Women and the Public Sphere in the Age of the French Revolution* (Ithaca: Cornell University Press, 1988), 27; and Chartier, *Cultural Origins*, 182–83. Arguably an appreciation of the highly charged moral atmosphere of the last decades of the Old Regime will allow us better to appreciate the resonance of the political pornography of the time. Emmet Kennedy has described libertinism as "the inverse of hypermoral sensibility," in *A Cultural History of the French Revolution* (New Haven: Yale University Press, 1989), 136; while Antoine de Baecque has observed that the political pornography of the early Revolution is characterized by "a tendentious use of every literary device to contrast the sick, impotent, and decadent old order with the regenerated new society"; see his "Pamphlets: Libel and Political Mythology," in *Revolution in Print: The Press in France, 1775–1800*, ed. Robert Darnton and Daniel Roche (Berkeley and Los Angeles: University of California Press, 1989), 168.

88. Anthony J. La Vopa, "Conceiving a Public: Ideas and Society in Eighteenth-Century Europe," *Journal of Modern History* 64 (1992): 84.

89. Thomas McStay Adams, *Bureaucrats and Beggars: French Social Policy in the Age of the Enlightenment* (New York: Oxford University Press, 1990), 219.

90. J. F. Lambert, *Démonstration au peuple du mal que lui ont fait les Jacobins et tous les clubs du royaume, de la nécessité d'une coalition paisible des bons citoyens de tous les partis contre les excès qu'on aurait à redouter de leur part, Indication d'un point central où aboutiraient à cet effet les lumières et les ressources, pour se propager ensuite sur tous les points de la surface de l'empire* (Paris, 1791).

of the Old Regime and that in 1789 just about everyone used the kind of language that was to become associated with the Jacobins.[91] What has been insufficiently recognized is that the Jacobin rhetoric of virtue is merely one aspect of the mentality and language of moral crisis that pervaded the intellectual climate of the late Enlightenment.[92] Dufourny's moralism, then, reflects a considerable degree of continuity between the late Enlightenment and significant strands of revolutionary discourse.

As presented here, Dufourny's political career contains a contradiction. On the one hand, he conceived of both the ends and means of politics in moral terms; on the other, he actively participated in and subsequently justified the Terror of 1793–94. One school of historians would argue that there is no contradiction here, that Dufourny's rhetoric of virtue, unified wills, and patriotism disposed him inevitably toward the kind of totalitarianism that found expression in the Terror. He was but another instrument of that absolute master of politics: the semiotic circuit.[93]

There are a number of reasons why, it seems to me, this explanation is inadequate. First, it is unable to explain why people who shared common assumptions about politics and spoke the same language in 1789 should subsequently have embarked on radically different political courses, as Dufourny and Lambert did. Second, it fails to explain why the Jacobins and Dufourny should have abandoned their irenicism for a policy of war and terror at one time rather than another. This is the great drawback of theories

91. Tocqueville, though he did not like it, recognized that the rhetoric associated with the Revolution was widespread before 1789. He observed that "the inflated sentimentalism, the exaggerated expressions, the incoherence, and the ungainly images, those constant citations from antiquity which were to be characteristic of the language of the Revolution were already habitual at this time [1787]." Alexis de Tocqueville, *The European Revolution and Correspondence with Gobineau*, intro., ed., and trans. John Lukacs (New York: Doubleday, 1959), 49 n.3.

92. Chisick, *Limits of Reform*, chap. 4.

93. Furet, *Interpreting the French Revolution*, 48. Furet, it is worth noting, has been uncommonly fortunate in his translator. In the original the passage in question reads: "Si la Révolution française vit ainsi, dans sa pratique, les contradictions théoriques de la démocratie, c'est qu'elle inaugure un monde où les représentations du pouvoir sont le centre de l'action, et où le circuit sémiotique est maître absolu de la politique" (*Penser la Révolution française* [Paris: Gallimard, 1978], 72). Elborg Forster has rendered this: "If the Revolution thus experienced, in its political practices, the theoretical contradictions of democracy, it was because it ushered in a world where mental representations of power governed all actions, and where a network of signs completely dominated political life" (*Interpreting the French Revolution*, 48). While faithful to the sense of the original, the translation moderates the extremeness of its tone, thus rendering it more accessible and credible.

based on atemporal structures: they are unable to account for the way a specific set of events works itself out and the contingencies that influence them. It is probably not too much to say that such theories are ahistorical, and so unable to come to grips with specific circumstances unfolding through time.[94] If the semiotic circuit were, as Furet maintains, the absolute master of politics, it would be sufficient for historians to study linguistics, and things would be very much simpler than they in fact are. Yet linguistic reductionism is as flawed as any other kind of reductionism, perhaps more so. In this context it is worth recalling Tocqueville's observation that "people fail to see the specific circumstances of the 1790s which helped to bring about the victory of the French revolutionary democratic government in 1792."[95] It is just possible that Dufourny, Robespierre,[96] Paine,[97] Burke,[98] Jaurès, Mathiez, Lefebvre, Soboul, Furet himself in an earlier work,[99] and others were right, and that one cannot understand either the Revolution or its most controversial episode without paying very close attention indeed to circumstance. People do of course have their beliefs and aspirations, and they can be carried away by rhetoric. Whether they are able to realize their ideals, and if so in what form, often depends on forces beyond their control or understanding. One may ignore these forces—or circumstances—if one so chooses, but then the result will not be history as we normally understand it.

Dufourny, one will not be surprised to learn, adhered to what Furet has called the theory of circumstances. He believed that the Revolution was forced away from its initial reform program aimed at constitutional reorganization and moral regeneration by the counterrevolution and war. It was either fight and win or return to the Old Regime. Conceptually, Dufourny's explanation of the Terror works on two levels, the one ideological-political (the values and reform program of the Revolution), the other pragmatic and

94. In his essay "The French Revolution is Over" in *Interpreting the French Revolution*, 61, Furet writes, "In so deducing the Terror from revolutionary discourse one lays oneself open to the objection that one is disregarding 'circumstances,' that godsend of historical causality." One does indeed. Furet does not inquire what alternate means the French government of 1793–94 might have used to restore order internally or to organize the war effort and fight the armies of enemy states. Yet the question is not without significance.

95. Tocqueville, *European Revolution*, 116.

96. Speech of 5 February 1794.

97. Thomas Paine, *Rights of Man*, ed. Eric Foner (Harmondsworth: Penguin, 1987), 60.

98. Edmund Burke, *Reflections on the Revolution in France*, ed. Conor Cruise O'Brien (Harmondsworth: Penguin, 1968), 89–90.

99. François Furet and Denis Richet, *The French Revolution*, trans. Stephen Hardman (London: Macmillan, 1970), 182–87.

extraconstitutional (counterrevolution and war). Since by itself an ideological response to a military threat was inadequate, the revolutionary authorities devised a pragmatic one through mass mobilization, centralized control of the economy, and the complex of legislation known as the Terror. Against this two-tiered explanation of the Terror most revisionists prefer a more unified and elegant account. If the political culture of France was responsible for 1789, they argue, then it must be held responsible for 1793 as well. The inner logic of the working of public opinion, the model of the general will, inadequacies in the concept of representation, the rhetoric of virtue, and the power of words and images—these are the things that caused the internally flawed if pacific ideology of 1789 to eventuate into the repression and bloodshed of 1793–94. Now if contemporaries are not always the best interpreters of their own actions, they are not necessarily the worst. They tend, on the whole, not to miss immediate and obvious aspects of their own experience. While the categories of political culture can be used to provide a model for the shift from the liberalism of 1789 to the violence and repressiveness of 1793, and while that explanation may be coherent, it may not provide the most comprehensive and convincing account of the events in question. There are two important areas that revisionists generally do not consider so closely as they might. One concerns the history of ideas.

To appreciate the key values in Dufourny's outlook in 1789 one must be reasonably familiar with the climate of opinion of the last decades of the Old Regime, and not just with the formal thought of that period, but with the texture of that thought. Concentrating on developing a new model to inform understanding and to direct research, emphasizing the function of the print media in the dynamic of an emerging political culture, and concerning themselves largely with the role of public opinion as a new principle of authority and with the formal expression of elites, adherents of the cultural interpretation of the Revolution tend to discount the findings of more traditional history of ideas.[100] And focusing on the break about to occur in 1789, these historians show particular interest in contestation.[101] Oriented in this way, researchers are not likely to be sensitive to the extent and significance of the moral discourse prevalent in the decades after midcentury; nor, geared up to explain radical change, will they be receptive to the

100. Chartier, *Cultural Origins*, 17–19.

101. See, for example, part 3 of Baker, *Political Culture of the Old Regime* and the articles of Baker, Censer, and Joynes, in Censer and Popkin, *Press and Politics in Pre-Revolutionary France*.

implicitly conservative intent of much of this discourse. Yet, I would argue, the overwhelming majority of writers and intellectuals active after 1750 sought to improve the lives of their fellow citizens, and conceived of doing so within the framework of the existing order, an order, it should be noted, that they generally regarded as viable.[102] Robert Darnton has recently pointed out that accounts of serious political contestation are curiously absent from the mainstream print media during most of the 1780s, the dominant subjects at the time being mesmerism and hot-air balloons.[103] Concurrently, there was much talk about social responsibility and the value of family.[104] Under rubrics such as "Traits de Vertus," journals described the exercise of socially cohesive values. The selfless and responsible beneficence of a widow and working mother of a large family, one Madame Menthe, was extolled in the pages of the *Journal Encyclopédique*, and materially as well as symbolically rewarded by a lodge of Paris Freemasons.[105] The same journal gave an account of the foundation of a *fête des Rosières*, which provided a way of encouraging "virtue" in young women of marriageable age.[106] These are instances of an extensive attempt to stabilize and strengthen the social fabric of the Old Regime, and are an important part of a picture that includes, to be sure, both mesmerism and significant political contestation. And while it is logical to see a contestatory mentality eventuating in revolution, one should not dismiss out of hand the possibility that a morally oriented, generally humanitarian, meliorative, and conservative outlook could, less directly, lead to the same result.

Dufourny's career also calls into question the effectiveness of the paradigm of political culture in dealing with properly social issues. Revisionists from Cobban, Taylor, and Furet on have consistently argued that the Revolution is better understood in political terms than social ones. The elaboration of the concept of political culture in which a highly specific notion of public opinion plays a central role, and the assumption of the autonomy of politics

102. Chisick, *Limits of Reform*, 266–70.

103. Darnton, *The Forbidden Best-Sellers of Pre-Revolutionary France* (New York: Norton, 1995), 240. Darnton had also brought attention to this situation in *Mesmerism and the End of the Enlightenment in France* (Cambridge: Harvard University Press, 1968), 41–42.

104. Censer, *French Press in the Age of Enlightenment*, 70–73. This often took the form of the denunciation of egoism and of bachelors who shirked their social and demographic responsibilities. See Chisick, *Limits of Reform*, 236.

105. Ibid., 231–33.

106. Ibid., 235. For a more extensive treatment of this subject see Sarah Maza, "The Rose Girl of Salency: Representations of Virtue in Prerevolutionary France," *Eighteenth-Century Studies* 22 (1988–89): 395–412.

has resulted in a shift of emphasis that has obscured certain issues. We have learned a great deal in recent years about writers, journalists, image-makers, and politicians—that is, the intellectual elites—who played roles in the Revolution, and this increase in knowledge is unquestionably useful. One consequence of this tendency, though, has been to provide an overly cerebral account of revolutionary politics, one that overlooks the role and condition of the lower classes.[107] Primarily oriented to problems of subsistence and less amenable to analysis in terms of symbolic representation, the lower classes play a small part in the work of most revisionists.[108] It is well to keep in mind Carlyle's dour observation that "this Sovereign People hath a digestive faculty, and cannot do without bread."[109] A portrayal of the Revolution from the shoulders up will not do justice to the large issue of popular participation. Nor will such an approach allow us to appreciate the concrete and informed description that Dufourny offered of the condition of the working population, or the way he engaged the problems involved in constructing a theory of democracy and a system of democratic practice.

If we accept that Dufourny's political vision was characteristic of its time and milieu, what conclusions should we draw? I think we are now justified in describing the Jacobin mentality as in a significant sense archaic. The focal points of Dufourny's political vision are virtue, the general good,

107. Two attempts to engage the problem of lower class participation in the Revolution from the revisionist point of view are Colin Lucas, "The Crowd and Politics between Ancien Regime and Revolution in France," *Journal of Modern History* 60 (1988): 421–57; and Brian Singer, "Violence in the French Revolution: Forms of Ingestion/Forms of Expulsion," in *The French Revolution and the Birth of Modernity*, ed. Ferenc Fehér (Berkeley and Los Angeles: University of California Press, 1990), 150–73. Arlette Farge has treated the problem of the political culture of the poor in *Subversive Words: Public Opinion in Eighteenth-Century France*, trans. Rosemary Morris (University Park: Pennsylvania State University Press, 1995).

108. In his admirable *The Structural Transformation of the Public Sphere: An Inquiry into a Category of Bourgeois Society*, trans. Thomas Burger (Cambridge: MIT Press, 1989), Jürgen Habermas provided the conceptual basis for the models of the public sphere and public opinion that are central to much revisionist historiography. In this work he closely linked cultural to political and socioeconomic developments. This latter element of his analysis has generally been ignored or rejected by revisionists. Baker, for example, treated the the public as a principle of authority, but was indifferent to it as a social construct in his article "Politics and Public Opinion under the Old Regime" (213–13). More recently he has written: "Little seems to be gained by attempting to analyze these political developments in the conventional Marxist terms used by Habermas in 1962"; "Defining the Public Sphere in Eighteenth-Century France," in *Habermas and the Public Sphere*, ed. Craig Calhoun (Cambridge: MIT Press, 1992), 192. One might argue that Habermas uses Marxist categories in a highly innovative way, and one may well question the wisdom of eliminating properly social factors from the analysis of culture.

109. Thomas Carlyle, *The French Revolution*, 2 vols. (New York and London: Colonial Press, 1900), 2:213.

humanity, liberty, equality, and fraternity. None of these values individually, nor the complex taken together, is compatible with the key dynamic of modern liberal democracy; namely, the notion of legitimized self, group, or class interest formally organized around political parties. The emphasis Dufourny places on individual volition and his tendency to reduce politics to moral choice puts him closer to Plato and Aristotle than to Malthus, Mill, or Marx. This was an emphasis he shared with probably the most famous of his fellow Jacobins. An important historian of the Revolution has maintained that "Robespierre belonged to the past, rather than the future, in holding that the application of fundamental moral principles in government was the only cure for political evils."[110] More recently the instability of French political culture at the end of the eighteenth century has been attributed to a blend of economic modernity and political archaism. Mona Ozouf has written of an attempt to restore "the archaic dream of full integration in the collectivity and unified public opinion," while Roger Chartier has characterized the Terror as a "return to archaic behavior patterns."[111] Albert Soboul has brought attention to the archaic character of sans-culotte economic aspirations.[112] And both George Rudé and Colin Lucas have commented on the traditional values and assumptions of the crowd before and during the Revolution.[113] It is perhaps ironical that an archaic Jacobin political ideal and morality complemented by a traditionally oriented and motivated popular movement should have provided the radicals of the French Revolution with the inspiration and courage to defeat the combined forces of Europe's old regimes—at least for a time.

110. Cobban, "The Fundamental Ideas of Robespierre," in *Aspects of the French Revolution* (New York: G. Braziller, 1968), 137.

111. Pierre Rosanvallon, "L'Utilitarisme français et les ambiguïtés de la culture politique prérévolutionnaire (position d'un problème)," in Baker, *The Political Culture of the Old Regime*, 437; Ozouf, "Public Opinion," 520; Chartier, *Cultural Origins*, 195.

112. See A Soboul, *Les Sans-culottes parisiens*, 457–96.

113. George F. E. Rudé, "The Pre-Industrial Crowd," in *Paris and London in the Eighteenth Century: Studies in Popular Protest* (New York: Viking, 1970), 22, and Lucas, "The Crowd and Politics," 430 and 438.

Part III

Conceptions of the Public Sphere in Eighteenth-Century France

6

"Sons of the Same Father"

Gender, Race, and Citizenship in French Saint-Domingue, 1760–1792

John D. Garrigus

By 1789 France's Caribbean colony of Saint-Domingue was home to the largest, wealthiest, and most self-confident free population of African descent in the Americas. Comprising close to half the colony's free population, these *gens de couleur* won civil equality with whites from the French Legislative Assembly in April 1792 and their political demands helped produce the Haitian Revolution. This article lays the foundation for a reappraisal of the actions of Saint-Domingue's free men of color in the French Revolution by drawing attention to the role of gender in colonial racial discourse before the fall of the Bastille.

After 1763 legal and social prejudice against free mulattoes and other nonenslaved people of African descent in Saint-Domingue was based on feminized stereotypes. Colonial writers began to describe free men and women of color as passionate, narcissistic, and parasitic. Because of these dangerous vices, elite white society increasingly excluded free people of even the most remote African ancestry. Tensions about the nature of white political power and cultural identity in Saint-Domingue produced this fusion of racial and gender categories. After the Seven Years' War new immigration from Europe and the increasingly "civilized" tone of elite colonial society raised the question of how "French" Saint-Domingue could become. Could a slave plantation colony produce a civic-minded public of the sort said to be emerging in France at this time?[1] Many colonial planters, magistrates, and merchants wanted to believe it could. The appropriation of metropolitan political discourse in an intense feud between the colony's *Conseils supérieurs* (high courts) and royal administrators led these elites to an explanation of how free Dominguan society differed from France. Using gender to solidify and expand the social category *gens de couleur,* placing it firmly outside French colonial society, white Saint-Domingue argued for its own freedom from ministerial despotism. Engendering the image of people of mixed blood answered troubling questions about white behavior in Saint-Domingue and seemed to guarantee that an orderly, rational colonial public could emerge. Feminized stereotypes reinforced the rejection of people of color who in nearly every other way, wealth, education, distance from slavery, even physical appearance, were indistinguishable from whites.

Before the dominance of sugar slavery in the 1700s, censuses of Saint-Domingue counted free men, women, children, and servants, not "whites" and "mulattoes."[2] In the colony's rough-and-tumble seventeenth-century

1. For the current historiographical debate on this issue see Joan G. Landes, *Women and the Public Sphere in the Age of the French Revolution* (Ithaca: Cornell University Press, 1988) and the following critiques: Keith Michael Baker, *Inventing the French Revolution: Essays on French Political Culture in the Eighteenth Century* (New York: Cambridge University Press, 1990); Baker, "Defining the Public Sphere in Eighteenth-Century France: Variations on a Theme by Habermas," in *Habermas and the Public Sphere,* ed. Craig Calhoun (Cambridge: MIT Press, 1991), 181–211; Roger Chartier, *The Cultural Origins of the French Revolution,* trans. Lydia G. Cochrane (Durham: Duke University Press, 1991); Dena Goodman, "Public Sphere and Private Life: Toward a Synthesis of Current Historiographical Approaches to the Old Regime," *History and Theory* 31 (1992): 1–20; David A. Bell, "The 'Public Sphere,' the State, and the World of Law in Eighteenth-Century France," *French Historical Studies* 17 (Fall 1992): 912–34; Daniel Gordon, "Philosophy, Sociology, and Gender in the Enlightenment Conception of Public Opinion," *French Historical Studies* 17 (Fall 1992): 882–911; Sarah Maza, "Women, the Bourgeoisie, and the Public Sphere: Response to Daniel Gordon and David Bell," *French Historical Studies* 17 (Fall 1992): 935–50; and Dale K. Van Kley, "New Wine in Old Wineskins: Continuity and Rupture in the Pamphlet Debate of the French Prerevolution, 1787–1789," *French Historical Studies* 17, no. 2 (Fall 1992): 447–65.

2. For example, the 1720 census of lands in the southern peninsula that had been under the control of the Compagnie de Saint-Domingue (Archives Nationales Section Outre-Mer, henceforth ANSOM, G¹509 No. 17) did not count free coloreds, but a 1713 general colonial

buccaneer society, race was not the obsession it would later become. Before the massive importation of African slaves for sugar work, children of mixed descent were apparently considered free from birth. Even in 1685, the metropolitan authors of the Code Noir were more concerned about sin than race and racial mixture. The code ordered the confiscation of mixed-race children and slave concubines, but stated that if a master married his slave mistress, she would be automatically free, as would the children of their union. Under the original terms of the Code Noir, ex-slaves enjoyed all the rights accorded to whites.[3]

As plantation slavery developed in the eighteenth century, colonial practice modified these laws to protect the hierarchy of "white" over "black" on which sugar profits depended. But concubinage between European men and African women was extensive and the sorts of master/slave marriages described in the Code Noir occurred as well.[4] Most European men left their wives and daughters behind in France and constituted new, ostensibly temporary, households with colonial women who shared their table, managed their domestic affairs, and often bore their children. By the 1720s many of these women were Caribbean-born, of mixed African and European ancestry. In this early period free men of color were often former slaves who were clearly "nonwhite." However, the social position of many free women of color was blurred by their relationships with white men. In the general census of 1730, for example, officials across Saint-Domingue reported the number of *mulâtres libres* but left the category *mulâtresse libre* blank for more than half the colony.[5] Evidence suggests that in the first half of the century, local authorities often included the wives, free mistresses, and racially mixed children of colonists in their enumerations of "white" society. Free women who owned property, could read and write French, and were faithful to the French church, were counted as white.

---

census did (ANSOM G¹509 No. 12). In the 1730 general census [ANSOM G¹509 No. 20], officials from the West province did not record numbers for free women of color, only for men in this class, though the North province provided data on both sexes. Only from 1739 (ANSOM G¹509 No. 21) do surviving general censuses systematically report the population of free men and women of color.

3. See *Le Code Noir* (Paris, 1767 [Basse-Terre, 1980]), 33–34, 55; and the interpretation in Alan Watson, *Slave Law in the Americas* (Athens: University of Georgia Press, 1989), 83–90.

4. Pierre de Vaissière, *Saint-Domingue: La société et la vie créoles sous l'ancien régime 1629–1789* (Paris: Librairie Academique Perrin, 1909), 65, cites the example from the 1730s of one of the richest planters in Saint-Domingue who began by marrying a free black woman who owned thirty slaves.

5. ANSOM G¹509 No. 20; however throughout the slave-owning Americas, women and mixed-race children were twice as likely as men to be freed, especially when there were few European women in the colony, as was the case in Saint-Domingue. Herbert S. Klein, *African*

Marie and Françoise Begasse were two such women. They were the legiti-mate daughters of a white planter in the coastal parish of Bainet. Born sometime around the beginning of the eighteenth century, the two sisters married ambitious French immigrants in the 1720s and produced, between them, more than a dozen children. As adults these men and women, like their mothers, owned property, abided by the law, attended church, and spoke, read, and wrote French well. By all documentary indications, local officials regarded Marie and Françoise Begasse as "white" up to the 1760s. They did not describe their skin color and did accord them the respectful titles of "Demoiselle" and "Dame." According to Moreau de Saint-Méry in 1730 Bainet had only twelve free people of color and 317 whites. But a visiting official touring the parish the following year said that there were few whites there, since most had married into wealthy families of color.[6] Indeed Marie and Françoise Begasse had a white father and a black mother. But only in the 1760s would the two women be consistently identified in documents as *mulâtresses libres*. With the establishment of the plantation economy, social categories in Saint-Domingue became increasingly based on genealogy rather than cultural identity.[7] In the 1730s men were more likely than women to be labeled "colored"; by the 1760s many whites argued that the free population of color was dangerously feminized.

The expansion of sugar also changed colonial attitudes about militia service. The hunters and pirates of the seventeenth century lent their sabers and muskets to French imperial strategy, reaping rewards in Spanish treasure. But by the 1740s colonists had bent their swords into sugar mills. Planters fought the royal administration over militia obligations and from the middle of the eighteenth century this issue was at the core of the debate about whether Saint-Domingue could have a "public" in the new sense of the word and whether people of color would be a part of that public.

Colonial governors, drawn from the royal army or navy, favored a strong militia as the basis of local government. Parish militia captains answered to

Slavery in Latin America and the Caribbean (New York: Oxford University Press, 1986), 227; Arlette Gautier, *Soeurs de Solitude* (Paris: Editions Caribéennes 1985), 172–74.

6. AN Colonie F³ 91, pp. 96–97; Census cited in Médéric Louis Elie Moreau de Saint-Méry, *Description topographique, physique, civile, politique et historique de la partie française de l'isle Saint Domingue*, ed. Blanche Maurel and Etienne Taillemite (1797); (Paris: Société d'histoire d'Outre-Mer, 1984), 1155.

7. For more on the Begasse and a longer development of this argument, see John D. Garrigus, "Blue and Brown: Contraband Indigo and the Rise of a Free Colored Planter Class in French Saint-Domingue," *The Americas* 50 (October 1993): 233–63.

the governor, collected taxes, kept the peace and often settled legal questions. But their neighbors resented this authority and Saint-Domingue's two *conseils* attacked the quasi-judicial role of these captains. The *conseils* were high courts that Versailles had originally staffed with ex-buccaneers and influential planters as a way of strengthening French rule. However, these magistrates came to see themselves as colonial *parlementaires,* and they led opposition to royal policies, especially the militia.[8]

Criticism of the militia system became a way for colonial judges to challenge the power of royal governors and their local appointees. Many magistrates and planters believed the *conseils,* not royal officialdom, should oversee local administration, so that the "rule of law" could replace the "arbitrary" power wielded by parish captains, colonial governors and, ultimately, Versailles.

Conflict over the militia system reached its zenith during the Seven Years' War. Colonists loudly insisted that the time and money they spent on defense duties were ruining their plantations. After Guadeloupe was captured by the British, Versailles was worried about Dominguan loyalty and agreed to disband the colonial militia. When hostilities had ended, parish captains would be replaced by a *syndic* chosen locally under *conseil* authority.[9]

Though much celebrated in the colony, this reform was short-lived. The duc de Choiseul's reorganization of French imperial defenses after 1763 reinstated the militia. In fact, the aftermath of the war transformed Dominguan society in at least three ways, leading to new attitudes about the free population of color. First of all, the reestablishment of the unpopular militia embittered the struggle between the *conseils* and royal administrators. Second, after the loss of Canada, Saint-Domingue more than ever became the focus of French immigration, commerce, and slave traffic. Peace accelerated the growth of the Dominguan economy but it also created a new class of angry white men—*petits blancs*—who were unable to fulfill their dreams of sugar riches. Third, peace brought more administrators and government functionaries to France's most valuable possession, changing the tone and tempo of urban society. Printing presses, theaters, public parks, and Masonic lodges were established in the colony. In short, white Saint-Domingue

8. Charles Frostin, "Histoire de l'autonomisme colon de la partie française de St Domingue aux XVIIᵉ et XVIIIᵉ siècles: Contribution à l'étude du sentiment américain d'independance" (Thesis, Université de Paris, 1972), 213; Pierre Pluchon, ed., *Histoire des Antilles et de la Guyane* (Toulouse: Privat, 1982), 83.

9. Moreau de Saint-Méry, *Loix et constitutions des colonies françaises de l'Amérique sous le vent* (Paris, 1784–90), 4:538–39.

began to build its own public sphere. These changes began almost immediately with the arrival of a new governor in 1764.

Charles Comte d'Estaing, charged with reinstalling the militia in 1764, was the first of a new style of administrator for Saint-Domingue. Earning ten to fifteen times the salary of his predecessors, d'Estaing installed himself in the colony with a large household staff, armorial dinner service, expensive wine and books, and an elaborate wardrobe.[10]

He also came equipped with his own ideas about how to reinstate the militia. The new governor believed that a lack of patriotism was at the heart of France's military problems and he tried to muster a new civic spirit in the colony. He established prizes, medals and new ranks, and renamed the militia La Legion Nationale. D'Estaing hoped this cultural re-engineering would popularize the institution and spare him a confrontation with colonial magistrates.[11]

He was disappointed. In 1764 and 1765 the Port-au-Prince *conseil* branded his militia reforms illegal. Printed placards, petitions, and pamphlets criticizing the governor circulated widely in the colony. D'Estaing was labeled a tyrant and his personal wealth was presented as evidence of corruption and his insatiable desire for power.[12] The *conseil* would not register his ordinance and Versailles called in another chief administrator in 1766.

This new governor, the Prince de Rohan-Montbazon, adopted the same ostentatious style. Like d'Estaing he was rebuffed by the Port-au-Prince *conseil,* which by now probably included twelve *avocats* sent from the obstreperous Parlement of Paris.[13] After several years of fierce political con-

10. Michel Vergé-Franceschi, "Fortune et plantations des administrateurs coloniaux aux îles d'Amérique aux XVIIe et XVIIIe siècles," in *Commerce et plantation dans la Caraïbe XVIIIe et XIXe siècles: Actes du colloque de Bordeaux, 15–16 Mars 1991,* ed. Paul Butel (Bordeaux: Maison des pays iberiques, 1992), 124.

11. AN C⁹ᴮ17, d'Estaing's MS. "Objets principaux que j'ai eu dans . . . l'ordonnance des milices," dated 15 January 1765; AN C⁹ᴮ17, d'Estaing's memoir entitled "Observations particulières" dated 14 June 1765, Nᵒ20bis; AN C⁹ᴮ17bis, 18 August 1765, letter from d'Estaing to Choiseul, the colonial minister.

12. Vergé-Franceschi, "Fortune et plantations des administrateurs coloniaux," 124; AN Col. F³179, p. 56. "Arrête du Conseil du Port-au-Prince qui nomme quatre commissaires pour faire le relevé des pouvoirs du Général et de l'Intendant; du 24 Janvier, 1765." However, the most public statements of this perspective came in the local assemblies convoked by d'Estaing's successor, the Prince du Rohan, in 1766. AN Col. F³180, p. 322.

13. On Rohan-Montbazon, see Vergé-Franceschi, "Fortune et plantations des administrateurs coloniaux," 124–25; AN Col. C9b18 "Copie de la lettre de Mgr le Duc de Choiseul à M. Etienne Batonnier de l'ordre des avocats. De Versailles le 3 mars 1766." This letter was apparently written in frustration at the difficulties that the Port-au-Prince *Conseil* raised for d'Estaing: "Le Roi étant, Monsieur, dans l'intention de rendre sédentaires les Conseils

flict, when explicit militia orders directly from the king finally arrived, antimilitia forces continued to blame the reform on Rohan's "tyranny." They refused to muster as ordered and were defeated by royal troops and loyal militia units in early 1769.[14]

These events confirmed the broad alignment of colonial and metropolitan political discourse down to the Revolution.[15] Magistrates and their supporters portrayed royal administrators as corrupt courtiers devoted solely to personal advancement. They debated why a civic spirit that might temper this despotism was slow to arise in Saint-Domingue.[16] Royal administrators also lamented the lack of public-spiritedness, which for them meant willingness to serve in the militia. With headstrong slaveowners, unemployed *petits blancs*, and few church or family influences, the colony was ungovernable, they reported.[17]

Despite these political struggles, or perhaps because of them, after 1763 observers generally agreed that white Saint-Domingue was becoming "more civilized," more French. In fact, accelerating slave imports were making the colony even more African, demographically. Nevertheless Moreau de Saint-Méry dubbed this the colony's "second age":[18] "Finally the light of civilization and *politesse* appeared after the peace of 1763, which brought army regiments, *officiers généreux*, lavish intendants, the fashionable of every station . . . the simple and steadfast ways of the colonists drew close to those of the home country."[19]

Saint-Domingue's *conseils* followed more closely than ever the style and pretensions of France's *parlements*. The populations of Cap Français, Port-

Supérieurs de St. Domingue et de les composer de Sujets instruits et éprouvés, j'ai proposé à S. M. de prendre douze avocats du Parlement de Paris pour remplir un pareil nombre de places de Conseiller qui sont vacantes dans les deux Conseils supérieurs. S. M. ayant approuvé . . . vouloir bien m'indiquer les sujets qui voudront prendre ce parti . . . "

14. AN Col. F³180, p. 340 "Lettre du Ministre à M. Le Chevalier Prince de Rohan sur le retablissment des Milices, 14 juin 1767"; AN Col. F³ 180, p. 363–64, "Lettre de M. le Prince de Rohan au ministre sur les milices . . . 10 Novembre 1767"; AN Col. F³181, pp. 142–44. See the account in Charles Frostin, *Les révoltes blanches* (Toulouse: Editions de l'Ecole, 1975).

15. On the ministerial versus magisterial tensions in prerevolutionary pamphlet literature, see Dale Van Kley, "New Wine in Old Wineskins," 454, 455.

16. AN Col. F³ 192, anonymous MS dated 1785, "Reflexions sur la position actuelle de St Domingue."

17. AN Col. F³192, "Reflexions sur la position actuelle de St Domingue"; AN Col. F³ 190, Cte Dautichamp, "Observations sur . . . St Domingue," MS dated 1781.

18. Moreau de Saint-Méry, *Description*, 31.

19. AN Col F³76, p. 151. See also Justin Girod-Chantrans, *Voyage d'un Suisse dans les Colonies d'Amérique*, ed. Pierre Pluchon (Paris: Tallandier, 1980), 118 n. 2. Jean Fouchard, *Les Plaisirs de Saint-Domingue: Notes sur sa vie sociale, littéraire et artistique* (Port-au-Prince:

au-Prince, and other port cities exploded in the 1770s and 1780s. New construction gave colonial cities a previously unknown air of permanence, even urbanity. Cap Français boasted parks, seventy-nine public buildings, public fountains, drainage, defenses, and hospitals. Theaters, Vauxhalls, booksellers, printers' offices, journals, social clubs, and Masonic lodges sprouted in the main ports and then in secondary towns. In the 1780s, Cap Français became home to a royally chartered scientific academy that could consider itself the peer of any in provincial France.[20]

This transformation of white urban society was superficially similar to changes occurring in France. The new press, improved postal service, and urban sociability mobilized popular opinion against the governor and intendant. Colonial writers began to refer to a "public" and the weight of its opinion.[21] Nevertheless, Saint-Domingue was clearly not France. Could a "public" of the sort emerging in France be created in a slave society?

For colonial administrators the militia controversies had proven how little "public-spiritedness" the white population possessed. The free population of color, however, assembled for monthly musters and hunted escaped slaves without complaint. Administrators had long recognized the military superiority of these amateur soldiers; in 1764 d'Estaing had proposed them as the core of his controversial Legion Nationale. Drawing on the neo-classical rhetoric of many military reformers, he had described free men of color as frugal patriots, loyal sons, and self-sacrificing citizens.[22] D'Estaing

---

Imprimerie de l'Etat, 1955), 28–53, cites Wimpffen, Hilliard d'Auberteuil, and announcements in the colonial press.

20. AN Col. F³76, p. 151; James E. McClellan III, *Colonialism and Science: Saint Domingue in the Old Regime* (Baltimore: Johns Hopkins University Press, 1992), 75, 78–81, 94–96, 106–8. He notes that "overall . . . the book collections in Saint-Domingue did not differ in character from those in bourgeois-professional and robe circles in France in the same period" (102). See his evocative description of Cap Français, 83–94. Figures on Cap Français are from Moreau de Saint-Méry, *Description*, 479–80. See also David P. Geggus, "Urban Development in 18th Century Saint-Domingue," *Bulletin du Centre d'histoire des espaces atlantiques* 5 (1900): 197–219; and Geggus, "The Major Port Towns of Saint Domingue in the Later Eighteenth Century," in *Atlantic Port Cities: Economy, Culture and Society in the Atlantic World, 1650–1850*, ed. Franklin W. Knight and Peggy K. Liss (Knoxville: University of Tennessee Press, 1991), 87–116.

21. See for example the affair of the Count deGravier, a parish militia captain accused of abusing his power, who then published a pamphlet to expose the facts of the case to the public; AN Col. F³191, pp. 198–265, especially p. 222. See also Moreau de Saint-Méry, *Description*, 415 and 1003.

22. AN Col. C⁹B17 MS. "Objets principaux" dated 15 January 1765; Moreau de Saint-Méry, *Loix et constitutions*, 4:820–24; Auguste Nemours, *Haïti et la guerre d'Independance américaine* (Port-au-Prince: Henri Deschamps, 1952), 29–31; on the importance of neoclassical imagery among military reformers in France, see Simon Schama, *Citizens: A Chronicle of the*

had planned to honor virtuous members of this class and allow the lightest-skinned families to be counted as white.[23]

His opponents, on the other hand, believed the free population of color was the core of colonial corruption. The reestablishment of the militia in 1769 demonstrated the power of colonial governors and military rule. Colonial writers and judges were more than ever struck by how weak social bonds were in Saint-Domingue. These reversals prompted whites to fashion another image of the colony's growing free population of color, drawing on the misogynistic rhetoric of some French opponents of royal despotism.

By the late 1760s both sides of the colonial political spectrum agreed that politics, family, and society in Saint-Domingue were corrupted by the weakness of "legitimate" bonds and by the force of pride and individual will.[24] But a number of writers associated with the *conseils* and opposed to military rule blamed the frailty of colonial society on the sexual power free and enslaved women of color exerted over white men. According to the Swiss traveler Girod-Chantrans,

> These women, naturally more lascivious than European women, flattered by their control over white men, have collected and preserved all the sensual pleasures [*voluptés*] they are capable of. *La jouissance* has become for them an object of study, a specialized and necessary skill [used] with worn-out or depraved lovers, who simple nature can no longer delight.[25]

In the 1770s and 1780s this feminine sexuality, described as "un-natural" in women of mixed ancestry, came to symbolize the "foreign-ness" of Saint-Domingue's free population of color. For Moreau de Saint-Méry,

> The whole being of a *mulâtresse* is given over to sensual pleasure and the flame of this goddess burns in her heart so as only to be

---

French Revolution (New York: Knopf, 1989), 169–74; Jean Chagniot, *Paris et l'armée au xviii siècle: Etude politique et sociale* (Paris: Economica, 1985), 656–57; André Corvisier, *Armies and Societies in Europe, 1494–1789*, trans. Abigail T. Siddall (Bloomington: Indiana University Press, 1979), 103. See also d'Estaing's own play, *Les Thermopyles, tragédie de circonstance* (Paris, 1791).

23. AN Col. C⁹ᴮ17 MS. "Objets principaux" dated 15 January 1765; Moreau de Saint-Méry, *Loix et constitutions*, 4:820–24; Nemours, *Haïti*, 29–31.

24. AN Col. F³192, "Reflexions sur la position actuelle de St Domingue"; AN Col. F³190, Cte Dautichamp, "Observations sur . . . St Domingue," MS dated 1781; AN Col. E 233, dossier "Jussan."

25. Justin Girod-Chantrans, *Voyage d'un Suisse*, 152.

snuffed out with life itself. . . . Even the most inflamed imagination
can conceive of nothing that she has not fathomed, concocted, experienced. Her sole vocation is to bewitch the senses, deliver them to
the most delicious ecstasies, enrapture them with the most seductive
temptations; nature, pleasure's accomplice, has given her charms,
endowments, inclinations, and what is indeed more dangerous, the
ability to enjoy such sensations even more keenly than her partners,
including some unknown to Sappho.[26]

As this ambiguous passage suggests, feminine sexuality, for Moreau, was
"both the danger and the delight" of men.[27] The work of other colonial
writers reveals more clearly the political fears generated by what Hilliard
d'Auberteuil described as an "empire based on *libertinage*" enjoyed by
women of color over white men.[28] An army officer and amateur poet Ga-
briel Bruey d'Aigailliers used Roman and Renaissance figures, and images
of corruption and disease, to portray women of color in these verses.

> Si je voulais en phrases ingénues
> Décrire aussi des sujets libertins
> Je vous peindrais des Messalines nues
> Entre les bras de nouveaux Arétins,
> Rivalisant de débauches honteuses,
> Vous les verriez ces couples gangrenés
> Plonger sans choix leurs âmes crapuleuses.
> Amour, pudeur, sentiments les plus doux
> Fuyez, fuyez ces rives dangereuses!
> Sous votre masque on s'y moque de vous.[29]

> If, in innocent sentences
> I were to describe those libertines
> I would paint for you naked Messalinas

26. Moreau de Saint-Méry, *Description*, 104; for similar stereotypes in the British Caribbean
see Hilary Beckles, *Natural Rebels: A Social History of Enslaved Black Women in Barbados*
(New Brunswick: Rutgers University Press, 1989), 147, and Barbara Bush, *Slave Women in
Caribbean Society, 1650–1838* (Bloomington: Indiana University Press, 1990), 14–17.
27. AN Col. F³76, p. 151.
28. Hilliard d'Auberteuil, *Considérations sur l'état present de la colonie française de Saint
Domingue, ouvrage politique et législatif* (Paris, 1776), 2:27.
29. Cited in Jean Fouchard, *Plaisirs de Saint-Domingue: Notes sur sa vie sociale, littéraire
et artistique* (Port-au-Prince: Imprimerie de l'Etat, 1955), 89–91.

In the arms of new Arentino,
Competing in shameful debauchery.
You would see these gangrenous couples
Aimlessly immerse their dissolute souls.
Love, modesty, the sweetest feelings,
Flee, flee these dangerous shores
For, beneath your mask, you are mocked here.

For the Baron de Wimpffen,

these Priestesses of an American Venus . . . have made sensual pleasure [*la volupté*] a kind of mechanical skill they have taken to the
highest perfection. Next to them Aretino is a prudish school
boy. . . . They combine the explosiveness of saltpeter with an exu-
berance of desire, that scorning all, drives them to pursue, acquire
and devour pleasure, like a blazing fire consumes its nourishment.[30]

The sexual power of free women of color over white men was especially
disturbing because of the public nature of that power. White men lived
openly with their black and brown mistresses and acknowledged their
mixed-race children. Though born in Martinique, Moreau de Saint-Méry
was shocked by Saint-Domingue's *mulâtresses*. "One is not protected . . .
by the public decency that preserves morality [even] in [Europe's] capi-
tals. . . . Publicity, I repeat, is one of the sweetest pleasures [of Saint-
Domingue's *mulâtresses*]." These women took money that should have gone
to legitimate families in France to satisfy their own "insatiable" desire for
rich fabrics and jewels.[31]

Contemporaries were troubled by what such behavior revealed about
colonial society as a whole, particularly about the inability of individual
colonists to sacrifice their immediate pleasures for a larger public good.
Montesquieu's *Spirit of the Laws*, widely read in Saint-Domingue by 1765,
discussed the physical and political effects of warm climates and warned of
the dangerous consequences of female vice.[32] The public freedom of women
was either a symptom of despotism that "feminized" men, or it produced

30. Cited in Pierre Pluchon, *Nègres et Juifs au XVIIIe siècle: Le Racisme au siècle des
Lumières* (Paris: Tallandier, 1984), 286.
31. Moreau de Saint-Méry, *Description*, 31–33, 105, 109.
32. AN Col. F³192, "Reflexions sur la position actuelle de Saint-Domingue." Montesquieu,
The Spirit of the Laws, trans. Thomas Nugent (New York: Hafner, 1949), 102; see book 7

social chaos. Those who hoped that the power of the governor and intendant would be tempered by rational public debate, or that the isolation and social violence of Dominguan life would give way to some form of recognizable community, saw the colony's free women of color as a reminder, even a reason, that Saint-Domingue could never be France.[33]

For Moreau de Saint-Méry and others the sensuality and narcissism of women of color was not only a property of their sex, but characterized the entire mixed-race population, female and male. In his encyclopedic *Description* of the colony Moreau devoted five pages to island-born white men and five to white creole women, but gave only one-and-a-half pages to "le Mulâtre." "La Mulâtresse," in contrast, received five-and-a-half pages. In his opinion "all the advantages given by nature to the *Mulâtre* are lavished upon the *Mulâtresse*." These defining characteristics were largely sexual; for the *mulâtre* as for the *mulâtresse*, "pleasure is his sole master, but it is a despotic master."[34]

Such passages illustrate that prejudice against Saint-Domingue's free population of color was not simply an extension of the racism that held nearly half-a-million colonial slaves in bondage. The new feminized definition of the free population of color incorporated French political clichés while providing hope that a rational public might yet emerge, if these corrupt beings could be effectively shut out.

After 1763 administrators and judges enacted a variety of measures to exclude this "vicious" class from Saint-Domingue's white world. Manumission was made more difficult and time-consuming, and female slaves were made twice as expensive to free as males. In 1773 free people of color were forbidden to use European names and were directed to take names of obvi-

---

chap. 8, "Of Public Continency," and chap. 9, "Of the Condition or State of Women in Different Governments." The interpretation is that of Joan Landes, *Women and the Public Sphere*, 35–38.

33. The views of colonial intellectuals were also influenced by the debate over American nature. Moreau de Saint-Méry believed that whites born in the colony had a physical and psychological constitution distinct from European-born men and women. In Philadelphia in 1798 Moreau wrote that the calculating and passionless teenage girls of that city engaged in masturbation and lesbian activities from an early age. Moreau de Saint-Méry, *Voyage aux Etats-unis de l'Amérique, 1793–1798*, ed. Stewart L. Mims (New Haven: Yale University Press, 1913), 302–3. See also Antonello Gerbi, *The Dispute of the New World: The History of a Polemic, 1750–1900*, rev. and enl. ed., trans Jeremy Moyle (Pittsburgh: University of Pittsburgh Press, 1973).

34. Moreau de Saint-Méry, *Description*, 103, 104.

ous African origin.[35] They were excluded form honorable professions and required to prove their freedom in all legal documents after 1778. They were forbidden to wear extravagant clothing, carry a sword, or sit with whites in churches, theaters, or music halls.[36]

The feminization of free colored stereotypes was not only a product of white attitudes and French political imagery; through the 1760s free women of color wielded far more economic power within their social category than did their counterparts in the white population. In one local census from midcentury, free colored women were four times more likely than white women to be heads of rural households.[37] Free women of color were at least four times more likely to participate in real estate transactions involving free people of color than white women were to be involved in similar transactions involving only whites.[38] In the 1760s women of color brought an average of 35 percent more property than their spouses to formally contracted marriages while white brides brought slightly less property than their grooms.

Yet, by the 1780s, a new free colored elite had come to the fore. This third or even fourth generation of mixed ancestry was wealthier than its

35. Moreau de Saint-Méry, *Loix et constitutions*, 5:448–49. This statute gave rise to a number of responses. Inversion of former names made Jean Décopin into Jean Pain Cordé, or Denis Pilorge into Denis Golerep. Others adopted other names from their family networks, so that Michel Depas, the free descendent of a Jewish commercial family at Bordeaux, became Michel Medina, after another prominent trading family. Others resorted to hyphenations, so that Michel Depas became Depas-Medina. Still others adopted African names or invented African-style names; the mulatto daughter of a militia commander was no longer Jeanne Maignan, but Jeanne Foedina. ANSOM, 14 December 1784, Gaudin reg. 742, Nippes, procuration.

36. Yvan Debbasch, *Couleur et liberté: Le Jeu du critère ethnique dans un ordre esclavagiste* (Paris: Dalloz, 1967), 94, 100–104; Moreau de Saint-Méry, *Loix et constitutions*, 4:225, 229, 342, 412, 466, 495; 5:384–85, 823; AN Col. F³243, p. 341; Col. F³273, p. 119; AN Col. F³91, p. 115; AN Col. F³189, decree of 2 June 1780.

37. ANSOM G¹509 No. 26.

38. In a sample of 4,882 notarial contracts from the 1760s, free women of color participated in 21 percent of rural land sales involving free coloreds, while only 16 percent of sales including whites involved a woman. In a 1780s sample of 2,679 notarial documents from the same districts free women of color were involved in 43 percent (68 of 160) of rural land sales involving their class, while white women accounted for only 11 percent (39 of 340). In the 1760s free women of color participated in 21 of the 28 sales of urban property that involved this class—75 percent. In the 1780s they were involved in 60 percent (53 of 88) of free colored urban sales, compared to white women who were in only 18 percent (29 of 165). In the 1760s and 1780s free women of color were involved in nearly 58 and 43 percent, respectively, of the leases of urban property in which free coloreds participated, compared to a female participation rate of only 21 and 4 percent among whites for the same periods. ANSOM, Saint-Domingue notarial archives.

predecessors, well-educated, light-skinned, and locally respected.[39] More-over, these elite families of color were increasingly led by men, not women. In the 1780s, free colored men brought far more property than free women of color to formal marriages, reversing the early trend.[40]

The emergence of this new generation of wealthy men of color in the 1780s did not alter the racial and gender imagery established after 1763. In the 1780s these men began to fight their exclusion from public life, challenging the stereotypes of racial pollution and tropical vice. They allied with Versailles against colonial whites and advanced a three-part argument that stressed their virtue and virility at every opportunity. Their economic virtue was demonstrated by their plantations and slaves; their social virtue was illustrated by their filial piety and obligations as husbands and fathers; and their civic virtue was seen in faithful militia service.[41]

White Saint-Domingue, which had been unable to prevent the reestablishment of the militia in 1769, responded by rejecting militia service as a sign of virtue. In March 1779, at the very moment Saint-Domingue's free men of color were volunteering for an expedition against the British in North America, the colonial press defined white colonial patriotism as commer-

39. See Garrigus, "Blue and Brown," and Garrigus, "Color, Class and Identity on the Eve of the Haitian Revolution: Saint-Domingue's Free Colored Elite as *Colons américains," Slavery & Abolition* 17 (April 1996): 20–43.

40. In the 1760s the average value of the property of nonwhite brides (slaves and free women of color) when listed, was 9,371 livres. For free colored grooms, the average was 6,881 livres. Among white couples, grooms listed more property than brides while the largest value a free man of color brought to marriage in the 1760s was less than half that of the largest recorded value brought by a free woman of color.

However, in the 1780s the average value of the property nonwhite brides brought to their marriages was 13,425 livres, while grooms from this racial category brought, on average, 23,497 livres. When Julian Raimond, a prominent indigo planter and man of color, married in 1782, he claimed to own nearly ten times what the wealthiest free man of color had claimed in the 1760s. Although the value of free colored bridal property also increased over this period, the wealthiest free colored bride of the 1780s brought only about 30 percent more in value than her counterpart of the 1760s. This data comes from the analysis of 4,882 notarial contracts for the period 1760–69 in the Nippes, St. Louis, and Cayes *quartiers* of Saint-Domingue and 2,679 contracts from these same districts in the years 1780–89.

41. See, for example, Raimond's manuscript memoirs to the colonial ministry from 1786, AN Col. F³91, pp. 171–83; these archival documents are copies of Raimond's text and none but the first are dated. The first bears the notation "1ᵉʳ mémoire de Raimond, en 7bre [September] 1786." See also his early preparations to bid for free colored representation in the Estates Generale in André Maistre de Chambon, "Acte notarié rélatif aux doléances des 'gens de couleur' de Saint-Domingue, (29 juillet 1789)," *Mémoires de la Société archéologique et historique de la Charente* (June 1931): 7–8.

cial, not martial.[42] The *Affiches américaines* extolled the idea that Saint-Domingue follow the example of Paris and several French provinces in presenting Louis XVI with a frigate of thirty-six to forty cannons. The newspaper contrasted this proposal with classical ideals of civic virtue and concluded that the ancients had been "harsh" and "severe":

> To the honor of humanity, undoubtedly one will never again see a barbarian and ferocious mother send her son to his death with a dry eye, see him again pale and bleeding without emotion and believe she owes this horrible sacrifice to the fatherland. . . . These awful traits, so long admired by our fathers, are not natural and make any respectable and sensitive soul tremble.[43]

Moreau de Saint-Méry, writing in the 1780s, affirmed that free colored military discipline did not contradict the image of the sensual and self-serving mulatto.

> It seems that then [in the ranks a mulatto] loses his laziness, but all the world knows that a soldier's life, in the leisure it provides, has attractions for indolent men. . . . A mulatto soldier will appear exactly to the calls of day, perhaps even to those of the evening, but it is in vain that one tries to restrict his liberty at night; [the night] belongs to pleasure and he will not indenture it, no matter what commitments he has made elsewhere.[44]

Such pronouncements helped white colonists reconcile their resentment of militia service with their fears of tropical corruption. But in France the ideal of the citizen-soldier was growing in popularity in the 1780s, with dramatic results in 1789 and thereafter. Although the wealthiest of Saint-Domingue's free families of color joined the white campaign to donate a frigate to the king in 1782, these same families and other less prosperous free men of color made military service a centerpiece of their claims for citizenship in the French Revolution. By 1789 their spokesmen had adopted a Rousseauean stance, blaming whites for corrupting colonial society and

42. See Garrigus, "Catalyst or Catastrophe? Saint-Domingue's Free Men of Color and the Savannah Expedition, 1779–1782," *Review/Revista Interamericana* 22 (Spring–Summer 1992): 109–25.
43. *Affiches américaines* (mardi 30 mars 1779): no. 13; BN 4, lc 12 20/22.
44. Moreau de Saint-Méry, *Description*, 103–4.

portraying themselves as natural men, *colons américains*, inherently virtuous and natively patriotic. As sons of French fathers, France was their *patrie* and Frenchmen were their brothers, literally as well as figuratively.[45]

The "feminization" of the free population of color had been designed to exclude them from the "civilized" colonial public. Yet by exaggerating the cultural gulf between whites and free people of color, such stereotypes ultimately worked in their victims' behalf. After 1789 the French Revolution's conflation of militia service, natural virtue, and universal brotherhood allowed Saint-Domingue's free men of color working in Paris and in the colony to expose prerevolutionary racial distinctions as artificial. Their victory over discrimination opened the way for the eventual inclusion of half-a-million slaves in the *liberté*, if not the *fraternité*, of the French Revolution.

This account of the construction and dismantling of racial categories corroborates two elements of the new scholarship on the origins of the French Revolution. First of all, conditions in Saint-Domingue clearly point to the emergence of a public sphere in the years 1763 to 1789. This development is perhaps even clearer in the colony than in France, since white inhabitants of this immensely profitable territory had so little in the way of "community" before the end of the Seven Years' War. Saint-Domingue was a place where the lives of African men and women were cheap, compared to the price of sugar and the ambitions of their masters. Frenchmen talked only of returning home the moment they set foot in the colony, though many never did. Nevertheless after 1763 the extraordinary rush to establish printing presses, theaters, post offices, Masonic lodges, urban parks, and other sites for elite sociability reveals the colony's appetite for the kind of "public" emerging in France.

Second, because the risks of this path were far deeper in Saint-Domingue than in the metropolis, the colonial story underlines the way contemporaries used gender to define this new public. Saint-Domingue's inhabitants were recognized to be black, white, and brown. Some prosperous people of mixed ancestry might even be recognized as white, early in the eighteenth century. But after 1763 those who hoped to create an effective colonial

45. On the citizen-soldier in prerevolutionary France, see Jean Chagniot, *Paris et l'armée au xviii siècle: Etude politique et sociale* (Pris: Economica, 1985), 611–13, 617. For free colored participation in the royal donation, see AN Col. F³91, p. 189. For free colored political claims in the early Revolution, J. M. C. américain, *Précis sur les gémissements des sang-mêlés dans les Colonies Françoises* (Paris, 1789); Abbé Cournand, *Réponse aux Observations d'un habitant des colonies, sur le Mémoire en faveur des gens de couleur . . .* (Paris, 1789); Abbé Grégoire, *Lettre aux philantropes, sur les malheurs . . . des gens de couleur de Saint-Domingue* (Paris, 1790); and any of the works published in Paris from 1789 to 1792 by Julien Raimond.

public sphere worried that this racial continuum would ultimately bring some free people of color into that sphere. They might even win a place over less-talented whites, calling the whole racial hierarchy into question. Drawing on metropolitan images, colonial reformers used gender—in addition to race—to explain the disturbing behavior of French male colonists who treated their mulatto and quadroon children like French sons or daughters. Mutually reinforcing gender and racial constructions barred people of color from elite status in a place where nearly half-a-million Africans and their descendents worked and died for the profit of roughly 40,000 French colonists.

7

Women and Power in Eighteenth-Century France

Actresses at the Comédie-Française*

Lenard R. Berlanstein

The writer and future revolutionary Louis-Sébastien Mercier proclaimed in a tract on the reform of theater that "the prestige which covers an actress renders her the most dangerous woman one can imagine."[1] His emphasis on her "prestige" underscores the prominence of actresses in prerevolutionary society and culture. The leading female artists at the Comédie-Française (and possibly at some of the lesser theaters) were surely among the most visible and celebrated women of their day. The queen and royal mistresses

*This article was originally published in *Feminist Studies* 20, no. 3 (Fall 1994): 475–506, and is reprinted here by permission of the publisher, Feminist Studies, Inc., % Women's Studies Program, University of Maryland, College Park, MD 20742.

I express deep appreciation to Sarah Maza, Jeffrey Ravel, and Jack Censer for their helpful comments on an earlier draft of this essay.

1. Louis-Sébastien Mercier, *Nouvel essai sur l'art théâtrique* (Amsterdam, 1773), 361.

aside, no other women could set high society and public opinion abuzz with rumors, news of changed fashion, and even with serious political debate. Mercier's concern with actresses' "dangerous" qualities also highlights the widespread condemnation of their visibility and influence. Actresses occupied a contested place in eighteenth-century French society, and commentary about them sometimes evoked the very principles upon which the social order was based. Although the public did not usually refer to female performers as "queens of the stage" until France ceased to have genuine queens, already actresses served as archetypes of womanhood.

Actresses at the Comédie-Française were unusual in having an official role in governing a cultural institution of dazzling international renown. The troupe of Europe's first theater made the basic production decisions itself, and actresses had the same rights and responsibilities as the male performers. The actresses at the Théâtre-Français present the rare case of women sitting side by side and on essentially equal terms with males in an important deliberative body, in this case the general assembly of the Comédie. The king thus entrusted women with the important task of giving theater to his people and representing in this way the splendor of the monarchy. Because the general assembly made decisions that affected the careers and prestige of the people who shaped public opinion in prerevolutionary France, actresses could not expect to wield power discreetly.

The authority actresses exercised at the Théâtre-Français makes them a valuable subject for addressing one of the livelier debates in gender history today—the place of "women in the public sphere" at the advent of the French Revolution. Until recently, scholars tended to inscribe the eighteenth century in a meta-narrative of progress for women's civic rights. The impact of Enlightenment culture, with its respect for the individual and its disrespect for tradition, supposedly disrupted a timeless patriarchal oppression and provided an arsenal of arguments from which feminists could draw.[2] A new wave of feminist scholarship has turned the meta-narrative on its head by reassessing what the Enlightenment meant for women and men. The work of Joan Landes is central to the revisionism: it presents a challenging argument that the cultural forces historians now accept as giving birth to the Revolution were gendered and effectively silenced

2. Peter Gay, *The Enlightenment: An Interpretation*, vol. 2, *The Science of Freedom* (New York: Knopf, 1969), 33–34; David Williams, "The Politics of Feminism in the French Enlightenment," in *The Varied Path: Studies in the Eighteenth Century*, ed. David Williams and Peter Hughes (Toronto: University of Toronto Press, 1971), 333–51; Samia I. Spencer, ed., *French Women and the Age of Enlightenment* (Bloomington: Indiana University Press, 1984).

women.[3] Landes explores the process by which a female/male dichotomy became the central distinction within the civic order, replacing degrees of rank; she singles out the political culture created by the Enlightenment and the Revolution as the source of the change. Rejecting the premise that the Enlightenment interrupted a timeless patriarchy, she argues that power was not yet truly gendered (masculine) before 1789. Absolutism had elevated the king so far above all other men that the rest seemed to share a subordinate position with females. Moreover, the Old Regime had created a legitimate space for women to exercise power. This was the absolutist public sphere, the arena for the spectacle and display of regal authority.[4] The existence of this legitimating space explains for Landes the coming into prominence of "a very impressive social institution" dominated by "public" women, the literary salon. Landes does identify a powerful current of criticism of influential women, part of an antiabsolutist, aristocratic discourse, but that very critique illustrates how closely public women were tied to the legitimacy of absolutism.

At this point, Landes turns to the work of Jürgen Habermas, which has exerted an enormous influence on the study of the eighteenth century and the Revolution in recent years. She accepts Habermas's view that a new sort of social organization, a "bourgeois public sphere," based on the informal association of private persons oriented to general interests, arose to challenge absolutism. However, Landes does not accept what she sees as Habermas's universalistic and gender-neutral understanding of the bourgeois public sphere. Her work is an attempt to redirect the entire discussion of the public sphere and starts with the recognition that "the exclusion of women . . . was not incidental but central to its incarnation." Landes proceeds to identify the discourse of the bourgeois public sphere with the thought of Jean-Jacques Rousseau. It was he who recast classical republicanism in such a way that a virtuous citizenry required the domestication and silencing of females, whose contribution to the polity could come only through being self-abnegating mothers. Advanced thinkers faulted the monarchy for opening a public space for women, which in their view could

---

3. Joan Landes, *Women and the Public Sphere in the Age of the French Revolution* (Ithaca: Cornell University Press, 1988). The analysis that follows is drawn principally from chap. 1. The thought of Joan Wallach Scott dovetails with that of Landes; see her "French Feminism and the Rights of 'Man': Olympe de Gouge's Declaration," *History Workshop Journal*, no. 28 (Autumn 1989): 1–21.
4. Benjamin Nathans, "Habermas's 'Public Sphere' in the Era of the French Revolution," *French Historical Studies* 16 (Spring 1990): 621.

never be legitimate. Landes insists that this political culture was victorious in the Revolution. Thereafter, even feminist thinkers could not conceive of a progressive social order in which women might, once again, occupy the public sphere. Landes concludes that "from the standpoint of women and their interests, enlightenment looks suspiciously like counterenlightenment and revolution like counterrevolution."[5]

These bold conclusions have, in fact, received extensive criticism from a number of perspectives. Dena Goodman finds Landes confusing the Habermasian category of the bourgeois public sphere with the "separate spheres" of the nineteenth century. Goodman places salon mistresses in the Habermasian public sphere and argues that most philosophes were highly supportive of the salon mistresses' activities.[6] Her claims dovetail with Daniel Gordon's study of the eighteenth-century discourse on "sociability," the art of conversing, being convivial, and producing pleasure through the exchange of ideas.[7] Philosophes, he notes, accorded a special place to women in enhancing sociability; indeed, they lauded women for being essential to it. From this perspective, Rousseau appears far outside the mainstream. Keith Michael Baker also discerns a narrowness in Landes's reading of the Enlightenment. He finds at least two different and competing discourses within the bourgeois public sphere, a republican one and a rationalist one.[8] The former, he admits, was "masculinist" in being organized

5. Landes, *Women and the Public Sphere*, 7, 204. The work of two other important scholars, Sarah Maza and Lynn Hunt, supports Landes, at least to an extent. Both start with the premise that narratives of family relations structured the political culture of the Old Regime. They see this model leading away from patriarchy and toward fraternity during the latter part of the eighteenth century. Maza draws the conclusion that the change made women's public role more problematical, and she endorses Landes's work. Hunt, however, argues that the Revolution made the exclusion of women more problematical by positing a rational, universal individual. See Sarah Maza's work: "Domestic Melodrama as Political Ideology: The Case of the Comte de Sanois," *American Historical Review* 94 (December 1989): 1, 249–64, "The Diamond Necklace Affair Revisited (1785–86): The Case of the Missing Queen," in *Eroticism and the Body Politic*, ed. Lynn Hunt (Baltimore: Johns Hopkins University Press, 1991), 63–89, and "Women, the Bourgeoisie, and the Public Sphere: Responses to Daniel Bell and David Gordon," *French Historical Studies* 17 (Fall 1992): 935–50. For Lynn Hunt's views, see *The Family Romance of the French Revolution* (Berkeley and Los Angeles: University of California Press, 1992), esp. 200–204.
6. Dena Goodman, "Public Sphere and Private Life: Toward a Synthesis of Current Historiographical Approaches to the Old Regime," *History and Theory* 31 (February 1992): 1–20.
7. Daniel Gordon, "Philosophy, Sociology, and Gender in the Enlightenment Conception of Public Opinion," *French Historical Studies* 17 (Fall 1992): 882–911.
8. Keith Michael Baker, "Defining the Public Sphere in Eighteenth-Century France: Variations on a Theme by Habermas," in *Habermas and the Public Sphere*, ed. Craig Calhoun (Cambridge: MIT Press, 1992), 181–209. Baker calls the alternatives "the rational discourse of the social" and "the republican discourse of political will."

around the ideology of republican motherhood. However, the latter, with its appeals to abstract, universal reason, was, at most, contingently antifeminist and could be the basis for the project of enfranchising women.

These positions lead to sharp disagreement about the meaning of the Revolution for women. Landes insists on the inevitability of Rousseauean doctrines dominating the debate over women. Baker, on the other hand, draws attention to the alternate political discourses available to revolutionaries and stresses that some favored women.[9] He assumes that 1789 produced a liberated public sphere in which women could take a visible and vocal place and which male revolutionaries could close only temporarily.[10] Goodman argues that the silencing of women in the Revolution, far from being the logical result of the essentially masculine nature of the bourgeois public sphere, was the consequence of the suppression of the public sphere by the government of the Terror.[11] At stake, then, is Lynn Hunt's question about whether the Revolution had an ungendered notion of the individual.[12]

Bringing the discourses on actresses' power into the debate is a useful step on several grounds. For reasons Goodman mentions, actresses provide a better focus for exploring "public women" than do salon mistresses. Moreover, actresses' collegiality with actors and their power over "men of letters" stimulated the people most responsible for shaping public opinion to reflect on the legitimacy of the situation. Writers came to think about the consequences of women having authority partly through the prism of actresses. We shall use their commentary to examine how women functioned in the absolutist public sphere and how their power was received within this sphere. We shall also seek to determine the response of the emerging bourgeois public sphere to actresses' authority. To the extent that there were arguments for and against that power, we shall be interested in how they were formulated and how their authors thought about men exercising the same influence. Finally, we shall take advantage of a dispute that erupted at the Théâtre-Français in the opening days of the Revolution to assess whether the Revolution was, in fact, masculine in its implications

---

9. Ibid., 207.

10. On women's street agitation during the Revolution, see Jane Abray, "Feminism in the French Revolution," *American Historical Review* 80 (February 1975): 43–62; Darline Gay Levy, Harriet Applewhite, and Mary Johnson, *Women in Revolutionary Paris, 1789–1795* (Urbana: University of Illinois Press, 1979); Catherine Marrand-Fouquet, *La Femme au temps de la Révolution* (Paris: Stock, 1989); Olwen Hufton, *Women and the Limits of Citizenship in the French Revolution* (Toronto: University of Toronto Press, 1992).

11. Goodman, "Public Sphere and Private Life," 16.

12. Hunt, *Family Romance of the French Revolution*, 201–4.

from the beginning. Ultimately, this study of Enlightenment reactions to accomplished women who visibly wielded power over men supports Landes against her critics. However, it also suggests some necessary modifications in her argument about patriarchy in the eighteenth century.

The Social Position of Actresses

The flourishing taste for theater in eighteenth-century France brought actresses to the center of cultural life. One scholar finds that "theatromania" raged among the social and political elite of the kingdom, as evidenced by the creation of private theaters among the high aristocracy and the passion devoted to amateur theatrics even within the royal family.[13] The theater consolidated its hold on the sociability of the highborn—so much so that contemporaries spoke of the lobbies of the Théâtre-Français or the Opéra as substitutes for an increasingly privatized royal court.[14] The aristocracy and its imitators flocked to the theater as a place to see and be seen; perhaps, they were even enjoying the spectacle more than ever, as one scholar has suggested.[15] However, the stage was a passion the highborn shared with other social strata, even the common people. An enormously diverse audience attended the bawdy performances at the improvised theaters of the fairs. So great was the interest that the seasonal spectacles evolved into permanent theaters, locating on the northeastern edge of Paris, the infamous "boulevard."[16] This was one manifestation of a dramatic growth in seating capacity at Parisian theaters during the course of the eighteenth century. The capital had about 4,000 seats available in 1700, about twice that many at midcentury, and nearly 13,000 on the eve of the Revolution. Behind this expansion, driven by the profit motive more than by official decree, was a

13. Jacques Boncompain, *Auteurs et comédiens au XVIIIe siècle* (Paris: Férrin, 1976), chap. 2.
14. Martine de Rougemont, *La Vie théâtrale en France au XVIIIe siècle* (Paris: Champion, 1988), 109, 165–68.
15. For an argument about the increasing enjoyment of operas, see James H. Johnson, "Musical Experience and the Formation of a French Musical Public," *Journal of Modern History* 64 (June 1992): 191–226.
16. Maurice Albert, *Les Théâtres des boulevards (1789–1848)* (Geneva: Slatkine, 1969); Robert Isherwood, *Farce and Fantasy: Popular Entertainment in Eighteenth-Century France* (New York: Oxford University Press, 1986); Michèle Root-Bernstein, *Boulevard Theater and Revolution in Eighteenth-Century Paris* (Ann Arbor: University of Michigan Press, 1984).

growth in a bourgeois and petit bourgeois audience.[17] The attraction of the stage expressed the uncertainties of an era of rapid cultural change as well as the widening options for behavior and identity.[18] With this burgeoning of interest in the theater, it was possible for actresses to become "celebrities," whose public and private lives fascinated worldly Parisians.

Actresses at the three royal theaters—the Académie royale de la musique (or Opéra), the Comédie-Italienne, and Comédie-Française—were, in legal terms, defined entirely by the absolutist public sphere. When they entered one of these troupes they became "the king's performers" and lost all prior familial and civil status. They were part of the royal household, and, as such, their persons were at the disposal of the Gentlemen of the Bedchamber. Officially, the performers made their debuts, performed, and retired by order of the gentlemen. Obstreperousness could earn players confinement in a special prison, the For l'Evêque.[19]

Although the monarchs of France had long bestowed special distinctions on performers, female and male, the Gallican church had designated them as outcasts. Christian thinking since the early Middle Ages had insisted on the scandalous nature of plays and on the moral dangers of attending them. The Gallican church classified actors as either excommunicates or as public sinners who were not worthy of taking the sacraments—the exact status was never settled. In either case, performers could not marry or be buried as Catholics unless they contritely renounced their profession. Their word was not acceptable in law courts. Philosophes frequently demanded that the royal government take steps to rehabilitate performers' status and insisted that the clergy treat actors like other artists. However, the kings declined to act on the grounds that society was not ready for such a change. Perhaps they were correct: just as secular voices arose to challenge the benighted attitudes of the clergy, a secular (republican) version of the denunciation appeared in the writing of Jean-Jacques Rousseau and his disciples.[20] Ultimately, the royal theaters in France were honored institutions, but they had the profoundly ambiguous status of being an honored vice.

---

17. Rougemont, *La Vie théâtrale*, 223.

18. This is the explanation William Bouwsma offers for the development of the stage in the sixteenth century. See his *John Calvin: A Portrait* (Cambridge: Harvard University Press, 1988), 177.

19. René Chancerel, *L'Evolution du status des comédiens* (Paris: Les Presses modernes, 1930); Paul Olangnier, *Les Incapacités des acteurs en droit romain et en droit canonique* (Paris, 1899); Franz Funck-Brentano, *La Bastille des comédiens* (Paris: Fontemoing, 1903).

20. Gaston Maugras, *Les Comédiens hors la loi* (Paris: 1877), 225–331; Marguerite Moffat, *Rousseau et la querelle du théâtre* (Geneva: Slatkine, 1970).

Whenever social elites became enthusiastic about the stage, as in the eighteenth century, sharp debate about its morality was inevitable.

The odor of sin had an impact on the recruitment of actors and actresses.[21] A poor young woman who had confidence in her talents would have to brave sharp objections from her relatives and community if she pursued an acting career. Not surprisingly, then, many actresses came from families already associated with theater. The closed recruitment suggests a world at least partly turned inward on itself, living by its own rules, and subject to its own mores. Those who came from outside the profession almost always had very humble origins. Many a star of the Parisian stage was the daughter of a laborer or a domestic servant, and somewhere between one-fourth and one-half of the women were born to unmarried mothers. Thus, the stage did not attract simply because it promised escape from a hard and insecure life of labor. It had an allure for women who were prepared to undertake an adventurous life and were willing to leave conventions behind.

Women who sought a theatrical career had to make their own way in the world, and they would find some of the most remunerative opportunities not so much on the stage as in the practice of aristocratic libertinism, known as *la vie galante*. Christian prescriptions of chastity and monogamy had never held much sway among the great ones. The lifestyle of male aristocrats was based on conspicuous displays of wealth, the pursuit of pleasure, spectacles of potency, and the competition for prestige. From about the time of the Regency (1715–18), aristocrats competed flagrantly and sometimes recklessly for the attention of actresses, opera singers, and dancers.[22]

Acting and aristocratic libertinism complemented each other in crucial ways. Beauty, charm, and sensuality facilitated the struggle for success. These were also the qualities that would allow an actress, who had few other assets except her talent, to obtain the "protection" necessary to establish a career at the best theaters. Yet, actresses' participation in *la vie galante* was

21. I am in the process of gathering data on the social origins of actresses based, in part, on the dossiers at the Bibliothèque de l'Arsenal. Much of the information is anecdotal in nature and is impossible to verify. Useful published sources of biographical information include Henri Lyonnet, *Dictionnaire des comédiens français*, 2 vols. (Paris: Librairie de l'Art du Théâtre, 1904); Emile Campardon, *Les Comédiens du roi de la troupe française* (Paris, 1879); and E. D. de Manne, *Galerie historique de la troupe de Voltaire* (Lyon, 1877).

22. Ludovic Celler, *La Galanterie au théâtre* (Paris, 1875); Adolphe Jullien, *La Comédie et la galanterie au XVIII siècle* (Paris, 1874); Erica-Marie Benabou, *La Prostitution et la police des moeurs au XVIIIe siècle* (Paris: Libraire académique Perrin, 1987), chap. 6; Camille Piton, ed., *Paris sous Louis XV: Rapports des inspecteurs de police au roi*, 3 vols. (Paris: Mercure de France, 1914).

not simply a matter of economic necessity, even if it began so. The celebrated performers did not distance themselves from scandal when they were materially secure. Female members of the Comédie-Française certainly earned more than any other group of self-supporting women in the eighteenth century. In the 1770s and 1780s a full member of the troupe could have a professional income of twenty thousand livres or more, as much as a substantial provincial nobleman. Instead of using their security to put an ignominious past behind them, they usually used their fame to demand more from lovers. In any case, no independent woman had less incentive to question and reject the patriarchal practices of aristocratic libertinism.

That the actresses at the Comédie-Française were, on the whole, a remarkable group of women there can be no doubt. They had entered a career requiring learning, cultural vision, literary judgment, and a dramatic excellence. These women endowed themselves with these qualities even though they began life with few cultural advantages and many disabilities. They made their own opportunities and advanced to the height of their demanding profession. Their position at Europe's first theater allowed them—entitled them to—intimacy with people at the pinnacle of the social order. Not even the king thought it beneath his dignity to attend to "his" actresses' concerns.[23]

Of course, we are not dealing with a society that accorded unambiguous admiration to self-made individuals, and still less to self-made women. The very phrase would have had a profoundly disturbing air. Yet, the lowly social origins and meteoric ascent of these women did not enter very much into the debate about their status. Commentators assumed that actresses would have humble births and, for better or worse, be "ambitious." What they were uncertain about was whether their personal achievements resulted from depravity or from exceptional artistic gifts. This question colored all discussions of actresses' use of authority and influence.

The Power of Actresses

As part of the royal household, the Théâtre-Français was, in principle, subject to the will of the Gentlemen of the Bedchamber. These great nobles

---

23. Denis Papillon de la Ferté, *L'Administration des menus: Journal (1756–1780)* (Paris, 1887), 109.

(the duc de Richelieu and the duc de Duras for much of the eighteenth century) had their *intendant des menus plaisirs* supervising the troupe on a daily basis. Nonetheless, the company was partly self-regulating and re-sisted commands from above rather successfully.[24] From an economic per-spective, the Comédie-Française functioned somewhat as a business partnership. Performers who passed through a successful probationary pe-riod became members *(sociétaires)* of the troupe and had to contribute a set amount of cash toward the working capital of the theater. The members were compensated with a share of the profits the theater yielded.[25] The central decision-making body of the troupe was the general assembly. It met at least weekly to carry on the important business of France's first theater. The assembly selected new plays for the repertoire, established the offerings for the current season, cast roles, approved new players, and budgeted productions.[26] Occasionally, a matter of principle would arise concerning the state of the theater or the profession, and the assembly would debate this, too. The positions of theatrical producer and director were as yet unknown, so the artists could do what they wished with the scripts as long as they could agree among themselves.[27]

The provisions for self-regulation at the Théâtre-Français were remark-ably free of gender distinctions. The rules *(règlement)* issued by the Gentle-men of the Bedchamber in 1719, codifying long-standing practices, specifically accorded the same deliberation and voting rights to females and males in the troupe. The main voting restriction concerned members of the same family in the assembly. The government was worried about voting blocs that might detract from the general interest, so it accorded only one vote per family. Even then, the rules did not specify the father or husband as the "natural" spokesperson for the family and allowed relatives with dissenting opinions to speak up.[28]

The members of the assembly, female and male, collectively exercised significant control over the kingdom's cultural life. The prestige of the stage dominated literary life in the eighteenth century. No wonder Voltaire told Jean-François Marmontel: "The theater, my friend, . . . is the most illustri-

24. Ibid., 8–38.

25. Louis Marcerou, *La Comédie-Française: L'Association des comédiens français* (Paris: Librairie de France, 1925).

26. Jules Bonnassies, *La Comédie-Française: Histoire administrative (1658–1757)* (Paris, 1874), and *Les Auteurs dramatiques et la Comédie-Française* (Paris, 1874).

27. Marie-Marguerite Allevy, *La Mise en scène en France dans la première moitié du XIXe siècle* (Paris: Droz, 1938).

28. The *règlement* of 1719 is reproduced in Bonnassies, *Comédie-Française,* 140–41.

ous career. There one can obtain glory and fortune in a day!"[29] Eighteenth-century writers assumed that it was desirable and perhaps even necessary to present their ideas in the form of plays to get them heard. A reading public for novels was growing, but writers knew that they could reach the social and cultural elite more directly from the stage. And there was no other stage like the Comédie-Française. The "House of Molière," it had a monopoly over producing the French classics and occupied the top of the hierarchy of theaters in the kingdom. It was rare for authors to dream of the glory described by Voltaire without aspiring to present a play on the stage of the Comédie.[30]

Men of letters knew that their careers and prestige were dependent on the actors and actresses in the Comédie. As we shall see, rejected authors were increasingly likely to express outrage and condemn the assembly's judgment publicly. Selecting new plays for the repertoire was one of the most important powers of the general assembly. In principle, playwrights sent a script to the *intendant* and had it read anonymously. After discussion, the performers cast a silent vote, using black and white chips, to ensure impartiality. The troupe presumably had an interest in selecting only the most stageworthy plays, because, as shareholders in the company, their earnings depended upon attracting an audience. The players were also sensitive to their duty, as the leading actors in the land and heirs to a grand tradition, to uphold lofty artistic standards. The actual practice of selecting new plays, however, left plenty of room for personal initiative and influence.[31]

Rather than submitting scripts to the troupe as a whole, playwrights made sure that they had supporters among the performers. It was common to send a script to a friend within the troupe, as Marmontel did with Mademoiselle Gaussin (Jeanne Gossem).[32] The authors hoped their sponsors would read the play with special verse so its value came through or would defend it warmly during the debate that followed the reading. This practice gave actresses an opportunity, rare for all but the best connected court women, to be "protectors" of men. Of course, protection implied mutual

---

29. Voltaire, cited in Jean-François Marmontel, *Mémoires de Marmontel* (Paris, 1891), 1:143.

30. Rougemont, *La vie théâtrale*, 241–47.

31. Royal officials continually tinkered with the voting procedure to reduce the role of influence and favoritism, probably to no avail. See Bonnassies, *Les Auteurs dramatiques et la Comédie-Française*, 46–50.

32. Marmontel, *Mémoires*, 1:42.

obligations. Actresses might insist that their clients provide them with desirable roles, ones that showed off their talents. Actresses sometimes agreed to sponsor a play only after their parts had been rewritten or the parts of their rivals on stage had been diminished. So common was this sort of patronage that authors wrote plays as "vehicles" for leading artists in order to ensure their acceptance.

Men of letters depended on favors from female or male players in other ways as well. A play became the virtual property of the troupe once it was accepted; therefore, the author had to hope that the troupe would set aside a sufficient amount of money to give the play an adequate production. The authors also had to hope that the cast would endow the production with the right spirit and values. Seeing that performers did not alter lines was another matter that called for good relations with insiders. The playwright's financial gains and visibility depended very much on the assembly scheduling that performances during the busy season, when seats were likely to be filled and the "right" people in them.

The assembly's debates gave actresses the opportunity to stake out positions, win over colleagues, and hold their ground when in a minority. This body did not function as an idealized democracy, with impartial members simply applying the dictates of reason. Some members inevitably had more influence than others. The most celebrated performers, those who considered themselves indispensable to the success of the troupe, insisted on having their way. Threats of quitting (in theory, impossible, because one could only retire by order of the Gentlemen of the Bedchamber) or simply of not performing made the assembly take note of an actress's wishes. Some performers achieved influence out of proportion to their talents by exercising skill at building coalitions or casting arguments in particularly persuasive ways. Nothing indicates that actresses deferred to actors in the often spirited deliberations.

That actresses could dominate this sexually mixed deliberative body and even force it to make audacious decisions is illustrated by the case of Mademoiselle Clairon (Claire-Hippolyte Léris). The illegitimate daughter of a seamstress, her early career in Rouen was accompanied by well-publicized sexual scandals. Indeed, future colleagues at the Théâtre-Français protested orders for her debut in 1743 on the grounds that she would bring dishonor to the troupe.[33] Yet, once admitted, Clairon proceeded to conquer not only

---

33. A four-part *chronique libertine* was published on Clairon under the title *Histoire de Mademoiselle Cronel, dite Fertillon, actrice de la Comédie de Rouen, écrite par elle-même* (La Haye, 1742). Throughout her life, Clairon had to defend herself against the charges in this

Mademoiselle Clairon exercised a great deal of influence over her colleagues at the Comédie-Française. Courtesy, Bibliothèque nationale de France, Paris.

the audience but also the general assembly by force of talent, intellect, strength of will, and political savvy. While she did manage to win approval for the scripts and roles that pleased her, Clairon was especially inclined to take a stand on the honor of her theater and her profession. She compelled her colleagues to rally to her cause. In 1762, she made them defy the duc d'Orléans on the grounds that his request violated the customs of the house. Clairon was devoted to removing the stain of excommunication from her calling; after one instance of clerical disapproval, she whipped up the passions of the general assembly so much that the *intendant* feared a strike by the troupe. She eventually launched a personal protest by leaving the stage until the government did something about the status of performers. She even forced the minister of the royal household to bring the issue before the council of state and demanded that the king receive a deputation of actors to explain the justice of the request. Clairon proved to be as stubborn as Louis XV and retired when the crown took steps she considered unsatisfactory.[34] For all her bravado, Clairon was not unique. Predecessors like Adrienne Lecouvreur, Mademoiselle Dangeville (Marie Botot), and Mademoiselle Gaussin had pushed their colleagues around even though they lacked Clairon's ideological fire.

The most controversial decisions in which the actresses participated usually concerned casting, for egos were involved and the rules were particularly unclear. In principle, playwrights selected the players for the roles they had in mind. However, this practice conflicted with rights performers held dear. Players were hired to perform character types *(emplois)* based on the classical repertory—first lovers, queens, soubrettes, ingénues, noble fathers, and so forth. The troupe members did not take lightly any attempts to reassign types; nor were they indifferent to seniority rights to a type. As new plays and new sorts of roles added complications to casting, the tensions mounted. The regulations assumed that goodwill and professional judgment would produce a consensus in the assembly, but cooperation was frequently lacking. The players insisted on knowing the role assignments before the vote on a script, a practice that was open to much abuse. Already,

work. On her life, see Edmond de Goncourt, *Mademoiselle Clairon, d'après ses correspondances et les rapports du police du temps* (Paris, 1889). Also, see her two-volume *Memoirs of Hippolyte Clairon, the Celebrated French Actress* (London, 1800). In her memoirs, Clairon never denied having affairs but insisted that they had nothing to do with money. This was not the case. See Francis Gribble, *Romances of the French Theatre* (London: Chapman and Hall, 1912), 103–4 for a list of twenty-two great names who were her lovers.

34. Papillon de la Ferté, *L'Administration des menus*, 76–77, 167, 183–88.

the regulations of 1719 warned of the "quarrelsome" nature of the meetings and the "sharp attacks" that were often made.[35] Harmony would not grow during the rest of the century.

By all accounts, actresses were ferocious infighters. Contemporaries attributed to them in particular the "intrigues of the wings" that made the Comédie a veritable snake pit. Of course, these claims contained strong elements of sexual stereotyping, and there is no reason to suppose that actors were any less aggressive. It is, nonetheless, true that actresses were at the forefront of the most vociferous struggle for preference during the century, the Vestris-Sainval Affair of the late 1770s.

Madame Vestris (Françoise-Rose Gourgand) and Mademoiselle Sainval (Marie-Pauline d'Alizari de Roquefort) were rivals. They had been brought into the troupe about a year apart, and tensions between them had been palpable from the first. Vestris was married to a celebrated dancer at the Opéra, but both partners had notorious extramarital affairs. Indeed, Vestris was protected by none other than the duc de Duras, one of the Gentlemen of the Bedchamber, who supervised the theater. When she complained to him about the poor roles she received, Duras went so far as to speak with Louis XV about the problem at a royal *lever*.[36] Both actresses used their power to bring siblings into the troupe against determined opposition. The rivalry came to a head in the summer of 1779, when Sainval forced the general assembly to protest the violations of her seniority rights in the face of Duras's obvious displeasure at the proceedings. Not obtaining satisfaction, Sainval had friends publish brochures in her favor to win public opinion to her cause. These pamphlets went too far, and the government responded harshly. One pamphlet made slightly veiled references to the sexual relations between Duras and Vestris. It also brought Marie Antoinette into the furor. The king exiled Sainval but did not count on the public taking up her cause. Audiences cheered Sainval's younger sister and hissed Vestris so forcefully that performances were disrupted even though the guard was doubled and tripled. Duras, present at one of the performances, was humiliated, and the general challenge to "royal despotism" could not be missed.[37] This affair opened up an era, lasting to the Revolution, during

35. Bonnassies, *Les Auteurs dramatiques et la Comédie-Française*, 29–31, 46. See Bonnassies, *Comédie-Française*, 140.

36. Papillon de la Ferté, *L'Administration des menus*, 14, 326.

37. Friedrich-Melchoir Grimm, *Correspondance littéraire philosophique et critique par Grimm, Diderot, Raynal, Meister, etc.*, ed. Maurice Tourneux (Paris, 1882), 12:279–80. 557–58; Louis Petit de Bachaumont, *Mémoires secrets pour servir à l'histoire de la républic des lettres en France depuis 1762 jusqu'à nos jours* (London, 1777–89), 14:127, 134, 140, 172.

which the theater audience did not hesitate to thrust itself into controversies of all sorts.[38]

The Vestris-Sainval affair illustrated the dovetailing of theatrical controversy with the rise of "public opinion."[39] Integral to this merger was the appearance of new artistic ideals with disruptive social implications and the growing aggressiveness of disgruntled playwrights. In this way, the decisions of the general assembly were becoming increasingly politicized in the last two decades of the Old Regime. We must turn to contemporary commentary on these decisions and examine whether the large role women had in them took on special relevance.

Interpreting Actresses' Power

The entire range of responses to actresses' power—usually from men—had a large amount of uniformity. Nonetheless, in order to fit the contours of the historiographical debate that launched this investigation, we must distinguish the discourse about actresses' power that came from within the absolutist public sphere and that which came from within the emerging bourgeois public sphere. In both cases, actresses' authority was seen as different from men's and, therefore, unwelcome.

Landes, as we have seen, argued that within the absolutist public sphere, certain women and men had influence over decision-making by virtue of their special status and privileges. Yet it pays to ask how open the absolutist public sphere really was to women's power. In fact, even among "the king's performers," females had a far less secure claim on the privilege to participate in the administration of their theater than did males. The royal decree that reestablished the Comédie-Italienne in France in 1716 gave its assembly all the responsibilities for self-administration that the one at the Théâtre-Français had, but it specifically prohibited the women in the troupe from voting or even deliberating.[40] Why the actresses at the Comédie-Française had the privilege is a matter of speculation. It may have been a matter of

38. Boncompain, *Auteurs et comédiens au XVIIIe siècle*, 210.
39. On this important subject, see Jeffrey Ravel, "The Police and the Parterre: Cultural Politics in Paris Public Theater, 1680–1789" (Ph.D. diss., University of California at Berkeley, 1991).
40. Emile Campardon, *Les Comédiens du roi de la troupe italienne pendant les deux dernière siècles* (Paris, 1880), 2:236.

continuing the prevailing practice, a favor to actresses of greater prestige, or an attempt to make the theater function more effectively. All we can say for certain is that actresses' place within the administration of royal theaters was contingent and contested, nor assured.

If the officials who wrote the regulations of 1719 for the Théâtre-Français did so in the hope of promoting efficiency and internal peace, they would have been disappointed with the results. The reports of Denis Papillon de la Ferté, who oversaw the general assembly between 1760 and 1780 as the *intendant des menus plaisirs*, testified to the disruptions they caused. The terms "vexations," "cabals," and "spirit of insubordination" filled his journal.[41] The *intendant* attributed the bulk of the problems to the actresses rather than the actors, although the latter group also included difficult individuals. Ferté singled out as the central obstacle to good order the actresses' use of powerful protectors—including his own superiors, the Gentlemen of the Bedchamber—to further their individual careers and fight their rivalries. In his opinion, the actresses were not afraid of sanctions and had "lost all sense of subordination."[42] Only occasionally (as in the case of Clairon, for example) did he recognize female power that did not entail ensnaring men in their intrigues. His was not the voice of aristocratic antiabsolutism, which Landes recognized as being hostile to women's influence; yet, he was appalled that women exercised power over the troupe.

Ferté did not hesitate to connect female sexuality with disorder. The *intendant* was distraught over the behavior of the Gentlemen of the Bedchamber. The familiarity that actresses assumed with the duc de Richelieu when the latter attended general assembly meetings shocked and embarrassed Ferté. When he once came upon Richelieu rehearsing lines with Mademoiselle Colombe (Marie Rombocoli), he was disgusted that "a great lord" would put himself in such a demeaning position.[43] The *intendant* did not blame his superiors except, perhaps, for their weakness. Ferté himself had a mistress who was an actress (at the Opéra-comique) and could understand the frailties of the flesh.[44] What he regretted was the ease with which actresses ensnared powerful men in their own quest for influence.

41. Papillon de la Ferté, *L'Administration des menus*, 77, 109, 118, 186, and passim. On the *intendant*, see René Farge, *Un Haut fonctionnaire de l'ancien régime: Papillon de la Ferté* (Paris: E. Leroux, 1912).

42. Papillon de la Ferté, *L'Administration des menus*, 326.

43. Ibid., 14–16.

44. Lorédon Larchy, *Documents inédits sur le regne de Louis XV, ou anecdotes galantes sur les actrices . . . de M. le lieutenant de police Sartine* (Paris, 1863), 197.

The *intendant* did not think systematically about nor comment very much on the power plays of the male performers although there is abundant evidence in his journal that they were troublesome subjects, too. The actors Préville (Pierre Dubus) and Molé (François) led cabals and took active roles in instigating and perpetuating the major affairs that brought the troupe's deliberations to a standstill. Ferté apparently took the actors' insubordination as more "natural" than that of the actresses. He sometimes referred to actors as "protectors" of this or that performer, thereby according them an authority associated with the highborn.[45] Never did Ferté conceive of a female artist as a protector.

Actors' strategies for asserting their will or advancing their careers were similar to those used by actresses. Both knew the route to the queen's chamber or to a lord's home, where they might plead their case to a sympathetic ear. Both used the threat of not performing, or performing poorly, as a way of protesting what they considered unfair treatment. Yet, while using these tactics, actors were just as inclined as Ferté to delegitimate actresses' exercise of power by linking it to the sexual manipulation of men. Molé denounced the intrigues of Mademoiselles Luzy (Dorothée) and Fanier (Alexandrine) even as he protected Mademoiselle d'Epiny (Claude-Hélène Pinet). When the general assembly was passing through one of its strident phases, the actors sent a letter to the *intendant* complaining that "the protected actresses, certain of impunity, do only what they want."[46]

Ultimately, perceiving actresses as voracious and achieving their ends through the weakness of men was a ubiquitous claim within the absolutist public sphere. Even those most culpable of offering their protection to actresses under compromising circumstances complained about the women's use of male influence. Thus, the duc de Duras defended the favors he accorded to Madame Vestris as the means of restoring a balance other actresses had disrupted through illicit protection. Actresses, too, used the charge against rivals. Not only Sainval but Clairon, too, produced a grave crisis at the Comédie by insisting that the troupe could not submit to the orders of the Gentlemen of the Bedchamber when female intrigue was behind a dishonorable command. This was at the root of the disruptive Dubois affair of 1765, during which the troupe accepted incarceration rather than perform with an actor whose lies under oath had dishonored them. Clairon led the charge to expel Dubois (Louis Blouin) from the company and steeled

45. Papillon de la Ferté, *L'Administration des menus*, 190.
46. Ibid., 188–91, 232.

colleagues for resistance when the Gentlemen of the Bedchamber insisted that he remain in place. Clairon maintained that the duc de Richelieu took the actor's side because his daughter (also in the troupe) sold her body for the lord's support. Clairon even used this incident to challenge the Gentlemen of the Bedchamber's right to interfere with the troupe's Parisian performances.[47]

The claim that actresses bought influence with male superiors for sex was less a description of women exercising power than a strategy for combating women's influence. The claim arose so often because actresses and actors were enmeshed in a situation with much potential for conflict. The collective responsibilities they bore allowed for much freedom in shaping individual careers. The rules and traditions that administrators like Ferté hoped would obviate the need for "influence" did no such thing. There were too many gaps and uncertainties about matters that performers, often high-strung anyway, considered vital to their careers. Male artists appealed to an order in which their influence was "natural" because it was supposedly based on their talents, making them essential to the troupe.[48] They would have spurned such claims from actresses and focused, instead, upon sexual intrigue. The simplifying interpretation did not do justice to the similar ways female and male artists exercised their power.

Nonetheless, the construction of actresses' power as illegitimate was strong enough *within* the absolutist public sphere to provoke a partial silencing of women. Probably at the behest of administrators like Ferté, the royal government took steps to curb female intrigue at its first theater. New regulations of the 1760s began to transfer some of the power of the general assembly to a small committee of performers, and in 1780 membership of the committee was restricted in a way that was not at all gender-neutral. It was to have seven actors (one as the secretary) and only two actresses.[49] The decree may not have been applied very effectively (later efforts at re-

47. Ibid., 326, 147–64; Grimm, *Correspondance littéraire*, 5:447–48, 6:256–59, 281.

48. Actors were also celebrated lovers; they seemed to have enjoyed much prestige among young aristocrats on this basis. The public was familiar with their affairs with actresses and courtesans. However, a discreet silence covered whatever relations they had with aristocratic women (and men). Not even the police reports, so explicit about actresses' affairs, named their highborn conquests. Whereas the sexual power actresses wielded was open and acknowledged, actors were able to have "private" affairs. See Jean-Baptiste Lafitte, ed., *Mémoires de Fleury de la Comédie-Française de 1757 à 1820* (Brussels and Leipzig, 1835–38), 1:193, 2:56–67, 276, 3:125; Gaston Capon, *Les Vestris* (Paris: Mercure de France, 1908), 100.

49. Bonnassies, *Les Auteurs dramatiques et la Comédie-Française*, 71. Presumably, the crown kept the two actresses on the committee only because their opinions on female roles were needed.

form paid no attention to it), but the intention was clear: females were to be constrained in the quest for good order. Thus, the power of actresses within the absolutist public sphere was never secure or matter-of-factly accepted. The king could easily envision fraternal governance for his theaters.

The organs of the emerging bourgeois public sphere were obsessed with theater and only to a slightly lesser degree with actresses. Any issue of the *Mercure de France* or the *Journal de Paris* might carry couplets from a star-struck young gentleman extolling the charms, grace, and talent of a woman he had seen on the stage and to whom he professed eternal devotion. Engravers turned to no subject so often as the lovely enchantress who was capturing audiences at the moment.[50] Such texts were important in turning actresses into icons, but they usually had little to say about their exercise of power. Yet, comments on this matter were common, too, because the Comédie was such an important cultural institution and because actresses' decisions had an impact upon playwrights. Whether from Grub Street or from the literary Establishment, playwrights had the inclination and opportunity to explain their professional victories and defeats to the world.[51] The potential for friction between performers and playwrights was one reason the actresses' power was debated in the Habermasian public sphere.

Playwrights entangled themselves in backstage intrigues even as they denounced undue influence when decisions did not go their way. Not having a play accepted or not receiving the best possible treatment from the players increasingly set the occasion for resorting to public denunciation. The most widely publicized cases of "abuse" identified actresses as the culprits. Even Voltaire, towering literary figure though he was, was not above taking vengeance on an actress for the presumed wrong she had done him. He was stung when his *Les Lois de Minos* was not produced until after the height of the season had passed and blamed the fiasco on the delays occasioned by Mademoiselle Raucourt (Joséphe-Françoise Saucelle).[52] Although Voltaire

50. Arsène Houssaye cites dozens of these references in *Princesses de comédie et déesses de l'Opéra* (Paris, 1860). On engravings, see Emile Dacier, *La Gravure en France au XVIIIe siècle* (Paris: G. van Oest, 1925), chap. 2.

51. On the notion of "Grub Street" writers, see the classic essay by Robert Darnton, "The High Enlightenment and the Low-Life of Literature in Pre-Revolutionary France," *Past and Present*, no. 51 (May 1971): 81–115.

52. Lafitte, *Mémoires de Fleury*, 2:13–17. Raucourt had created a sensation in Paris by flaunting her supposedly irreproachable virtue. Voltaire ended this phase in her career by exposing her blemished past in a widely circulated letter. On the actress's colorful life, see

Rôle de Medée
Mᴸᴸᴱ. RAUCOURT

„ Hécate le desire et je te le commande,
„ Nuit, Stix, Hécate, Enfers, terribles Déités.
„ J'ordonne; obéissez ....

Mademoiselle Raucourt was notorious for her extravagances, homosexual affairs, and contacts in high places. Courtesy, Bibliothèque nationale de France, Paris.

was eager to raise the public status of actresses, he did not hesitate to publicize Raucourt's vices.

Sharper attacks were more likely to come from the obscure playwrights who thirsted for fame; and in fact, they channeled their discontents into a general attack on the Théâtre-Français during the 1770s. Like other state institutions, the Comédie came under a crescendo of criticism when the young Louis XVI dismissed the Maupeau parlement in 1774, signaling a diminished resolve to stifle dissent. A diverse group of disgruntled writers, whose ideas spanned the entire political spectrum, cooperated informally to subject the Comédie to ridicule. They asserted that the performers used their power to do little more than defend their privileges, restrain innovation, and reward bad art. Nina Rattner Gelbart has called this group the *"frondeur* journalists"* because, in identifying the Comédie as part of the Establishment, they used their pens to strike at royal authority.[53] For every Mercier, who was guided by a principled vision of a regenerated (and masculine) social order, there were many others whose hostility barely disguised frustrated personal ambition. Of course, actresses were the targets of their patriarchal rage.

Charles Palissot de Montenoy, a writer scorned by the literary establishment for his antiphilosophe views, was among these disaffected playwrights.[54] He intentionally created a cause célèbre to promote himself and, not surprisingly, found it useful to attack the power of actresses. Palissot had written a play of questionable worth, *Les Courtisanes* (1775), which the general assembly rejected twice. Friedrich-Melchoir Grimm wrote in his *Correspondance littéraire* that the play was "without interest, without gaiety, and filled with indecent details."[55] Yet, Palissot was able to create a considerable stir by charging that actresses had scuttled a play that would have been morally uplifting simply because it cut too close to their lascivious mores. He portrayed actresses as being dangerous not only to the stage but also to public morality.

Jean de Reuilly, *La Raucourt et ses amies* (Paris: Daragon, 1909); and Hector Fleischmann, *Le Cénacle libertin de Mademoiselle Raucourt* (Paris: Bibliothèque des Curieux, 1912).

53. Nina Rattner Gelbart, "'Frondeur' Journalism in the 1770s: Theater Criticism and Radical Politics in the Pre-Revolutionary French Press," *Eighteenth-Century Studies* 17 (Summer 1984): 493–514, and *Feminine and Opposition Journalism in Old Regime France: Le Journal des Dames* (Berkeley and Los Angeles: University of California Press, 1987), chap. 6.

54. On Palissot, see Hervé Guénot, "Palissot de Montenoy, un ennemi de Diderot et des philosophes," *Recherches sur Diderot et sur l'Encyclopédie*, no. 1 (October 1986): 59–63.

55. Grimm, *Correspondance littéraire*, 9:64.

Palissot campaigned with savvy against the decision of the Comédie, taking advantage of these ambiguities. He quickly sought and received the approval of the royal censor after the second rejection so as to refute the assembly's claim that the play was unacceptable on moral grounds. Using his reputation as an antiphilosophe, he won the "dévot party," pious courtiers, to his side. The satirical pamphlet he produced, *Gratitude Expressed by the Women of the World to the Actresses of the Comédie-Française for Rejecting "Les Courtisanes,"* caused a sensation and even won the support from the archbishop of Paris. Indeed, the actor Fleury (Abraham Bénard) reported in his memoirs that the archbishop paid for publishing the brochure.[56] Pressured by so many devout voices, the king ordered his actors to present the play. Skillfully manipulating the issue of morality, Palissot triumphed over the actresses and got his way.

Whether or not Palissot actually believed that the actresses were the source of disorder at the Comédie, he made the point before an entertained public. Other maverick playwrights came to his defense even when they despised his support of the status quo. Mercier did so from the opposite side of the political spectrum. Alexandre du Coudray, who also wrote obscure plays touching on the bad morals of performers, lent support with a *Lettre à M. Palissot sur le refus de son comédie "Les Courtisanes."* This was another attack on actresses for protecting indecency.[57]

Philosophes' disagreements with Palissot did not usually extend to the subject of actresses. Neither Grimm's *Correspondance littéraire* nor Pidansat de Mairobert's *Mémoires secrets*, for example, gave any credence to his claims in this affair. On the other hand, the two newsletters of enlightened opinion could be just as likely as Palissot (or, indeed, as *intendant* Ferté) to interpret the behavior of actresses in terms of sexual license.[58] This was how the *Correspondance littéraire* explained the failure of Diderot's *Le Fils naturel.* This play was the foundational example of a new aesthetic, the

---

56. Bachaumont, *Mémoires secrets*, 8:3–11; Lafitte, *Mémoires de Fleury*, 2:242–46.

57. Bachaument, *Mémoires secrets*, 8:10.

58. On the general fear of women's sexuality expressed in newsletters like the *Mémoires secrets*, see Jeffrey Merrick, "Sexual Politics and Public Order in Late Eighteenth-Century France," *Journal of the History of Sexuality* 1 (Winter 1990): 68–84. On the contested authorship of the *Mémoires secrets*, conventionally attributed to Louis Petit de Bachaumont, see Louis Olivier, "Bachaumont, the Chronicler: A Questionable Renown," *Studies on Voltaire and the Eighteenth Century* 143 (1975): 1161–79. On the milieu that produced the philosophical newsletters, see Dena Goodman, "Enlightenment Salons: The Convergence of Female and Philosophical Ambition," *Eighteenth-Century Studies* 22 (Spring 1989): 329–50.

bourgeois drama, based on intimate emotions and privatized situations.[59] The *Correspondance littéraire* noted that the actor Molé, an advocate of bourgeois drama, accused Madame Préville and her husband of undermining the play's effect with their poor performances. The actress reacted bitterly to the remark and refused to perform her role again, forcing Diderot to withdraw the hapless work from the stage. The newsletter found a sexual motive at the root of Madame Préville's peevishness, although it would have been just as easy to attribute it to anger at being criticized. Grimm speculated that Préville's hostility derived from an "unfortunate adventure in licentiousness" with Molé. The *Correspondance littéraire*, like the voices from within the absolutist public sphere, linked actresses' power and their sexuality and accentuated the unfortunate consequences.[60]

The anonymous "public" certainly learned and expressed this lesson in the Vestris-Sainval affair. A satirical commentary printed in the *Gazette de France* (27 September 1779) equated the dispute with a naval battle (while England and France were currently engaged in warfare). On one side was the flotilla of "Queen Venus," Madame Vestris; and on the other side was the flotilla of "Queen Melpomène," Mademoiselle Sainval. The article surveyed the forces deployed by each side, with each player designated as a "captain." The notes on the captains were replete with double entendres and insiders' gossip. Significantly, the actresses' notes made reference to their physical attributes. The comment on Louise Contat, for example, cited her as being "quite petty" but still having "only a small renown for her conquests." By contrast, actors were described in terms of their acting ability, and the comments about them were less acrid.[61] The satire signaled that the public expected actresses to be behind the intrigues that demeaned the Comédie—and even the monarchy.

Playwrights and the public were clearly anxious about the fate of the first theater of Europe being in the hands of actresses. Their complaints would find a partial resolution in the reorganization of the general assembly that the monarchy ordered in 1780. Well before this, however, Rousseau had brought to the forefront another discourse on actresses' power. In certain ways, it was a continuation of the debate over the Christian rejection of theater, but Rousseau transposed the controversy into an entirely different

59. Scott Bryson, *The Chastised Stage: Bourgeois Drama and the Exercise of Power* (Saratoga, Calif.: ANML Libri, 1991), chaps. 1–2.

60. Grimm, *Correspondance littéraire*, 9:378–79.

61. The broadside was reproduced in Bachaumont, *Mémoires secrets*, 14:192–95.

realm. His *Lettre à D'Alembert sur les spectacles* of 1758, written in the context of the celebrated debate over establishing a theater in Geneva, was concerned not with Christian morality but rather with the impact of the stage on a sovereign people.[62] The goal Rousseau had in mind was the formation and maintenance of a democratic culture, in which virtue resided in the people themselves, and he aggressively concluded that the theater was inherently dangerous to a people needing to exercise reason. The claim proved to be problematical for advanced thinkers of the day, but it still shaped subsequent discussions of theatrical reform. It brought writers, especially Rousseau's radical disciples, to consider another sort of power actresses exercised, their influence over the moral judgment of male spectators. Ultimately, the Rousseauist discourse on actresses encouraged shrill statements about women on the stage, but the representations of women with power it produced were only partly innovative.

Rousseau's denunciation of the theater repeated many of the arguments that Catholic opponents had long hurled, focusing on the frivolities and sensuality of the plays, the immoral behavior of performers, their duplicity, and so on.[63] The distinctive element in his argument was the assumption that public virtue required the domestication of women. The opposition between women as nature intended them to be and women as they appeared on stage had not received so much attention in Christian denunciations of theater. Denying that plays could inspire virtue, he charged that playwrights inevitably endowed female characters with a wisdom and superiority that properly belonged to men. "In augmenting with so much care the ascendancy of women," he asked rhetorically, "[will] men be better governed?" Rousseau was also more insistent than most Catholic writers that the institution of the theater was hopelessly condemned by the private vices of the performers. Unlike some of his disciples and even his critics, Rousseau denounced evenhandedly the transgressions of actresses and actors. He put money at the roots of players' debauchery. Because they were profligate

62. There have been many attempts to interpret Rousseau's attitudes toward women. Most add a degree of complexity to his hostility. See, for example, Victor Waxler, "Made for Man's Delight: Rousseau as Antifeminist," *American Historical Review* 81 (April 1976): 266–91; Joel Schwartz, *The Sexual Politics of Jean-Jacques Rousseau* (Chicago: University of Chicago Press, 1984); Paul Thomas, "Jean-Jacques Rousseau, Sexist?" *Feminist Studies* 17 (Summer 1991): 195–217. For Rousseau's views on theater, see David Marshall "Rousseau and the State of Theater," *Representations*, no. 13 (Winter 1986): 84–114.

63. On this source of denunciation, see Jonas Barish, *The Antitheatrical Prejudice* (Berkeley and Los Angeles: University of California Press, 1981); and Moses Barras, *The Stage Controversy in France from Corneille to Rousseau* (New York: Institute of French Studies, 1933).

and constantly in debt, they were continually open to criminal temptations. Although he believed that actresses were "inevitably suspect because they rejected the natural modesty of their sex," he did not hold them to a higher standard than actors, nor did he claim that they had fallen lower. Their unnatural will to display themselves, coupled with adverse circumstances—an education based on coquetry, constant exposure to amorous roles, the need to wear revealing costumes, and pressure from an adoring entourage of young men—prepared actresses to sell their bodies for gold. But for performers of both sexes, Rousseau concludes that "prohibiting [them] from being vice-ridden would be like prohibiting them from becoming ill!"[64]

Rousseau's disciples, especially Louis-Sébastien Mercier and Nicholas-Edme Rétif (or Restif) de la Bretonne, were haunted by the questions Rousseau posed about the place of theater in a democratic culture. Their answer, however, was not to suppress the stage but rather to subject it to a radical transformation. They argued for the regeneration of theater so that it would be compatible with the needs of a sovereign people. Making theater into a school of virtue would require a new aesthetic as well as constraints—sometimes severe ones—on actresses' freedom. Mercier and Rétif were among the playwrights who condemned the classical stage as hopelessly tied to the artificiality and vice of the absolutist public sphere. They championed bourgeois drama as the sort of theater that would not have the faults Rousseau claimed were inherent in all plays. Drama would promote authentic, transparent, and virtuous relations in society. Playwrights would be "legislators," in Mercier's view, raising public morality by encouraging the audience to identify with the characters and celebrate the triumph of virtue in a privatized world of ordinary citizens. However urgent they believed the artistic reform to be, the advocates of drama never doubted Rousseau's point that the corruption of performers could easily vitiate its moralizing impact. Noble speech in the mouth of a harlot would only render the audience cynical, a situation that had to be avoided at all costs. Mercier and Rétif offered harsh prescriptions for controlling actresses' influence over spectators.

Mercier despised the troupe of the Comédie for its indifference to the moral state of the people and believed that the dramas he had submitted unsuccessfully to the general assembly might help to regenerate society.[65]

64. Jean-Jacques Rousseau, *Lettre à D'Alembert sur les spectacles*, ed. Max Fuchs (1758; Lille and Geneva: Giard, 1948), 63, 65–149.

65. Henry Majewski, *The Preromantic Imagination of L.-S. Mercier* (New York: Humanities Press, 1971); Bryson, *Chastised Stage*, 49–51, 51–53, 56–59.

His anonymously published *Nouvel essai sur l'art théâtrique* of 1773 laid down guidelines for the sort of moralizing theater that Rousseau had not imagined. Most of the work was an attack on classical theater and an argument in favor of bourgeois drama. Mercier did not discuss performers until the end when he focused on the depravity of actresses and affirmed that a stage that encouraged virtue would require ostracizing and humiliating them.

A one-time editor of the *Journal des dames*, Mercier has been labeled a "feminist" because he sometimes encouraged women to cultivate their talents.[66] Yet, he was so troubled by the behavior of actresses that he went so far as to champion the Gallican condemnation of performers—indeed, to see it as necessary for a democratic culture. Proclaiming that "through the centuries, women of the theater have caused frightful ravages to public morality," Mercier was more concerned with actresses' influence outside the theater than within. He painted their seductive powers over young men in terms more lurid than most clerical writers had, wondering if there were many families whom actresses had left solvent. Not only did lust destroy young men's ability to think clearly, but actresses' empire over men taught innocent women that virtue was not worthwhile as males flocked around the harlots of the stage. To remove the official opprobrium from actresses—Mercier was not at all concerned that it also fell on actors—would be to remove the last reminder that innocence deserved to prevail. He also recalled with apparent approval the practice among ancient Romans of having actresses reappear on stage in the nude after each performance "either to efface the impression their veiled charms had made or to confirm the disdain which opinion had for this profession."[67]

At the heart of Rétif's radical thought was also a bipolar model of femininity and masculinity, so it is no wonder that he shared Mercier's horror of actresses' depravity.[68] His corpus of writings often referred to the erotic impact of the stage on male spectators.[69] *La Mimographe* of 1770 (subtitled, "Ideas of a Virtuous Woman on the Reform of the National Theater") defined the reform project primarily in terms of radically restructuring the private lives of performers. Indeed, Rétif proposed going beyond the Romans in humiliating actresses. His book, one of five in a series on women's

66. Gelbart, *Feminine and Opposition Journalism*, 212–13.

67. Mercier, *Nouvel essai*, 347–72.

68. Mark Poster, "The Concepts of Sexual Identity and Life Cycle in Restif's Utopian Thought," *Studies on Voltaire and the Eighteenth Century* 73 (1970): 241–71.

69. Pierre Testud, *Rétif de la Bretonne et la création littéraire* (Geneva: Droz, 1977), 313–65.

place in society, began as an epistolary novel. Madame d'Algan, a virtuous, well-born woman, bemoans her fate since her husband ran away with an actress. Her demand for the complete suppression of theater (Rousseau's position) allows Rétif to launch into a long counterproposal for the radical reform of acting. Most of the book outlines plans for replacing professional performers, the source of so much trouble, with citizen-actors. Public schooling would inculcate a love of drama, and citizens would specialize in one role and come to identify with it to such an extent that they would emulate the noble sentiments that professional performers presently feigned. The rules Rétif devised for the citizen-actors reflected very clearly the fears he had about actresses' private lives. They would be under the close supervision of twelve directors and directresses, chosen among citizens of irreproachable conduct. The directors could never call actresses to their homes for a consultation; contact had to take place through a directress or through the performer's parents. In Rétif's utopian vision, the theater wings, rather than being open to intrigue and licentious contacts, would become tightly controlled environments. The sexes would be segregated, and even then, only the performers' parents would be permitted behind stage.[70]

Toward the end of *La Mimographe*, Rétif fretted that he had not gone far enough in undermining the physical enticements female performers exercised over spectators and proposed a new strategy for thoroughgoing vilification. Actors, recruited from the royal foundling homes *(Enfants trouvés)*, would become slaves, living in segregation from the rest of society under draconian discipline. Rewards would be tied not only to their talent but also to their obedience to severe codes of conduct. To ensure that both the public and performers understood the outcast status of the players, there would be an annual ritual of humiliation not unlike the Roman one Mercier described with approval. Artists would appear on stage, bound in chains, and an official would denounce the faults each had committed that year. The ritual was intended especially for actresses, "whose faces and talents might inspire vanity and whose attractiveness might have caused ravages among the spectators."[71]

---

70. Nicholas-Edme Rétif de la Bretonne, *La Mimographe* (Amsterdam, 1770), 17–44, 175–232. Sometimes there was not much distance between "utopian" thinking about the stage and reality. A royal order of 1732 (frequently repeated) closed the wings of the Opéra to all but performers.

71. Ibid., 448–66. Moffat, *Rousseau* (272) interprets the revolting proposals to mean the opposite of what they literally say—that they were a plea for rehabilitating the status of actresses. This argument is implausible because it fails to consider the positions Rétif de la

Rousseau's discourse on the moral effects of the stage on a free people unleashed powerful currents of patriarchal rage among disciples seeking to foster a democratic culture. Reflection on the moral lessons actresses taught led to denunciations of their seductiveness. This is exactly what Landes would have expected. Yet, Rousseau's antifeminism was only one among many. There was much continuity with the rhetoric that came from within the absolutist public sphere and from more temperate elements in the bourgeois public sphere. In all cases, the power of actresses, whether over the theater itself or over men in the audience, was equated with their appealing bodies and with their participation in *la vie galante*. Actresses thus posed a challenge to reason and virtue which actors did not.

In the face of these denunciations, where were the arguments in defense of actresses? Landes's critics would have expected them from the philosophes (usually of the High Enlightenment) who disagreed strongly with Rousseau's conclusions on the dangers of the stage. From them, if at all, there should have been praise for actresses' contribution to sociability; on those grounds, philosophes might have seen their opinions as essential to the life of the theater. However, no such defense was forthcoming. The writers who challenged Rousseau (and, by implication, the Gallican position as well) were preoccupied with his claim that plays would not be moralizing. Their thought on actresses was less developed, not because the problem appeared unimportant to them, but, rather, because they conceded most of Rousseau's complaints. They differed from Rousseau in that they had solutions for the grievances that he regarded as inevitable. But these solutions sometimes paralleled the sexual repression that Mercier and Rétif advocated.

Jean-François Marmontel's response to Rousseau's *Lettre à D'Alembert sur les spectacles* set a pattern for later pamphlets by concentrating on how plays could be morally instructive. Turning to the vices of performers at the end of his tract, Marmontel agreed with Rousseau that their conduct was appalling, but in his view, this was the result of the defamed status of actresses. If the king would lift their excommunication, then women with high moral standards would consider the career.[72] The playwright did not even begin to grapple with the point that the crown would make a few years later, when Clairon pushed the issue: the prejudice against the profession was so deeply rooted as to be beyond changing for the moment. Jean

---

Bretonne takes in his four other books on women. Rétif de la Bretonne's comments were "utopian" but not ironic.

72. Jean-François Marmontel, "Apologie du théâtre," in his *Contes moraux* (Paris, 1767), 2:162–271.

D'Alembert's eagerly awaited reply to Rousseau also conceded the problems that Rousseau found in performers. Like Marmontel, he held the low status of acting to be the cause rather than the consequence of the libertine inclinations of actresses. D'Alembert put his confidence in an official prize given to actresses for good behavior. "When one accords distinctions to virtuous actresses," he dared to predict, "the profession will be characterized by the most upright morality." The superficiality of his solution suggests that he ultimately despaired of finding a viable one.[73]

Whereas D'Alembert chose to reward virtue, some of Rousseau's other critics ironically anticipated the thinking of Rétif and Mercier in advancing a moralization based on repression. One pamphlet written by a performer prescribed a theater with actor-citizens as suitable for Geneva. The nonprofessional players in this proposal would be under the strict supervision of a director and four commissioners, who were empowered to incarcerate them to prevent unacceptable behavior. To eliminate temptations for the female performers, they would not be allowed to wear jewelry at any time off the stage, and merchants would be prohibited from extending them credit.[74]

Another provincial actor and playwright, L.-H. Dancourt, took up Rousseau's point that performers' vices were rooted in the quest for gold. However, Dancourt located the problem in actors' peripatetic and insecure existence, which caused women to sell their bodies. His solution was to suppress the self-regulating nature of acting companies and subject performers to local supervisory boards charged with overseeing morality and assigning roles purely on the basis of talent. Why this board would perform any better than the Gentlemen of the Bedchamber is not a question the author explored.[75] Despite the logical gap, the argument continued to resonate in defenses of the theater. On the eve of the Revolution, Jacques Mague de Saint-Aubin placed his trust in a new sort of theatrical administration, which would be responsible for the pay and conduct of the performers. He also thought that a drama school (which in fact had recently come into being) would allow the directors of the theater to avoid the influence of powerful protectors and select actresses on the basis of talent, not intrigue.[76]

73. Jean D'Alembert, *Lettre de M. D'Alembert à M. Jean-Jacques Rousseau sur l'article Genève tiré du VIIe volume de l'Encyclopédie* (Amsterdam, 1759).

74. P.-A. Laval, *P.-A. Laval, comédien, à J.-J. Rousseau, citoyen de Genève, sur les raisons qu'il expose pour réfuter M. D'Alembert* (La Haye, 1758).

75. L.-H. Dancourt, *L.-H. Dancourt, arlequin de Berlin, à M. J.-J. Rousseau, dit de Genève* (Amsterdam, 1760).

76. Jacques Mague de Saint-Aubin, *La Réforme des théâtres* (Paris, 1787), 26–54.

Thus, the opponents of both Rousseau and of the Christian denunciators of theater had little to say in favor of the virtues of actresses; still less did they accord their official power within the Comédie any legitimacy. An appreciation of women's contributions to the art of conviviality was qualified by the fear that actresses' vices endangered the moralizing potential of theater. The ungendered performer was rarely to be found in the discourses of the bourgeois public sphere before 1789. But what about thereafter?

Fraternity and Patriarchy in the Revolutionary Theater

Keith Michael Baker argues that the revolutionaries of 1789 faced a number of political options regarding female citizens. He finds that rational and republican ideologies competed with one another on at least equal footing.[77] By this assessment, the silencing of women was not inevitable or even imagined until circumstances produced the triumph of a republican discourse of unified political will. And even then, the triumph was only temporary. This was not, however, how the male performers at the Comédie-Française saw the situation as the Revolution began. They seemed convinced that women should and would be excluded from power from the first. The conflict over actresses' authority that erupted at the Théâtre-Français in December of 1789 was, to be sure, a small event. Yet, it does uphold the claim that the Revolution was made against women in the public sphere.

The last month of 1789 was a troubled moment, indeed, for the Comédie. Its monopoly over presenting serious plays was under attack as never before, and playwrights clamored to obtain more rights over their works. Moreover, a political rift between pro- and counterrevolutionary players threatened to pull apart the troupe. This division surfaced during the infamous *Charles IX* affair. The incendiary play by Marie-Joseph Chénier about the Saint Bartholomew Day massacre had quickly become a favorite of the Patriot party but embarrassed many actors, who saw it as an insult to the monarch. Demands from Mirabeau and other revolutionary leaders to feature the play led to confrontations within the company, with the young François Talma, about to launch a legendary career, leading a small group of artists against a larger group of colleagues who apparently wished

---

77. Baker, "Defining the Public Sphere," 206–7.

that July 14 had never happened.[78] The reactionary tenor of the Comédie presented increasing problems as the National Assembly made its plans for the theater. The National Assembly removed the Comédie from the royal household and placed it under the supervision of the Commune of Paris. Friction with the mayor (Jean Bailly) soon intensified. Just as the revolutionary authorities considered making the Comédie the "Theater of the nation" the troupe voted to retain the title "actors of the king."[79]

In this atmosphere of trouble and uncertainty, a number of actors petitioned the National Assembly and the Commune for far-reaching changes in the administration of the troupe entailing a formal gendering of power. They asked that their female colleagues be prohibited from voting within the general assembly. The petition also identified the moral situation of actresses as a grave problem for the theater. It requested the firing of all actresses who produced illegitimate children or otherwise caused a public scandal, although there was no parallel concern for scandals originating with actors. Finally, the petition "encouraged" all actors who were married to actresses who were not faithful—and there were several in the troupe— to "repudiate" them, presumably for the sake of public morality.[80]

This extraordinary petition seems to have been initiated by Dugazon (Jean Gourgaud), one of the prorevolutionary actors and a close ally of Talma. Whereas Talma was confrontational, Dugazon worked to smooth over differences and preserve as much collegiality as possible. His principal goal seems to have been keeping the Comédie together and out of political trouble. We do not know how many signed, but it is likely that most males accepted the proposals, as they were meant to help the troupe through an impasse. The petition was surely intended to reassure the revolutionary authorities and place the Comédie in the best possible light. The timing of the petition makes that apparent. The move to exclude actresses emerged as tensions between the troupe and its new master, the Commune, had reached a level of crisis. The petition also anticipated the debate that was about to preoccupy the National Assembly on the suitability of actors (along with Jews and Protestants) becoming citizens.[81] The wish to tran-

---

78. Arthur Pougin, *La Comédie-Française et la Révolution* (Paris, n.d.), 6–50.

79. Noelle Guilbert and Jacqueline Razzonnikoff, *Le Journal de la Comédie-Française, 1787–1799: La Comédie aux trois couleurs* (Paris: Sides, 1989), 61–75.

80. La Comédie-Française, *L'Influence de la révolution sur le Théâtre-Français: Pétition à ce sujet adressée à la Commune de Paris* (Paris, 1790), 10–14.

81. The debate took place on 24 December 1789. See *Réimpressions de l'ancien Moniteur* (Paris, 1854), 2:464. A letter from the secretary of the troupe to the National Assembly stated

scend an outcast status had long engaged the troupe. Evidently, the petition was meant to prove that the Comédie was not hopelessly reactionary, that it could enter into the spirit of the Revolution and regenerate itself into an institution that the nation could respect. Actors believed—on ideological or pragmatic grounds—regeneration required the silencing of women.

To assess whether Landes is correct about Rousseauist thought being behind the silencing, it would be helpful to seek the precise ideological sources of the petition. However, the task is futile. Anxiety about actresses' authority was the common coin of both the absolutist public sphere and the Habermasian public sphere. To assume a dominant Rousseauean influence would be arbitrary, especially because no hint of a complementary approach to gender roles is evident. In truth, the actors found many reasons to attribute grave failings to a theater that gave decision-making power to women. Moreover, they believed that the revolutionary leaders, about to regenerate the nation, saw things this way, too. Eager to improve relations with the Paris Commune and with the National Assembly, actors sought the mantle of reform by excluding their female colleagues. They did not have to be Rousseaueans to appeal to a fraternal model of government in which women were made virtuous by being placed under the control of males.

In the end, the petition had no impact because efforts at administrative reform were overtaken by other events. The troupe, subjected to fierce internal divisions, soon split in two. The National Assembly suppressed the monopoly over serious plays, creating financial disorder. Eventually, a masculinization of power did come to pass but not exactly as the actors had foreseen it. The self-regulating features of acting companies were weakened. Not only were theaters put under increasingly heavy police supervision; they also came under the control of administrators who had the authority to give orders to salaried players.[82] Despite its negligible effects, the actors' effort at masculinist reform illuminates the large potential for gendering power in the early days of the Revolution. The incident suggests that from the beginning a fraternal conception of power prevailed. The sovereignty

---

that the performers "would be pleased if legislation, reforming abuses that have appeared, would make the theater once again a worthy influence on mores and on public opinion."

82. Actresses' power at the Comédie eventually became lost to collective memory. By the 1880s, the chief administrator of the theater found it improbable that women had ever had an official voice in decision-making. See F. W. J. Hemmings, "Playwrights and Play-Actors: The Controversy over the *Comité de lecture* in France, 1757–1910," *French Studies* 43 (October 1989): 417.

of the people was not compatible with immoral actresses making decisions
for a cultural institution of the first order of importance. This, at least, was
the principle to which the actors adhered in trying to reconcile their theater
with the new regime. And it did not even take several years of general
political involvement and street agitation by women to make actors believe
that the authorities were ready for the silencing of females.

Conclusion

A Clairon or a Sainval could not complacently assume the same freedom
to exercise power as their male colleagues; nor did they assume an inevitable
subservience to men. Well-practiced in being resourceful, actresses had constantly to negotiate and test the limits of their authority. As quintessential
women in the absolutist public sphere, they were lightning rods for controversy. Several distinct discourses had made the private lives of actresses
the central question about the potential for exemplary theater. Actresses'
participation in the administration of the Théâtre-Français, although sanc-
tioned by royal decree, was exceptional and accepted only with regret.
Intendant Ferté, no less than a Rétif, conceived of actresses' power in terms
of their seductive bodies and offstage license. Public opinion, even of the
"rationalist" variety described by Baker, used the very same representation
of actresses with power under the Old Regime. To be sure, female players
won widespread praise for their talent and beauty and often inspired a
devoted following. Yet, it does not follow that enlightened men were comfortable with talented females having authority. Faced with accomplished
women who exercised power, sometimes directly over them, enlightened
men tended to worry about the illegitimate influences their charms encouraged. In either sphere, reflection on powerful women quickly led to anxiety
about pornocracy.

Thomas Laqueur has proposed that women's bodies were defined only
in relation to men's; and, therefore, understandings of the former were
unstable and problematical.[83] The same principal seems to apply to women's
power. Royal officers, philosophes, and democratic dreamers concurred in
viewing actresses' influence over men as dangerous because a sexual link

83. Thomas Laqueur, *Making Sex: Gender and the Body from the Greeks to Freud* (Cambridge: Harvard University Press, 1990), 22.

might be involved. Such a link was unthinkable as far as actors were concerned, not because they were chaste, but because actors had a right to a discreet private life that did not reflect on their professional activity. Males were free to exercise power through patronage, rational argument, or professional indispensability to the troupe. Actresses might use these very channels of influence, but because they were defined by their private behavior and by sexuality, the sense of legitimacy was absent.

On the whole, the various responses to actresses' authority support Landes's claim that the Enlightenment and the Revolution were essentially masculinist. At the same time, this study also poses two important qualifications. First, Landes's vision of a relatively ungendered public sphere surrounding the absolute monarch seems unsustainable. Rather, there was a huge and forcefully articulated difference in the degree of legitimacy enjoyed by privileged men compared with that of privileged women. The males were seen as using power rationally; women intrigued for domination. It follows from this reconsideration that the notion of a counterrevolution against women, staged particularly by the radicals of the Enlightenment, is dubious. The absolute monarchy was also highly suspicious of actresses' authority and took steps to curb their power in the few cases they had any.

Because the absolutist public sphere did entail engendered power, we also have to rethink Landes's argument about the distinctive place of the late eighteenth century and of the Rousseauean discourse in the process of silencing women. This study points to the enduring significance of patriarchy. To be sure, the emergence of a cult of domesticity and of the complementary representation of the sexes in the eighteenth century contributed to the gendering of power.[84] Voices from the bourgeois public sphere simultaneously grounded the rights of man and sexual difference in nature. Yet, the change was cumulative, not transforming. It reinforced antifeminist attitudes without breaking with the past (just as Rousseau added to the traditional discourse of Christians against the theater). Peter Gay, even while characterizing the philosophes as feminists, found in their thought an "age-

---

84. On the development of complementarity, see Londa Schiebinger, *The Mind Has No Sex? Women and the Origins of Modern Science* (Cambridge: Harvard University Press, 1989), chap. 8. On the English side, see Catherine Hall and Leonore Davidoff, *Family Fortunes: The Men and Women of the English Middle Class, 1780–1850* (Chicago: University of Chicago Press, 1987). For an interesting, speculative effort to put the distinctive aspects of eighteenth-century misogyny into a long-term perspective on patriarchy, see Kenneth Lockridge, *On the Sources of Patriarchal Rage* (New York: New York University Press, 1992), chap. 5.

old fear of women, the antique superstition that women were vessels of wrath and sources of corruption."[85] Before Marie Antoinette came to bear the sins of her sex, actresses did.[86] Their extraordinary talent and the pleasures they evoked only reinforced the prejudices of patriarchy.

85. Gay, *The Enlightenment*, 33.
86. Hunt, *Family Romance of the French Revolution*, chap. 4. Chantel Thomas, *La Reine scélérate: Marie-Antoinette dans les pamphlets* (Paris: Seuil, 1989).

8

The Public Divided

How Contemporaries Understood Politics in Eighteenth-Century France

Jack R. Censer

Despite the ever-increasing interest in the political opinion of the eighteenth-century French public—sparked by François Furet, Jürgen Habermas, Robert Darnton, and many others[1]—there have been relatively few systematic analyses of the readily available range of political news. Rather, the tendency has been to highlight one or another aspect, a limitation I seek

1. A list of works on the political culture of eighteenth-century France could easily be longer than this essay. For representative works by these important figures, see Jürgen Habermas, *The Structural Transformation of the Public Sphere*, trans. Thomas Burger (Cambridge: MIT Press, 1989); Robert Darnton, *The Forbidden Best-Sellers of Pre-Revolutionary France* (New York: Norton, 1995). François Furet has collaborated with Keith Michael Baker, Colin Lucas, and Mona Ozouf, on probably the single most important effort: *The French Revolution and the Creation of Modern Political Culture*, ed. Baker, 4 vols. (Oxford: Pergamon, 1987–94).

to remedy in this essay. Beginning with the state-dominated *Gazette de France*, this essay travels from the least to the most adventurous foreign Francophone press circulating within France and finally considers the *nouvelles à la main* (manuscript newsletters). Most obviously omitted are the pamphlets, which, although disseminating news, generally had as their main purpose commentary. In contrast, though not lacking a viewpoint, the newspapers and newssheets nominally purported to deliver news and were also somewhat constrained by expectations that they would. Also omitted is oral communication, ever so important, but virtually unrecoverable. Perhaps the rise in respect in the eighteenth century for the written over the spoken compensates for this lacuna.

The focus then is on news organs; even if they cannot tell us all the news that eighteenth-century French people had at their disposal, they do tell a lot. Considering at least this range of sources allows reconstructing the news and understanding how it might condition other events. Moreover, by wending our way through a hierarchy of papers, one can begin to imagine a layered public, possessing very different levels of information. A topography of the public may begin to emerge. Also, as we shall see, the differences among these media reveal much about the strengths and weaknesses of royal power.

The specific topics selected for this study of news are the very important national political events of the first five months of 1776. In this period, Turgot hit the height of his activist career, issuing in early January his "Six Edicts," which among other actions abolished both guilds and the *corvée* (a system that forced peasants to work on the roads). Although the country apparently favored these reforms, the parlements—especially the Parisian one—did not, violently objecting to the destruction of the privileges of masters and others and to the edicts that liberated production from guild control. They determinedly waged war against Turgot, and eventually because of this opposition and other related reasons, the king dismissed his chief minister in May 1776.[2] The coverage of these events cannot be said to typify all eighteenth-century reportage; clearly this was a particularly tumultuous period and government controls over the press were at this time relatively lax.[3] Yet, as will become apparent, some generalizations may be

2. On Turgot, see Edgar Faure, *La Disgrâce de Turgot, 12 mai 1776* (Paris: Gallimard, 1961); Douglas Dakin, *Turgot and the Ancien Regime in France* (New York: Octagon, 1965).

3. Jack R. Censer, *The French Press in the Age of Enlightenment* (New York: Routledge, 1994), 138–83. See these pages for a chronology of the fluctuations in government policy from 1745 to the Revolution.

made. Furthermore, even if this period possesses anomalies, its particular significance provides its own justification.

Although private individuals wrote the *Gazette de France,* the state controlled it. Predictably, its account was very supportive to the monarchy. The entire crisis received no mention at all for seven weeks until the February 26 issue, when the paper noted that the parlement had approved a Turgot edict concerning the Caisse de Poissy, a relatively unimportant matter reforming tax collection. Without any reference to opposition, the *Gazette* lauded the value of this change for the general population. Two small notices (8 and 11 March 1776) reported that the king had heard complaints from the justices (remonstrances), but they were buried among other notices of parlementary events. While these squibs, by reference to remonstrances tacitly admitted opposition, they focused on the orders of "His Majesty."

After a brief silence, the issues of 18, 22, and 25 March substantially presented all six royal edicts and the *lit de justice* (a ceremony required for parlementary acceptance when the court refused to register laws). These accounts largely consisted of the minutiae of these new regulations and the royal justifications for them. For example, along with the details concerning the suppression of the *corvées,* the paper provided the king's rationale, especially concerning the benefits to agriculture and commerce. The article specifically noted the inefficiencies engendered when cultivators were forced to work at road duty that took them from more important tasks: such circumstances also produced shoddy work. Somewhat subversive in all these justifications was the king's repeated portrayal of his acts on behalf of the public weal. Such remarks seemed to move him away from the more certain absolutist moorings of silence toward the activity of enlightened despotism—potentially shaky footing for a divine-right king. On the contrary, such remarks linked his politics with the popularity of the Enlightenment. At worst, such subtleties in monarchical arguments might lessen but surely did not undermine the paper's positive buildup of royal action.

The reporting of the actual interchange at the *lit de justice* was a little more challenging to royal power. When the assembly had begun, the *Gazette* simply mentioned that the first president gave the reasons for parlementary opposition, but then stated that this official finished by begging the king "to see in this conduct of his own parlement only the purity of its sentiments and its inviolable love of his sacred Person" (22 March). Evidently, the paper did not yet note the attack on policies in this speech, but the report on Seguier, the *avocat général* of the parlement, very tentatively spelled out a complaint. This magistrate averred that his fidelity forced objections. Moreover, the *Gazette* briefly indicated that in his justifications he critically noted that these edicts would result "in a total subversion of commerce" (22 March). Yet the parlements' relative lack of interest in trade seemingly lessened the intensity of the criticism.

Other than the fact that this was a remonstrance, the account gave little direct attention to the opposition. Perhaps the report on the close of the session was problematic for the monarchy. After the keeper of the seals adjusted one edict regarding the sale of tallow, Louis XVI ordered all six registered and expressed a willingness to remediate any difficulty. He stated: "My intention is not to make matters worse; I only wish to reign by justice and through the laws" (22 March). Furthermore, Louis argued that the good harvests after 1774 proved the value of earlier laws liberalizing the grain trade. In all this the king again pictured himself the servant of his own country to be held accountable to the success, morality, and legality of his legislation.

Still none of this reflected the virulent parlementary attack on Turgot. And much of what was included was self-justificatory for the government, even if the long-term effects of the rationale employed might contribute to untoward results. Perhaps the full denial of the opposition came in the complete failure to mention Turgot's dismissal. All along, the king, not ministers, figured in the pages of this paper. Incredibly though, nothing was said about the sack of Turgot, and therefore nothing emerged on the power of the opposition to undermine the monarch's ministers.

Beyond the French border were foreign papers that found more freedom abroad yet much of their audience in France. These periodicals varied a great deal, but in their coverage of France the most important factor was the protection from Bourbon interference that their host government could give them. Thus, some were relatively tame, others obstreperous. We can understand reasonably well what they had to say about the events of 1776 if we look first at the *Courrier d'Avignon,* one of the most constrained, and then at the *Courrier du Bas-Rhin,* located at or near the far end of the most liberated papers.[4]

4. Jeremy D. Popkin, *News and Politics in the Age of Revolution: Jean Luzac's "Gazette de Leyde"* (Ithaca: Cornell University Press, 1989); René Moulinas, *L'Imprimerie, la librairie et la presse à Avignon au XVIIIe siècle* (Grenoble: Presses universitaires de Grenoble, 1974); François Moureau, "Les *Mémoires secrets* de Bachaumont, le *Courier du Bas-Rhin* et les *bulletinistes* parisiens," in *L'Année 1768 à travers la presse traitée par ordinateur,* ed. Jean Varloot and Paule Jansen (Paris: Editions du Centre national de la recherche scientifique, 1981), 58–79; François Moureau, "*Courier du Bas-Rhin* (1767–1809?)," in *Dictionnaire des*

Despite the enormous influence the French could use to quash news coming out of Avignon, the paper published there told a story that in some ways went considerably beyond the *Gazette de France*. At first, however, utter silence characterized both papers. The *Courrier* broke the story on 6 February, some three weeks before the *Gazette* but still a month after the event began. The paper announced that three new edicts were expected including the suppression of the guilds and *corvées*. This report proves rather disingenuous and extremely limited as the editors, and indeed surely most of the literate public, had known the general nature of the decrees for some time. This information as well as an elliptical reference in the 9 February issue went beyond the *Gazette*, but only barely. Likewise another report on 20 February indicated: "They have presented yesterday for [parlementary] registration different Edicts and Declarations whose content remains unknown to the public." Only very basic material was available.

Beginning with the 27 February issue, the *Courrier* began to outstrip its governmental competition by airing the views of the opposition. At first extraordinary caution reigned as the editor evidenced when discussing some of the resistance: "If these *Mémoires* [by the guilds] had not been desired to become public, we would give a circumspect résumé. But even with such great interest we still will limit ourselves to what the parlement has stated when this gets to us." As reserved as was this claim, it still went far beyond the *Gazette*'s approach.

The independence staked out by the *Courrier* included some real bite as the paper throughout the month of March thoroughly aired the magisterial version. For example, judicial justifications occupied much more space than royal ones in the account of the *lit de justice* (29 March). While the *Gazette* only referred to the remarks of the first president of the Paris court, the *Courrier* detailed his rationale, including a defense of the *corvée* that insisted that even though this duty fell disproportionately on the laborers, the nobility and clergy deserved exemption as they already contributed enormously to public need. Such a class-centered defense, implying an embarrassing royal failure to protect the elite, the *Gazette* had ignored. Despite the inroads of philosophic thinking, members of the public, even contradictorily to their other Enlightenment values, would still have found wanting a king who did not protect the first two estates from unfair treatment. While the *Courrier* was wary of much editorializing and reported the parlementary

journaux, 1600–1789, 2 vols., ed. Jean Sgard (Paris: Universitas, 1991), 1:301–5; and Censer, *French Press*, 15–53, 138–83.

statements of fealty to the king, it also lauded the justices more than the central administration. Its articles described speakers as giving interesting, intelligent, and committed responses.

Yet, with the reporting on the *lit de justice* complete, the *Courrier* retreated to its earlier siding with the monarchy. The little news that appeared cited the diligence of the government (23 April).

The dismissal of Turgot once again opened the coverage (24 May). The account is worth citing in full:

> The retirement of M. Turgot has made a great sensation, not astonishingly at a time the hopes and projects of so many are awakened. The influence of the minister of finance is so considerable that his fall resembles a crisis. His probity and disinterestedness are not problematic, and that is much in his favor. Some people who previously believed that the system of government depended on him regarded these changes as devastating; but the enlightened wisdom of the king and the vigilance of the minister who now holds the reins has reassured the public in this respect.

Despite the optimism of the last phrase, this report, by labeling the affair a "crisis," aired difficulties that the *Gazette* had absolutely ignored. And indeed, the *Courrier* had included some more uncertain coverage before the more consistent monarchial tone set in later issues.

The *Courrier du Bas-Rhin* adds complexity to this picture. While the *Courrier d'Avignon* broke with the *Gazette* by showing more problems for the monarchy and even siding with the justices at times, the German-based paper gave a far franker account. Nonetheless, the editorial leanings of the paper emphasized support for Turgot's program.

The *Courrier du Bas-Rhin*, although geographically farther removed than the Avignon paper, beat the coverage of the latter paper by placing a story in the 13 January edition, more than a month before any substantial reporting in the *Courrier d'Avignon*. Although the details of edicts were not published in the German paper until February, very significant coverage of the debate emerged in the 20 January edition.

Indeed, the king's formal battle with the Parlement of Paris made its way into the *Courrier du Bas-Rhin*. Despite its aforementioned tendency to side with the monarchy in this debate, the paper presented in complete form the rationale and justifications of the parlement, including remarks potentially damaging to the king. Where the *Courrier d'Avignon* had summarized the first president's speech, this newspaper quoted it liberally. Included in this oration was the claim that the elimination of the *corvée* had caused universal consternation. And since the king no longer wished to rule by force, wondered the president aloud, why was he doing this? Furthermore, "this edict, by the introduction of a kind of perpetual and arbitrary imposition on wealth [taxes to replace the *corvée*], carries an inevitable bias to the property of the poor as well as the rich. It attacks the natural election of the nobility and clergy whose distinctions and rights provide constitutional support to the monarchy" (10 April). Such an attack, summarized in the Avignon paper, was more explicit in this longer form and raised the issue, long rejected by the king, that the nobility was a body on which the monarchy depended for its legal existence. Moreover, as the article continued, it cited the argument that as the king did not rule absolutely, the parlement possessed the right to complain. Printing such claims as the constitutionality of the Second Estate and parlementary privileges publicized basic contentions of royal opposition through much of the century.

The richness of this coverage—more than the Avignon paper even though the leanings of the German editors likely discouraged reports—climaxed in some ability to forecast events. A report dating from 19 February in the 28 February issue accurately predicted there would probably be a *lit de justice* to force registration of the edicts. Surely, continued the paper, the parlement would reject the law, invoking as the argument that, with the destruction of the guilds, the public would not be able to rely on the quality of various products. Furthermore, on the eve of the sack of Turgot (22 May; report dated 13 May), the *Courrier* foresaw this as likely to occur.

Yet such forewarnings proved few; indeed, the actual dismissal of the minister received scant attention. Most of what readers learned appeared in the 25 May issue:

> The dismissal of M. Turgot is very real; although he did not expect it at all, he was not disconcerted and received the news philosophically. Dictating a letter when he heard the news, he remarked that his successor would complete it. The clergy, the high nobility, the magistracy, the world of finance were overjoyed, while those in the countryside will surely differ. Everyone knows he has worked for the general benefit, and his greatest shortcoming has been overconfidence in hypocritical subordinates who countermanded his effectiveness.

The brevity of these reports plus the enigmatic reference to disloyal subordinates help demarcate the boundaries of the coverage in the *Courrier du Bas-Rhin*. Publishing information in advance on the *lit de justice* and the firing of Turgot as well as gossip about his problems required the paper to possess or be able to use inside information from the institutions running France. Evidently, this kind of news, because of royal repression or lack of investigative reporting, was in short supply. On the other hand, what was clearly available, as the discussion of the *lit de justice* has already implied, was much material relating to formal discourses, prepared explicitly for wider audiences. It was in this area, for the most part, that the Bas-Rhin organ established its superiority over its more southerly compatriot.

Interestingly, in this case, however, the German periodical used its independence to back up Turgot's efforts on behalf of the monarchy by publishing much more on the administration than its adversaries. While contemporaries as well as present-day scholars have pointed out the contradiction between these reforms and the king's theoretical moorings,[5] the *Courrier du Bas-Rhin* avoided this, first praising the minister but also his master. Indeed, the initial phase of the *Courrier*'s coverage concerned a pamphlet by Condorcet endorsing the suppression of the *corvées* (20 January). Wrote the philosophe: "Bless the benevolent minister who has delivered us from the double burden of the *corvées* and its administrators." Condorcet insisted that people simply wanted to work, existing by the sweat of their brows. As a tax, the *corvée* was too regressive. In the future, well-paid workers would be cheaper in the long run. Moreover, the edition of 2 March noted that the king stood fully behind the governmental innovation. "One sees by this trait that goodness does not supersede firmness in the young monarch. He'll rid us of obstacles, obstructing the national weal."

Not only did the *Courrier du Bas-Rhin* uphold the monarchy; it also printed materials that directly attacked its opposition. Condorcet argued: "The *corvées* have two great protectors, avarice and stupidity" (31 January). In February the paper itself suggested that those fighting the abolition of the old road-repair system had been receiving immense royal pensions. The implication here evidently was that opponents had already been corrupted by great wealth. Finally, the paper leveled charges specifically against the parlement. After the *lit de justice*, the *Courrier* (23 March) wrote: "In

5. See, for example, Peter Gay, *The Enlightenment: An Interpretation*, 2 vols. (New York: Knopf, 1966, 1969), vol. 2, *The Science of Freedom*, p. 496.

general everyone is discontented that the parlement joins in underhanded dealings, with the most problematic kinds of remonstrances. One suspects that the *esprit de corps*, self-interest itself, inspires it, while more essential works should occupy it."

Through the preponderance of the coverage, the *Courrier du Bas-Rhin* thus sustained monarchical efforts. Ironically, although more revealing than the Avignon periodical, the contents of the German paper proved more supportive to royal goals.

Such complications make difficult any general conclusions about how the foreign press supplied news about the 1776 crisis. In general, other research suggests that during periods of relative governmental tolerance of the press (and evidence surely indicates 1776 was such a period) this freedom to publish was used to favor opposition. Certainly, the *Courrier du Bas-Rhin* had done so in other circumstances.[6] Perhaps then, the German paper clearly illustrates the sharper image of politics conveyed in the foreign press while its changeableness over royal goals ought to be regarded as anomalous. Likely, in most lax periods—for example, most of the 1760s—both factors generally operated. When linked together they could produce far more criticism than the *Courrier* and especially the *Gazette*. Nonetheless, even this exception proves interesting because it shows a side often overlooked by scholars who stress the downhill slide of the monarchy into the Revolution. In fact, such press coverage reminds us that some papers presented the monarchy as still doing well, even under the feckless Louis XVI. Despite the early unpopularity of the deregulation of the grain trade, others besides the *Courrier du Bas-Rhin* applauded Louis's later moves.[7]

Turning to the *nouvelles à la main* raises methodological difficulties. Despite the problems in studying the printed periodical, selecting them is simple compared to choosing these hand-copied newssheets. With so many lost forever and the discovery and cataloging of those remaining just beginning,[8] no comparative collection is available and it may remain thus. For the purpose of this broad sketch, it may be reasonable to rely upon printed works that claimed to have previously circulated as *nouvelles*. In this case, I selected the *Correspondance secrète*, the *Espion anglais*, and the *Mémoires*

6. Moureau, "*Courier du Bas-Rhin*," 304.

7. Censer, *French Press*, 38–53.

8. For the most complete inventory to date, see François Moureau, "Clandestinité et ventes publiques: Le Statut du manuscrit," in his *De Bonne Main: La Communication manuscrite au XVIIIe siècle* (Paris: Universitas, 1993), 165–75.

secrets to use collectively as a group representing their brethren.[9] One questionable assumption is whether these sources—now printed—resembled their manuscript form or any other *nouvelles*. Despite Jeremy Popkin's argument that clearly these printed materials were rearranged by publishers, he shows that even the *Mémoires secrets*—the most-suspect *nouvelles*—bore a passable relationship to the handwritten copy that was afloat in eighteenth-century France.[10] It seems reasonable that the others did too. Whether they were representative remains open, but the problem of recovering a large-enough sample of originals for comparison makes resolution of the question difficult at best.

As for expressing views on the Turgot controversy, the *nouvelles à la main* resembled the foreign press with its array of opinions. Likely this media at least kept pace when periodicals' coverage turned harsh. But the significant difference between print and manuscript lay not so much in the views expressed but in the way they were presented. First and foremost, the newsletter writers clearly set forth the events. While newspaper journalists might comment or editorialize briefly, these remarks remained few enough so that discerning a paper's perspective required readers to sense the tilt in the amount of coverage. For example, comprehending the *Courrier du Bas-Rhin*'s coverage meant sensing the balance between favorable and unfavorable accounts as well as being guided in their understanding by stated opinions. In contrast, the *nouvelles* clearly imposed a vision on what was transpiring, at least on individual reports as they were communicated. This pattern of commentary, of course, sharpened whatever opinions existed, but was generally subversive: its level of frankness erased the principle that situations could remain ultimately ambiguous. This notion of clarity created a system that supported the audience's right to know at the expense of the authorities' ability to obfuscate.

Examples of characterizations abound in their pages. The *Mémoires secrets* (21 March 1776) described the speeches of the *lit de justice* in critical

---

9. Fr. Metra, *Correspondance secrète, politique & littéraire. Ou Mémoire pour servir à l'histoire des cours, des sociétés & de la littérature en France depuis la mort de Louis XV*, 16 vols. (London, 1787–89); *L'Espion anglais ou Correspondance secrète entre Milord All'Eye et Milord All'Ear*, 10 vols. (London, 1785); and Louis Petit Bachaumont, *Mémoires secrets pour servir à l'histoire de la république des lettres en France depuis MDCCLXII jusqu'à nos jours. Ou Journal d'un observateur*, 36 vols. (London, 1777–89).

10. See "The *Mémoires secrets* and the Reading of the Enlightenment," in *The* Mémoires secrets *and the Culture of Publicity*, ed. Jeremy D. Popkin and Bernadette Fort (Oxford: Voltaire Foundation, forthcoming). Because Popkin indicates the publishers were employing *nouvelles à la main* as an Ur-text, their synopsis possessed some relationship.

terms. According to the writer, the whole affair was not so well done as had been anticipated. The speech of the king's keeper of the seals was "cold and boring. It was a vague résumé of the preambles of the Edicts [of Turgot] and a dry enumeration, which lacked nobility of expression, of the diverse acts of legislators." The speech of the parlementary leader critiqued the *Mémoires secrets,* lacked energy, and proved trivial, even false. Even the best offerings of this opposition incurred attack. The *Espion anglais* was customarily more direct than the other newssheets in its views. Instead of providing summaries and quotes from various events, this newsletter only explained what transpired. Common as well were both unflattering and positive opinions. In an explanation of the *lit de justice* favorable to the government, the journalist referred to the parlementarians as "limited, timid, some old men accustomed to routine (letter 11)." Conversely, Louis XVI "exudes benevolence and possesses the purest and most enlightened love of humanity."

Not only were the *nouvelles à la main* able to achieve greater forthrightness in presentation, they could report a significantly wider range of topics. The foreign press could cover much of the events already dispersed to at least a part of the public, but did far less when it came to the more shrouded. Such was the specific *métier* of the manuscript news carriers. They too failed at prediction but their accounting covered a wider angle. The *Correspondance secrète* (25 April) divulged the contents of closed interchanges between parlement and king.

> The parlement which leaves no occasion to mortify M. Turgot has brought up an affair from Angoulême. . . . It's a question of usury in which Turgot had . . . helped the perpetrators receive a decision from the Conseil. The parlement wanted to attack this . . .; the Sorbonne joined here to condemn this canonically. The king angrily stated that *he prohibited deliberation and declared that this procedure undermined the authority of the Conseil.* However they have ignored him.

Even more shrouded news was the exposé in the *Mémoires secrets* of Maurepas's machinations to unseat Turgot (4 June). This newsletter explained that even though Maurepas had helped to maneuver the *controller-général* out of office, he hypocritically had extended his regrets about the dismissal. By ambiguously responding, Turgot, without verging into improprieties, made it clear that he understood the true nature of his opponent's activities.

Evidently at each level of publication from the governmental press to manu-scripts, the form of presentation became more open. The foreign press covered a wide range of subjects and at times critically; the particular weapon of the *nouvelles à la main* was its coherence. These two approaches proved problematic for the monarchy, whose closed, upbeat approach in the *Gazette de France* reveals that it too believed that candor and criticism were no friends of royalty. By comparing all three sources one can begin to see—just from the specific cases in the first half of 1776—what the public received as information.

But to evaluate this range of information, one might first specify further the roles of the various media. A recent study has, in fact, opened a debate about whether there was really much difference in content between the foreign press and manuscript newsletters.[11] I maintain that not only was there a difference, but that that difference was significant: increased candor constituted an increased threat. And during periods of governmental re-strictions, the difference among the media seems even more likely. Would not an aroused government have turned more on printed organs whose very arrival indicated an open administrative consent? If so, in such times the *nouvelles à la main* would become even more different. All this specula-tion requires more study of different times including those of greater gov-ernmental intervention. Further, this mention of variations in governmental attitudes may raise again the question of the reliance on printed "*nouvelles,*" published years after the events involved. Perhaps authorities allowed selec-tion and embellishment not tolerated at the time, so that the actual news-letters were far tamer, much like the foreign press. Yet it is useful to remember that the difference between the *nouvelles* and the newspapers depends mainly on different degrees of forthrightness. So endemic was this characteristic in virtually every entry of the *nouvelles* that it seems integral to the genre. Yet another completely separate point revealed in this essay is that the governmental *Gazette de France,* seemed to operate, not so much by lies, but by sins of omission. Finally, both *nouvelles* and gazettes made little attempt to predict much about future developments.

These differences in various publications also allow a better understand-ing of the structure of the public. No scholar has been more influential in focusing on the early modern political public than Jürgen Habermas, espe-cially in his *Structural Transformation of the Public Sphere.* In his work the alternative nonroyal sphere of politics consists of a zone occupied by a

11. François Moureau, "La Plume et le plomb," in Moureau, *De Bonne Main,* 5–16.

bourgeoisie unified by its independence. Even when scholars include the nobility in this zone, they emphasize that whatever the social difference, these two groups coalesced. In opinion and outlook they became one.

The very existence of variations among the media suggests, even if it cannot define, a sociology of this alternative public sphere. The *Gazette de France* was very cheap and reached a wide audience.[12] Slightly more expensive was the *Courrier d'Avignon*, specializing in a southern readership. Less accessible were other foreign newspapers.[13] We know very little about the price structure and circulation of the *nouvelles à la main*, but the best evidence suggests that they were far more difficult to obtain, although this remains unclear.[14] Of course, reading clubs, street readings, the ability to rent sheets, sharing of all sorts, and more important the oral transmission of news among friends must have overcome some of the deficiencies of distribution.[15] Yet outside Paris and other major cities, access to the news must have had far fewer of these alternatives. Thus, the price differential of the printed media, more expensive as controversial approaches mounted, suggests that wealth level—and thus to a lesser extent, social class, which highly correlated to wealth—related to different degrees of political knowledge. Eventually urban/rural and north/south divisions would also be important. It is the job of scholars to begin to sketch a topography of the public that these divisions can only begin to indicate.

What all this digression over the structure of both media and public has done is to permit a better appreciation of the availability of news than simply repeating the hierarchy of media. We now see that this range likely varied greatly by income, geography, and the like. Using that insight, con-

---

12. Gilles Feyel, "La *Gazette* au début de la guerre de Sept Ans. Son Administration, sa diffusion (1751–1758)," in *La Diffusion et la lecture des journaux de langue française sous l'ancien régime*, ed. Hans Bots (Amsterdam: APA–Holland University Press, 1987), 101–16.

13. Gilles Feyel, "La Diffusion des gazettes étrangères en France et la révolution postale des années 1750," in *Les Gazettes européennes de langue française (XVIIe–XVIIIe siècles)*, ed. Henri Duranton, Claude Labrosse, and Pierre Rétat (St. Etienne: Université de Saint-Etienne, 1992), 82–98.

14. See the contrast between the more restrictive view of Larry Bongie, "La Nouvelles à la main: La Perspective du client," and the expansive Moureau, "La Plume et le plomb," both in Moureau, *De Bonne Main*, 5–16, 135–42. Habermas himself believed that the *nouvelles* were strictly private communiques (*The Structural Transformation of the Public Sphere*, 20–21), but this goes beyond the more pessimistic account of the circulation of these newsletters. Furthermore, Moureau's evidence, with more forthcoming, makes virtually untenable the understanding of the *nouvelles* as thoroughly private.

15. Paul Benhamou, "Essai d'inventaire des instruments de lecture publique des gazettes," in Duranton et al., *Les Gazettes européennes*, 121–29.

nected to the contents of various presses, one can hypothesize a little more about the information in the public. For those parts of the public highly dependent on the official press, evidently not much troublesome information arrived. Here one may hypothesize that orality played a major role. First, it provided glimmers of information generally unavailable but this was surely not the main fare for that part of the public removed from other sources. Orality, acting as a form of interpretation, had to be very, very prevalent. The lack of material, supplemented by creating a word-of-mouth system, must have made the penetration of information and data very slow. Understanding had to be fashioned on little evidence. Oral communication could not supply the details either of battles or laws. At the other end of the spectrum, with everything available, news likely took on a largely modern form with written—if not printed—information communicated by journalists to a waiting public. And at least in the periods of laxity, a great range of information proved available. The oral, now relatively unnecessary, was less significant. Nonetheless, the written remained slow because the foreign papers took a while to gather news and arrive; generally the same may be said for handwritten versions. And here the lack of prediction left room for contemporaries to speculate. But lots of news appeared and orality surely diminished significantly. My proposals for the nature of available news still founder on the inability to map who belonged in these two groups and those in between.

These formulations about the accessibility of news do suggest more generally a new way to do political history. For example, they can contribute to understanding of the fall of Turgot. Any examination of this subject necessitates including his favorable press treatment and the possibility of a variably informed public opinion. In fact, this case study points toward the writing of the political history of the Old Regime as a complex account, focusing on the internal workings of institutions, the presentation to the public of conflicts, and the knowledge and reaction of society. Instead of a narrative of what happened to politicians and then the societal response, one must factor in public responses in a more complex manner. The narrative will take on a postmodern air in which events occur, various publics react in different ways and temporal rhythms, and all feed back into formal political events. Essentially, multiple cause and effects replace a more simple model.

Finally, this study of the periodical holds broad insights about the ability of the French government to master the whirlwind of the Enlightenment by advocating and taming it, as was attempted by counterparts in Prussia,

Russia, and Austria. The Turgot ministry was the most aggressive French effort. But examine the case study of the *Gazette de France* with its particularly elliptical and optimistic tone. No doubt the candor generally challenged the monarchy, but in the prevailing circumstances, circumlocution had its price. Assuming the rest of the press as the government accepted it—frank though harboring a mixture of views—would the government paper have been better served by a more candid approach that retained what it could of the positive analysis? Would not an enlightened minister try this approach? As pointed out, straightforward reporting conflicted with the theory of monarchy relying on obfuscation. The *Gazette* could not risk mimicking the extraordinarily direct approach of the *nouvelles*. Yet it could have dropped its unrealistic avoidance of difficult subjects in the manner of the foreign gazettes, which surely provided a respectable level of detached reporting. And in this period, quite positive for the monarchy, an opportune occasion for more honest coverage seems to have arisen. Where the *Gazette* was the prime source of news, some advantage would have been lost, yet the enlightened government would have been compensated for its candor by an ability to compete in the more informed public sphere, which likely influenced matters more. It might have been met with considerable acquiescence. Yet the *Gazette de France* slavishly continued past approaches that must have earned it scorn. One can hardly resist the conclusion that this myopia was related to a fatal rigidity present in the government in 1776. One might suggest that allowing the foreign press to circulate, with its mix of openness and some good as well as bad news, revealed royal flexibility. But this does not excuse the blindness regarding the *Gazette*. Whatever the successes that Turgot achieved, the royal administrator seemed ill-prepared to capitalize aggressively upon them and drive his points home. If Turgot was so hesitant, what of the less innovative? Ultimately the story uncovered here illuminates all the broad band of political actors from the king to the public that would shortly unseat him.

Notes on Contributors

CHRISTINE ADAMS is assistant professor at St. Mary's College of Maryland. Her research and publications in the area of family and gender history in pre- and postrevolutionary France explore the history of familial relations, class, and social identity. In 1995, she received a grant from the National Endowment for the Humanities to study the Society of Maternal Charity of nineteenth-century France.

LENARD BERLANSTEIN is professor of history at the University of Virginia. His work has ranged over the eighteenth and nineteenth centuries in France, and includes studies of the professional classes in *The Barristers of Toulouse in the Eighteenth Century* (Baltimore: Johns Hopkins University Press, 1975) and the working classes in *The Working People of Paris, 1871–1914* (Baltimore: Johns Hopkins University Press, 1984) and *Big Business and Industrial Conflict in Nineteenth-Century France: A Social History of the Paris Gas Company* (Berkeley and Los Angeles: University of California Press, 1991). He has recently turned his attention to gender history and the history of French theater women from the Old Regime to the fin-de-siècle.

JACK CENSER is professor of history at George Mason University. After first studying the revolutionary press in *Prelude to Power: The Parisian Radical Press, 1789–1791* (Baltimore: Johns Hopkins University Press, 1976), Censer has published widely in the history of the Old Regime press. His most recent book, *The French Press in the Age of Enlightenment* (New York: Routledge, 1994), is an attempt at synthesis in this dynamic area of research.

HARVEY CHISICK teaches history at the University of Haifa in Israel. One of the first historians to approach the Enlightenment "from below," his publications include *The Limits of Reform in the Enlightenment: Attitudes Toward the Education of the Lower Classes in Eighteenth-Century France*

(Princeton: Princeton University Press, 1981), *L'Education élémentaire dans un contexte urbain sous l'Ancien Régime: Amiens au XVIIe et XVIIIe siècles* (Amiens: Ansel, 1982), and more recently, *The Production, Distribution, and Readership of a Conservative Journal of the Early French Revolution: The* Ami du Roi *of the Abbé Royou* (Philadelphia: American Philosophical Society, 1992).

CISSIE FAIRCHILDS is professor of history at Syracuse University. Her first book, *Poverty and Charity in Aix-en-Provence, 1640–1789* (Baltimore: Johns Hopkins University Press, 1976), drew attention to the problem of poverty in Old Regime France, while *Domestic Enemies: Servants and their Masters in Old Regime France* (Baltimore: Johns Hopkins University Press, 1984) was one of the first historical studies of servants in the eighteenth century. Her current research focuses on consumerism in prerevolutionary France, a country usually considered on the periphery of the commercial revolution.

JOHN GARRIGUS is associate professor of history at Jacksonville University. A specialist in the history of the French Caribbean, Garrigus examines how conceptions of state and society—and race and gender—shaped the emergence of Haitian identities and politics. He was awarded the 1994 Tibesar Prize from the Conference on Latin American History for his article "Blue and Brown: Contraband Indigo and the Rise of a Free Colored Planter Class in French Saint-Domingue." He is currently working on Saint-Domingue during the French and Haitian revolutions.

LISA JANE GRAHAM is assistant professor at Haverford College and specializes in the political culture of Old Regime France. She received the 1994 Walker Cowen Memorial Prize for an "outstanding original work of scholarship" in eighteenth-century studies. Her manuscript "If the King Only Knew: On the Margins of Absolutism in Eighteenth-Century France" will be published by the University Press of Virginia.

OREST RANUM, professor at the Johns Hopkins University, was appointed in 1994 to the International Chair at the Collège de France. An extremely prolific scholar in the history of Old Regime France, especially the seventeenth century, his most recent publication is *The Fronde: A French Revolution, 1648–1652* (New York: Norton, 1993). Previous works include *Artisans of Glory: Writers and Historical Thought in Seventeenth-Century France* (Chapel Hill: University of North Carolina Press, 1980) and *Paris in the Age of Absolutism: An Essay* (Bloomington: Indiana University Press, 1979), among numerous other books, articles, and edited volumes.

Index

www.ingramcontent.com/pod-product-compliance
Ingram Content Group UK Ltd.
Pitfield, Milton Keynes, MK11 3LW, UK
UKHW031049110225
454912UK00002B/38